"This book provides great insights int
career development needs of differe
be dipping into it frequently and rec
Elisabe
Global Financia.

"An excellent addition to your toolbox if you want to develop a much deeper understanding around how to engage in authentic conversations with employees about their careers. Centring around the principle of a 'whole-person' approach and the importance of focusing on people's strengths, it's a must-read for all progressive people leaders looking to create a positive team/organisational culture."

Gary Kindon, HR Director Teva Pharmaceuticals

"Practical, rich, and every bit as holistic as the approach itself, this handbook already feels like the definitive word on career coaching as a discipline - and is invaluable for anyone coaching in this area, whether professional coaches, or professional managers supporting their teams."

Richard Goff, Chair, The People Director Partnership

"This book offers important new thinking to help line managers and coaches understand the impact of career reflection for individuals at every life stage. The idea that any valid career conversation should address the 'whole self' is a vital one and a key part in understanding how much work contributes to life experience. Highly recommended."

John Lees, author of How To Get A Job You Love

"Rob and his colleagues have gifted us the fruits of all their experience to support coaches, line managers and organisations in delivering high quality, research-led career support for clients at different life stages with specific career needs. The combination of case studies, practitioner research, career tools and reflective questioning makes this a highly valuable resource based in real-world career coaching in organisations in the 21st century."

Janet Sheath, Birkbeck College, University of London

"This book fills an important gap in the market, offering practical guidance to managers and employers who want to support the career development of their employees. The chapters are full of gems, written by specialists who draw on their own experience as career coaches, alongside evidence and models from the academic literature. Practical exercises, suggestions and case studies bring the ideas to life, and readers are offered a range of frameworks, tools and skills to help make their career conversations meaningful and effective. Empathic, holistic career support is more important than ever, and this book elegantly shows us how we can do it."

Julia Yates, *CPsychol, SFHEA Associate Professor, Deputy Head, Psychology Department, City, University of London*

"This was an excellent read, full of fresh and challenging concepts, laid out to make them relevant and relatable to anybody interested in creating a modern working environment. I've seen the workplace change drastically since 2020. This book really helped me to look at how we can improve relationships with our employees to ensure that each individual attains maximum satisfaction from their work and the organisation enjoys the full benefit of each employee."

David Whitmarsh, *CEO Standard Gas Technologies*

"Employing organisations often expect managers to have career conversations with individual employees, but rarely equip them to do this effectively. This handbook offers practical frameworks and tools for givers of career support, acknowledging the challenges facing a diverse workforce at different life stages in different situations."

Wendy Hirsh, *Principal Associate, Institute for Employment Studies, Visiting Professor of Career Development, University of Derby*

The Holistic Career Coaching Handbook

Exclusion from the workplace not only has devastating effects on individual well-being and public health, but also limits organisational development and social cohesion. This book promotes an understanding of the strengths of people with diverse attributes, transforming a sense of being overlooked by employers to being a valued asset.

This handbook provides tools for people to respond respectfully to the way employees experience their working lives. It guides the reader to realise the potential strengths of employees, regardless of their background, life situation, mental health or neurological condition, and appreciate the impact of emotions on their contribution to and experience of work. Other books look at organisational reasons for motivation; this book addresses the emotional effect of significant change outside the workplace that has an impact on motivation at work. Chapters cover neurodiversity, parental coaching, Career Returners, menopause and the impact of different life stages.

This practical book uses cases and summaries throughout and has chapters on creating a successful programme of career support, together with 15 original Career Tools. It is particularly relevant to Human Resources, Learning and Development, and line managers, and anyone wanting to develop effective in-house career coaching for employees.

Rob Nathan is a Chartered Psychologist and the founder of Career Counselling Services. He is the co-author of *Career Counselling* and has pioneered holistic career coaching training in the UK and globally.

Tamsin Crook is an ICF Accredited Career Coach at Making Careers Work, with an MSc in Career Management and Coaching, and has a particular focus in working with neurodivergent clients.

Frances Cushway has been supporting women through career transitions since she trained as a Career Coach in 2006 while working for the BBC. She founded The Maternity Coach in 2019.

Gilly Freedman is a Psychologist and Accredited Executive Coach. She trains line managers in career coaching and also specialises in training and supporting doctors.

Kate Mansfield transitioned from a career in Recruitment to Career Coaching and is now a Director of Career Counselling Services. She coordinates CCS's work with employers.

Aretha Rutherford is a Visiting Lecturer at Birkbeck University. With expertise in neurodiversity and career development, she combines academic knowledge with creative strategies to support diverse professionals.

The Holistic Career Coaching Handbook

A Guide for Managers and Employers

Rob Nathan

LONDON AND NEW YORK

Designed cover image: Getty Images

First published 2025
by Routledge
4 Park Square, Milton Park, Abingdon, Oxon OX14 4RN

and by Routledge
605 Third Avenue, New York, NY 10158

Routledge is an imprint of the Taylor & Francis Group, an informa business

© 2025 Rob Nathan

The right of Rob Nathan to be identified as author of this work and of the chapter authors for their individual chapters, has been asserted in accordance with sections 77 and 78 of the Copyright, Designs and Patents Act 1988.

All rights reserved. No part of this book may be reprinted or reproduced or utilised in any form or by any electronic, mechanical, or other means, now known or hereafter invented, including photocopying and recording, or in any information storage or retrieval system, without permission in writing from the publishers.

Trademark notice: Product or corporate names may be trademarks or registered trademarks, and are used only for identification and explanation without intent to infringe.

British Library Cataloguing-in-Publication Data
A catalogue record for this book is available from the British Library

Library of Congress Cataloging-in-Publication Data
Names: Nathan, Robert, author.
Title: The holistic career coaching handbook : a guide to providing the right environment for all employees to thrive / Rob Nathan.
Description: Abingdon, Oxon ; New York, NY : Routledge, 2025. | Includes bibliographical references and index.
Identifiers: LCCN 2024046559 (print) | LCCN 2024046560 (ebook) | ISBN 9781032816647 (hardback) | ISBN 9781032802350 (paperback) | ISBN 9781003510475 (ebook)
Subjects: LCSH: Vocational guidance. | Career development.
Classification: LCC HF5381 .N283 2025 (print) | LCC HF5381 (ebook) | DDC 331.702—dc23/eng/20241121
LC record available at https://lccn.loc.gov/2024046559
LC ebook record available at https://lccn.loc.gov/2024046560

ISBN: 978-1-032-81664-7 (hbk)
ISBN: 978-1-032-80235-0 (pbk)
ISBN: 978-1-003-51047-5 (ebk)

DOI: 10.4324/9781003510475

Typeset in Calibri
by Apex CoVantage, LLC

Contents

About the Authors viii
Acknowledgements xi

This Book's Scope and Structure 1

1 The Nature of Holistic Career Coaching 7

2 Early Career: Work Expectations and Experience of People in Their Twenties 18

3 Mid-Career: The Impact of Experience 38

4 Later Career: Opportunities and Challenges Faced by Older Workers 62

5 Supporting Neurodiversity in the Workplace 109

6 Supporting the Transitions of Career Returners 170

7 Supporting Parents in Their Careers Through Parental Leave and Beyond 217

8 Talking About the Menopause at Work 279

9 Creating a Successful Programme of Career Support 316

10 Conclusion 340

11 Career Tools 346

Index 409

About the Authors

Rob Nathan

Rob has pioneered holistic career coaching and career coach training in the UK and globally. He is the co-author of two previous books: *How to Survive Unemployment: Creative Alternatives* (with Michel Syrett) and *Career Counselling* (with Linda Hill). He is the Founder and CEO of Career Counselling Services, where he combines one-to-one career coaching with supporting employers to build sustainable career development support for their employees. He loves working with diverse groups and continues to work extensively with the United Nations.

Tamsin Crook

Tamsin Crook is an independent ICF accredited career coach at Making Careers Work, with a particular focus in working with neurodivergent clients. Prior to this, she worked within HR and Learning and Development roles in the private, public and voluntary sectors. She has an MSc in Career Management and Coaching, has co-authored research into ADHD career strengths and successes, and is currently studying for MSc Psychology, and ongoing neurodiversity coaching development programmes.

She has three teenage boys and a dog to wrangle, so finds relaxation and focus in her work, gardening, and walking with friends.

Frances Cushway

With a degree in Psychology and PGC in Career and Talent Management, Frances Cushway has been supporting women through career transitions since training as a Career Coach in 2006. She founded The Maternity Coach, which works with a broad range of organisations to support the transition to parenthood, and trains coaches to work as Maternity Coaches. Her work has been recognised by the CDI where she has been a finalist for Career Coach of the Year. She is married, with two daughters, and takes refuge from the madness of the work–life juggle in local coffee shops and Pilates classes.

Gilly Freedman

Gilly is a Career Coach, Accredited Executive Coach, Course Tutor and qualified Coach Supervisor with a Masters in Psychology. She is Principal Career Coach at Career Counselling Services where she works with a wide range of clients and organisations, as well as specialising in coaching doctors. She trains HR and line managers in career coaching skills and has wide international experience. Relaxation involves running with her dog, Wilma, and piano accompaniment.

Kate Mansfield

Kate is a Director and Career Coach at Career Counselling Services (CCS). She is a passionate advocate of women's careers and was for many years Lead Coach at Women Returners (now Career Returners). Kate is a Lead Tutor on CCS's Accredited Career Coach Training and coordinates their extensive career conversations and career development work with employers.

Kate is also a qualified Coach Supervisor with Oxford Brooks and has a Postgraduate Diploma in Career and Talent Management from Kingston and an MSc in Organisational Behaviour from Birkbeck. She is married with two children and two cats and is familiar with the challenges of mid-life work and family juggling! This has fuelled her motivation to help women find ways of combining meaningful work and life choices, and to look after themselves in the process!

Aretha Rutherford

Aretha Rutherford is a visiting lecturer on Birkbeck University's Career Coaching and Coaching Psychology programme. She founded the coaching company Pattern and is an Associate Coach at Genius Within, a specialist neurodiversity training, research, and coaching consultancy. She was also the former Head of Coaching and Development at neurodiverse employment consultancy Exceptional Individuals. With an MSc in Career Management and Coaching and an MA in Design and Branding Strategy, her academic background informs her creative and strategic approach to career development. She enjoys visiting art galleries and museums, collecting vintage children's books, is an avid textile designer, and adores spending time in green spaces with her beautiful Australian Labradoodle.

Acknowledgements

Many, many people have given their time in supporting the idea as well as the writing and completion of this book. Huge appreciation goes to Rebecca Marsh at Taylor and Francis, whose calm reassurance and confidence in the material kept all of us on track and able to complete this work in time.

Colleagues, friends, clients, graduates of our courses all contributed their time in reading chapters, providing case studies, being interviewed and, above all, being excited by our ideas and believing in the value of the project. We include Adoption UK, Almuth McDowall, Angela Roshier, Anna Thornley, Anton Fishman, Atinuke Awe, Bob Crowe, Career Returners, Charlotte Ball, Daniela Corallo, David Whitmarsh, Deana Murfitt, Debra Parsons, Ed Warner, Elisabeth Rudman, Fertility in the Workplace, FDM Group, Franziska Otto, Gavin Wells, Gary Kindon, Helen Klarich, Helen Law, Ian Dinwiddy, Jan Stancliffe, Janet Sheath, Jenny McLaughlin, John Lees, Josie Davies, Jude Harvey, Julia Yates, Julianne Miles, Karen Danker, Kirsty Tifft, Lesley Salem, Lindsay Hickey, Lucy Standing, Mansfield Building Society, Mark Hocken, Michael Friedler, Motionspot, Neurodiversity Entrepreneurship Association, Olivia Omideyi, Over the Bloody Moon, Rachel Wright, Richard Batley, Richard Goff, Rob Edwards, Roberta Barker, Sarah Mavius, Sheena Bailey, Stella Amor, Stephanie Rix, Susie Leafe, Tracy Meller and Wendy Hirsh.

To our editorial team at Routledge, a big thank you to Rebecca March, Grace Collier and Laura Whelan.

And finally, but most importantly, we could never have completed this book without the constant support and encouragement of our families, whose willingness to allow us the space and peace we needed to focus on the research, writing and much re-writing of the text, never wavered.

As a co-writing team, and as a close group of professional colleagues, we have buddied with each other to provide counterpoint, critique, edits, edits and more edits, but above all a commitment to each other's wellbeing in the honouring of this important piece of work.

Tamsin Crook, Frances Cushway, Gilly Freedman, Kate Mansfield, Rob Nathan, Aretha Rutherford

This Book's Scope and Structure

Rob Nathan

The Need for This Book

Several years ago, I was talking with a senior manager who recently completed an exit interview with a middle ranking employee. He was astonished to find out how bored this person had been in his back room administration role, and how he had been compensating by building electronic devices in his shed at home. 'If only I'd known' this manager told me, 'I could have made good use of his skills'. What he implied was 'if only I'd spent time getting to know him'.

A simple message. But one that is often overlooked. In the quest for operational efficiencies, pressures to perform to the highest professional or commercial standards, plus the norms of some organisational cultures, make it hard for people's strengths, skills and experience to be noticed and used or developed in the workplace.

Covid-19, with all its pain and trauma, together with rapidly advancing technologies, acted as a catalyst which challenged the wisdom of the 'work-face'. People have reflected and realised that the link between work and 'life' matters enough to take action to ensure a healthy work–life balance. This has unleashed the recognition that people bring their whole selves to work. And, when labour markets compete not just for scarce technical skills but also for valued interpersonal strengths, it also makes business sense, for large and small organisations alike, to invest time to really get to know the qualities, aspirations, values and needs of the people who keep the business going. This is similarly the case when layoffs become more common, as these same people may not only be ambassadors for the employer but also could supply valued skills and strengths when times improve.

Managers are in the front line. Often pressed themselves to perform with limited resources, they may forego the need to spend quality time with their teams. We at Career Counselling Services (CCS) have trained thousands of managers and leaders to use a few simple frameworks and tools which we believe are a very good use of time and ultimately will save the squandering of talent, motivation and engagement. We have always taught a holistic approach to giving career support.

Underpinning this training is the mindset required towards listening; it is a mindset that sees the purpose of listening as learning, rather than responding. This book is a response to the welcome zeitgeist of wanting to understand more deeply what people bring to the workplace, how their diverse strengths and experiences add value, and how to respond in a way that optimises their engagement and satisfaction, and recognises that tough personal times are not just temporary, but also may yield valuable qualities that are not immediately obvious.

This practical handbook is based on the authors' individual and combined experience as career coaches and career coach trainers. We all support individuals in their career reflections, and some of us have specialised in coaching Career Returners, neurodivergent people, and those with career challenges before, during and after parental leave. We combine coaching with the sensitive use of Career Tools, a selection of which are available at the end of the book.

Inevitably, and perhaps paradoxically, a book that has 'holistic' in its title cannot cover every topic or the experience of every individual, yet we hope that the reader will find that the principles outlined here, together with the broad range of case studies, are sufficiently useful to apply to a wide range of people, cultures and life situations which are brought to the workplace, and which may impact upon engagement, motivation and performance.

Please feel free to dip into one or two chapters, or read all the way through.

Chapter 1 describes the nature and scope of holistic career coaching, and how it differs from the way career coaching is usually approached. It positions the book's premise as the ability and will to show empathy, and that this can be enhanced by increasing knowledge and understanding of what people bring to work which may not always be visible. It sets out that managers, employers and coaches can contribute to realising the potential strengths, aspirations and talents of employees, regardless of their background, their life situation, age, mental or physical health, and by appreciating the potential impact of life situations on their contribution to and experience of work. It describes the holistic approach to supporting people who may otherwise be overlooked.

Chapters 2, 3 and 4 cover three stages of life. Chapter 2 – the expectations and experience of people in their twenties – looks at why this age group matters to employers, the strengths they bring, myths associated with this group, and explores whether there is a difference between people's priorities in their early and late twenties. Examples, research and cases illustrate the prevalence of a 'developmental' or 'quarter-life' crisis. I will report on my own primary research, where I asked 20 people under 30 for their views on what engages them at work, and what would drive them away. As with all the chapters, there are guidelines and tips for managers and other career supporters on ways to best respond, questions for reflection and indication of the Career Tools in Chapter 11 which may help.

Chapter 3 looks at the impact of experience of people in 'mid-life', a term I prefer to 'mid-career' as many people now have more than one career. The chapter challenges the notion of the somewhat mocking term 'mid-life crisis' and looks at the dichotomies sometimes felt in mid-life between 'young and old', 'destruction and creation' and 'attachment and separation'. The chapter explores the idea that happiness seems to get harder in mid-life. From the manager's perspective, the chapter will describe some of the common mid-life questions people often bring to career conversations, and the steps managers and employers can take to optimise work engagement during this potentially volatile period.

In Chapter 4 Gilly Freedman looks at people 55 and over, and the impact of longevity, the desire for continued work and the steps employers and managers can take to acknowledge the needs, strengths and contributions older workers can make. There are benefits both to the business and to individuals of continued contribution. Gilly spoke to 40 people age 55 and over, and came up with several categories which the chapter describes: flexibility, opportunity to mentor, respect for experience and expertise, doing meaningful work, learning and personal growth. Cases are accompanied by questions for reflection, contributing to understanding what people in this older worker group might be experiencing. The chapter also challenges some of the biases against the contribution older workers can make, as well as suggesting tips for managers who conduct career conversations with older workers.

Tamsin Crook and Aretha Rutherford look at the experience of neurodiversity in Chapter 5. Using an intersectional approach, their insights will enable managers and coaches to understand more deeply the different ways in which neurodivergent people (NDers) navigate the workplace, communicate and build relationships. Insights from neurodivergent employees, and organisational case studies illustrate how employers can support NDers to identify and build on their strengths, to mitigate some of the challenges, and work towards thriving in their roles. They also look at the unique impact of late diagnosis of neurodiversity, which is something that we are seeing more of as awareness and understanding has increased.

Career Returners is Kate Mansfield's focus in Chapter 6. She looks at the impact of a career break on women and men, the business case for gender diversity, and addresses the talent pipeline gap for mid- to senior-level women. Kate's extensive experience working with Career Returners has made her alert to some of the common assumptions and biases levelled at this group, for example, that skills become obsolete and career breaks are only taken by mothers. Cases and examples illustrate the many strengths returners bring which may often be overlooked because of inaccurate assumptions. Kate will indicate the kind of career support that managers can give to set up returners for success.

In Chapter 7 Frances Cushway looks at why it is so important to take a holistic approach to supporting parents in their careers and why nurturing parents can bring huge benefits at both a team and organisational level. For this chapter, Frances conducted original research at The Maternity Coach, and shares key findings and case studies alongside published research. The chapter looks at the role assumptions and biases play in the experience of parents returning to work and what can be done to challenge these attitudes and behaviours. Cases illustrate the lived experiences of parental leave and how this impacts their career on their return. Frances also unveils some of the hidden strengths parents bring to their careers, which can bring a huge benefit to their organisations. Managers will benefit from an insight into what they can do to support parents to enable them to thrive in their careers after parental leave and beyond.

In Chapter 8 – on talking about the menopause – Kate Mansfield highlights the need for managers to create the psychological safety for team members to talk about their experience of the menopause and its impact upon their motivation and performance at work. It underlines both the physical symptoms and emotions that every woman might go through. 75–80% of women are in work and it is vital that managers recognise both the normality of this phase and any temporary impact on performance. Cases are cited of examples of women who have found how talking about their experience of the menopause contributed to their engagement at work.

Chapter 9 focuses on the important and practical steps employers and managers can take to maximise the benefits of a programme of career support. Beginning with a focus on organisational culture, the 15-step Holistic Model for an Attractive Workplace is described, along with some key factors for success taken from a CCS Employers Survey of 2021, including an emphasis on the shared responsibilities of the manager, individual and employer to ensure that any programme of career support is both successful and sustainable. Moving to the manager's role, the importance of mindset is described along with a simple and practical four-stage framework of career conversations, and a description of ways in which managers can elicit strengths and skills in a career conversation. The chapter closes with some manager guidelines, an indication of the questions people may bring to career conversations and the many possible positive outcomes.

Chapter 10 draws together some of the key themes of this book and gives a summary of practical ways in which managers and coaches can impact the motivation, engagement and performance of their teams. This leads on to Chapter 11 – on the Career Tools – where the reader can find a selection of easy to use tools, together with a link to a free online seminar to learn how best to debrief one very useful tool and integrate it appropriately into the career coaching.

Chapter 1

The Nature of Holistic Career Coaching

Rob Nathan

What Is Holistic Career Coaching?

We define Holistic Career Coaching as *a process which enables people to identify and utilise their resources to make career-related decisions and manage career-related issues*[1]. The term 'resources' refers to those qualities within the person, such as skills, strengths, personal qualities, self-belief, experience, motivations and values, as well as external resources such as networks, infrastructure, finance and support from others (including people who believe in you). Offering a holistic 'career-related' approach implies the need to acknowledge and respect any emotion or personal issue which arises in a work-based conversation, but also to know the limits of this approach and to refer someone for more specialised help if the personal issue becomes the dominant consideration.

Holistic career coaching is different from what has often been understood as a career conversation. The latter may involve talking about aspirations along with a focus on development or progression, but with little or no attention to what the person may be experiencing that is apparently external to the workplace. Since this can include challenges to mental and physical health, family responsibilities, significant transitions and personal crises, managers and coaches cannot ignore the potential impact on motivation, engagement, well-being and performance.

The role of a manager is not an easy one. This book aims to make it a little bit easier.

Why Holistic Career Coaching?

The World Health Organization (WHO) paper on mental health at work[2] pointed out the following:

- Decent work is good for mental health.
- Poor working environments – including discrimination and inequality, excessive workloads and job insecurity – pose a risk to mental health.
- Globally an estimated 12 billion working days are lost every year to depression and anxiety at a cost of US $1 trillion per year in lost productivity.
- There are effective actions to prevent mental health risks at work.

The WHO lists a number of risks to mental health at work. They include:

- Underuse of skills or being under-skilled for the work
- Lack of control over job design or workload
- Organisational culture that enables negative behaviours
- Limited support from colleagues or authoritarian supervision
- Conflicting home/work demands

In addition to the short-term negative impact of these risks, people who leave employment because of any of the above factors may experience a decline in self-confidence and an increase in anxiety with a longer-term impact on their ability and will to gain re-employment. This influences their individual lives, their families and the economy.

To protect mental health the WHO paper suggests, among other items,

> Manager training (should) recognise and respond to supervisees experiencing mental distress, build interpersonal skills like active listening and foster better understanding of how job stressors affect mental health and can be managed.

This book provides the tools for managers and anyone having career conversations in organisations to realise the potential strengths, aspirations and talents of employees, regardless of their background, life situation, mental or physical health, and appreciate the impact of emotions on their contribution to and experience of work. It is thus a holistic approach to supporting people who may otherwise be overlooked.

A Strengths-Based Approach to Career Conversations

The relationship between employer and employee has changed beyond recognition. Since Covid-19, the boundary between work and non-work has been challenged, as many employees have reflected on their priorities and values, and decided to challenge the traditional separation of work and home. Some labour markets have moved in the direction of favouring employees, and employers have chosen, or been forced, to acknowledge the whole life considerations and well-being of their employees, if they are to keep them engaged and motivated. Employers also need to create the right environment to get the best out of their people to deliver the organisation's objectives. As one colleague put it: 'everybody has the potential to do something amazing – understanding their strengths to deliver gives them energy and propels the business forward'.

Some employers have seen the value of offering career support to their employees, as they need their employees to develop. It is an area that consistently comes up as lacking in the ubiquitous annual or biennial employee survey. One response has been to train up cohorts of managers, representatives from Human Resources, cross-organisation career mentors or in-house coaches to have career conversations. Often that training focuses on coaching techniques and tips for a good *career* conversation.

Yet how equipped are those trained to respond to the wider needs of the people they manage or coach? How capable are they to tap into the strengths of someone with, for example, neurodivergent qualities and strengths? Our culture at work has traditionally focused on looking at what is *wrong* or *deficient* in a person's performance, rather than looking for their strengths, and the work environment that enables those strengths to flourish. People who thus do not fit into a cultural norm may start to concur in the belief that they do not have a great deal to contribute, and consequently their performance and engagement decreases. What a waste.

Research has suggested that high-functioning teams need six positive comments to balance each negative one[3]. When deficiencies, gaps and development needs are highlighted at the expense of strengths, the lack of recognition and praise can go a long way to undermining a person's self-belief. This is especially true if someone doesn't fit the cultural norm, or has their own unique approach to work tasks and challenges. This book aims to challenge this excessive emphasis on deficiencies, with evidence, cases, tools and resources to support a strengths-focused approach.

The Impact of Transitions

Holistic career support acknowledges that emotion may be part of a career conversation, sometimes positive and at other times less so. Several situations addressed in this book require time to adjust to the change. This means that a person's strengths may be temporarily impaired or just not visible. There are many examples of change which can impact a person's confidence and realised strengths. The examples below are in no particular order, and are far from exhaustive:

- New or increased caring responsibilities
- Returning after parental leave
- Recent health diagnosis
- Relationship breakdown
- Returning to work after significant break
- The onset of menopause
- Experience of discrimination
- Rejected for promotion
- Redundancy
- Change in partner's work status
- Personal crisis

The work of William Bridges[4] distinguishes between the word 'Change' and 'Transition'. Bridges describes change as a tangible or physical event, such as moving to a new job, getting married, losing a loved one or changing location. Transition is the emotional 'work' or psychological adjustment needed to adapt to and accept the change. This is why it is so rare to be able to 'hit the ground running'. We need time and support to ease the transition.

Bridges described three stages we go through in response to an external event. Colleagues at work may only see the outer version of the person who may be going through a significant transition or development stage. These stages are shown in Table 1.1.

Each stage brings with it a number of possible emotions. Bridges summarises these in three zones: Endings, the Neutral Zone and New Beginnings. The Neutral Zone can be most confusing and unsettling, and it is likely that managers will have a number of people in their team going through an unsettled time, whether caused by a move to a new role or department, an organisational re-structure or a significant personal event. Table 1.1 describes the kind of emotions that can be experienced during the different stages.

Table 1.1 The three zones of William Bridges' Transition model

Endings	Neutral Zone	New Beginnings
Elation	Confusion	Hope
Excitement	Impatience	High energy
Relief	Frustration	Enthusiasm
Sadness	Fear	Confidence
Loss	Loss of confidence	Anxiety
Shock	Depression	Self-doubt
	Creativity	
	Energy	

Often the time and support needed to enable the transition to happen with all its lumps and bumps is not given. By allowing the emotional ups and downs of transition to be acknowledged and accepted, managers are more likely to foster a feeling of support and consequently belonging and engagement.

Life Stages

To give some wider context to career and life, there have been some useful descriptions of the different stages that people go through. Chapters 2, 3 and 4 address the kind of considerations, challenges and dilemmas facing people during early, middle and later career stages. The way that 'career' is experienced, however, may be highly individual, and some of the metaphors indicated below may resonate with the reader. Stages and career metaphors all imply some kind of movement or transition. Change is one of the few things that everyone experiences, although the way they do so is vastly different.

It is natural to expect that emotions during times of change can be felt strongly (even though they are not always expressed). William Bridges' Transitions model mentioned above is a useful way of enabling us to gain insight into what people might be experiencing at different times.

Life stages, and their associated tasks, were identified as far back as 2,500 years ago, as quoted in *The Sayings of the Fathers* (*The Talmud*). Fourteen ages of man were indicated, each with its own developmental tasks. Shakespeare outlined seven ages of man in *As You Like It*. Since the 1970s, there has been a plethora of stage theories, the most influential including Levinson et al.[5], Super[6] and Sheehy[7].

More recently, Sullivan and Mainiero[8] came up with the Kaleidoscope theory of careers. Chapters 6 and 7 on Career Returners and parental coaching describe this model in relation to those specific groups. Sullivan and Mainiero suggested that the changing career priorities of an individual over their life-span can be described by the interplay of three factors:

- **Authenticity** – ensuring that your role and working environment are consistent with your values, ideals and sense of identity.
- **Balance** – ensuring that you achieve an optimum equilibrium between work and non-work (note this is not just balance between work and family life but between work roles and any other roles a person may be engaged in).
- **Challenge** – ensuring that your working life is stimulating and that you are progressing or developing.

They identified two main career patterns:

- **Alpha pattern careers** – starts with a desire for *challenge* prominent, later a desire for *authenticity* becomes more significant, eventually a desire for *balance* begins to take on more importance.
- **Beta pattern careers** – also starts with a desire for *challenge*, then a desire for *balance* comes forward, then a desire for *authenticity*.

Change Is Not as Predictable as Stage Theory Suggests

Any stage theory over-simplifies the reality of the individual sitting in front of us. Stages can be seen as somewhat prescriptive and predictable, especially when focused on so-called marker events, such as leaving school, getting a first job, starting at university, taking an apprenticeship, graduating, finding a partner, childbirth, all of which may affect us, but in *different* ways. But, recent experience has shown that significant and perhaps an increasing amount of change occurs in a person's life and not necessarily at certain predictable ages or stages.

Learning

For example, people do not finish learning when they leave school, as they almost certainly need to continue learning to keep developing their skills and knowledge. In recent years, the '70-20-10' indicator of different ways of learning has become better known and can act as a catalyst for people to find a range of ways to learn which are beyond formal classroom learning. According to the 70-20-10 guidelines[9] people learn and grow from three types of experience, with a ratio of:

- 70% experiences and assignments
- 20% relationships
- 10% structured coursework and training

Although there is a lack of solid evidence to support the truth of this framework, I have found it a useful way to open people's eyes to the myriad ways of learning, and thus to look on any project or work experience as containing potential learning opportunities.

Unhelpful Generalisations About Life Stages

Certain myths have probably developed about the kind of tasks, attitudes and behaviours expected of people in each stage. For example, men in their forties are supposed to go through the 'male menopause'. Such generalisations can act as an unhelpful pressure. If young adults under the age of 25 are supposed to have a high drive to succeed, or people in their late twenties are expected to be 'settling down', people who find themselves with a low desire to achieve at 22 or a desire to travel at 29 may feel guilty for feeling different from what they believe others expect of them, or they might think that something is wrong with them. Are there in fact any common denominators that distinguish a particular age or stage of life, and which can thus give managers clues as to how best to respond?

A way to increase empathy for every person is to deepen the knowledge and understanding of what someone might be experiencing at a particular stage of life, with a certain mental or physical condition, or who reacts with strong emotions to a recent or current event. This book hopes to provide the basis for this understanding and the guidelines to enable managers to do just that.

People see and experience their careers in very different ways and sometimes it can be useful to use a career metaphor to acknowledge that very individual perspective.

Career Metaphors

Inkson[10] described careers according to nine metaphors:

- *Career as a legacy:* Focuses on what we inherit and what we want to pass on.
- *Career as a craft:* This emphasises the role of the individual in constructing their own career.
- *Career as seasons:* This has a similarity to seeing career as a series of stages of a person's life.
- *Career as a fit:* The notion of matching and round pegs in round holes (now dated).
- *Career as a journey:* This sees career as movement between places and time. Traditional vertical journeys have given way to careers characterised by lateral and even 'squiggly' movement.
- *Career as relationships:* This focuses on the social nature of the career journey and the influence of relationships on career movement.
- *Career as theatre:* This sees career as a series of roles we take on, and sees career almost as a performing art, the actors being employers, employees, supervisors, co-workers, professional associations, unions and 'psychological contracts'[11].
- *Career as economic resource:* Terms such as 'Human Resource Management' beg the question who owns career: the individual or the employer.
- *Career as a narrative or story:* Where the 'red threads' that run through our life and career can enable us to construct a coherent narrative to ourselves and others.

In our work as career coaches, we often find that when people are approaching a birthday with a zero, they may begin to reflect on their life and question their current commitments and next steps. Sometimes it is useful to share the list of metaphors, and ask them to choose the metaphors which resonate with them. One of the most popular choices is 'Career as narrative'. It is often one where career coaching can be so useful, in enabling the person to see the 'red threads' that run through their life as a whole, and begin to appreciate that the strengths and qualities they have gained in their whole life have contributed to the story of who they are. These qualities may have developed from personally satisfying achievements, enjoyable events, moments of flow and 'being in the zone', and also life experiences which may have been highs or lows. (See Chapter 11 on Career Tools.)

The 'Squiggly Career' metaphor[12] has gained popularity in recent years. It describes careers as unpredictable, and probably more like a Climbing Frame, where, to progress, you may have to move laterally, rather than vertically, and not in any pre-defined way.

As you read through the chapters of this book, you might find it useful to think of each member of your team and their likely career metaphor preference. Perhaps you will consider showing them the list? It could be a good conversation starter.

Notes

1 Nathan R, Hill L. *Career Counselling*. Sage; 2006.
2 www.who.int/news-room/fact-sheets/detail/mental-health-at-work
3 https://medium.com/@Praiseworthy/harvard-research-finds-employees-need-a-6-1-positive-feedback-ratio-to-perform-their-best-8f14160a8fbd
4 Bridges W. *Transitions: Making Sense of Life's Changes*. Da Capo; 2020.
5 Levinson DJ. *The Seasons of a Man's Life*. Ballantine; 1981.
6 Super DE. A life-span, life-space approach to career development. *Journal of Vocational Behavior*. 1980;16(3): 282–98. https://doi.org/10.1016/0001-8791(80)90056-1
7 Sheehy G. *Predictable Crises of Adult Life*. Bantam Doubleday Dell; 1984.
8 Sullivan S, Forret, ML, Carraher SM, Mainiero, LA. Using the Kaleidoscope Career Model to examine generational differences in work attitudes. *Career Development International*. 2009;14(3):284–302. doi:10.1108/13620430910966442.
9 https://trainingindustry.com/wiki/content-development/the-702010-model-for-learning-and-development/

10 Inkson, K. Images of career: Nine key metaphors. *Journal of Vocational Behavior*. 2004;65(1):96–111. https://doi.org/10.1016/S0001-8791(03)00053-8
11 Herriott P, Pemberton C. *New Deals: The Revolution in Managerial Careers*. J Wiley; 1995.
12 Tupper H, Ellis S. *The Squiggly Career*. Portfolio Penguin; 2020.

Chapter 2

Early Career

Work Expectations and Experience of People in Their Twenties

Rob Nathan

Introduction

This chapter focuses on people in their twenties. It illustrates, through extracts from relevant research, my own client experience, real cases and the lived experience of this group, their vulnerabilities and strengths. The experience of a 'developmental crisis' is not uncommon and often occurs at the 'quarter-life' stage. Interesting research results (Robinson[1]) point to clear gender differences in what contributes to such a crisis.

The chapter also looks at why this age group matters to employers, the strengths they bring and myths associated with this group, and explores whether there is a difference between priorities of the early and late twenties.

Finally, it indicates ways in which managers and coaches can best respond, with longer case studies and some questions for reflection and discussion (I use these regularly on manager training programmes). The chapter ends with suggested tips for managers. At various points in the chapter I suggest certain Career Tools which will be found in Chapter 11.

The aim of this book is to equip anyone with responsibility to support, motivate and develop people at work to do so with understanding, empathy and sensitivity. It is easy to overlook the fact that people bring with them to work their whole life experience, past and present. While previous generations may have accepted a clear division between work and 'personal life', survey data prepared for this chapter and my own experience as a career coach suggest this is not the case today. There has been a revolution that has challenged the boundaries between work and non-work, which may have been fuelled by a combination of Covid-19 and rapidly accelerating technology. As one interviewee put it: 'I started work in 2018, before the pandemic, worked 9–5 and commuted, like everyone else. Then along came Covid and being online became the norm'.

Young people are at the front line of challenging approaches to work which do not always seem reasonable. If employers want to motivate, engage and retain this group of people, it is vital they appreciate their lived experience, and accept them as 'whole people'.

Research for This Chapter

I interviewed and surveyed 30 people, asking which were the most important areas for them in their work, and to what extent they were currently being met.

The results showed a large differential between the degree of importance placed on financial and job security and the degree to which it was being met. There was also a discrepancy between the importance placed on security by individuals and just how important employers (a sample of ten) considered these factors to be for this group. Out of 14 factors, individuals considered financial and job security as 4th and 7th, whereas employers saw them as 13th and 14th.

In answer to the question: *what is the one thing that would make you really excited to take a job?*, growth and development, learning and progression featured but so did culture, atmosphere and alignment of values.

But in answer to the opposite question, *what is the one thing that would make you quit a job*, the blame fell fairly and squarely on the shoulders of bad management, lack of recognition, abuse and a toxic environment.

The other areas individuals saw as insufficiently met at work may shed some light on what may be contributing to what Oliver Robinson[1] referred to as feeling trapped in a job. They were:

- Physical and mental health
- Having the flexibility to balance work and personal life
- Being treated fairly

It is interesting to note that these three factors would all fall under the Herzberg category of 'Hygiene' factors. In 1968, and re-written in 2003[2], Frederick Herzberg developed his theory of 'Motivation and Hygiene Factors of Job Satisfaction'.

Herzberg's findings revealed that certain characteristics of a job are consistently related to job satisfaction, while different factors are associated with job dissatisfaction (see Table 2.1).

The conclusion he drew is that job satisfaction and job dissatisfaction are not opposites.

- The opposite of *Satisfaction* is *No Satisfaction.*
- The opposite of *Dissatisfaction* is *No Dissatisfaction*.

Remedying the causes of dissatisfaction will not create satisfaction. In other words, by granting more and more comfort factors (such as well-being initiatives), employers are stopping dissatisfaction – for a while – but not contributing to satisfaction.

Table 2.1 Herzberg's factors for job satisfaction and dissatisfaction

Factors for Satisfaction	Factors for Dissatisfaction
Achievement	Company policies
Recognition	Supervision
The work itself	Relationship with supervisor and peers
Responsibility	Work conditions
Advancement	Salary
Growth	Status
	Security

Thus, if managers create a healthy work environment but do not provide members of the team with any of the satisfaction factors, the work they are doing will still not be satisfying. This may placate people instead of actually motivating them to improve performance.

To motivate teams, managers should focus on satisfaction factors like achievement, recognition and responsibility. These intrinsic satisfiers are to be found in the way the work itself aligns with an individual's values, motivators and aspirations.

Of course there will always be a variety of factors which influence the way people experience work. Lucy and Briony had a vulnerability in their first work roles which went unrecognised and unsupported.

> I felt very unsupported in my first role as a teacher, my manager was highly critical and there were a lack of positive training opportunities to develop skills, and a culture of workplace bullying.

It is interesting to note from Briony that being 'emotional' was seen as a weakness.

> Particularly as a young female employee at the start of my career (age 21) I felt that my age negatively impacted my work life, and that I was not trusted, seen as emotional (which was seen as a weakness) and singled out for my clothes being inappropriate, despite them being in line with guidance and similar to those worn by others.

Flexibility and fairness came out repeatedly from the survey and seemed to underline the importance that this group places on whole life considerations:

- I work compressed hours that allow me to study alongside my job.
- I was granted ad hoc paid compassionate leave to support my father in law in illness.

- My condensed hours mean I have an extra half day with my son each week.
- My manager allows me to flex my office hours, . . . this is such a massive benefit to me as a mum trying to juggle work and family life.
- If we have a doctors' appointment, we can just take an hour out of the day.
- Some tasks work better in the office such as being creative. Others I need the quiet of home to concentrate. Flexibility extends not just the place of work but also hours. It boils down to trust and giving people the autonomy to decide. There needs to be a good reason for demanding people come into the office.

The Quarter-Life Crisis

The transition from school or college to work is not straightforward. Decision making may be haphazard and, although this can be a time of learning about the world of work, it may coincide with multiple changes. Look out for examples of multiple changes in the case of Atif below.

Atif was experiencing his first role after university, so he had to manage that transition to his first proper work position. He received little or no support and found himself in a role he did not enjoy. There was little sign that anything positive would be coming from the analytical work he undertook, and he never felt valued or recognised. Even later, when he was successful in gaining a new role, he was very much left to his own devices.

> Atif joined an NHS Trust as a Graduate in HR having studied HR Management at University and found himself based in the recruitment team of a quite dysfunctional People Directorate where a blame culture existed and the structures were very hierarchical. Recruitment did not inspire Atif and he did not particularly enjoy analytical work. The recruitment team themselves were too busy trying to fill vacancies to be able to support him, so he was given quite mundane transactional

work. He was asked to call ex-staff to complete a leavers survey as turnover in the Trust was very high.

This uncovered quite a lot of negative feedback which he was asked to collate, analyse and present to the senior HR team. Atif had the impression that no action would be taken from any of his findings.

During this time he moved into a house with some of his old university friends which meant his commute was increased from a 30 minute drive to an hour and a half each way.

Atif successfully completed his graduate course in the Trust and he applied for the first suitable HR vacancy that was advertised (People Promise Manager). He felt frustrated in this new role as many in the organisation did not understand its purpose or scope and his direct manager (the Deputy Director) took a very hands off approach giving him space to 'make the role his own'.

The following questions are ones we use on our career conversations training courses to build empathy and understanding of people's lived experience:

- What emotions do you think Atif was experiencing?
- What was done to help Atif to adjust to his new surroundings?
- What could Atif's manager have done more of to support his transition?

Think back to when you were growing up. What were your hopes for the future? Perhaps you were one of the few people who knew what they wanted to do, stuck to it and made a success of it. But this would not have been the norm. Maybe you knew you didn't want an office job or to be part of a faceless bureaucracy. Or you saw yourself as different, and had a vague notion you wanted to do 'something creative', without knowing what that meant? From my experience as a career coach, young people often talk about their early ideas coming from their families. This is in spite of the huge influence of social media and the infinite availability of information.

Alvin Toffler wrote *Future Shock*[3] in which he described that the pace of change and the sheer amount of information bombarding us has outstripped our ability to absorb, process and reason our way to understanding and using this knowledge. Incredibly, Toffler wrote this *before* the internet crept from the side lines into the mainstream of our lives. So, to process and make sense of this knowledge explosion, and to translate it into a life or career decision, people may seek yet another website, stocked full of information, but still end up confused, perhaps even more so. This reminds me of stories from clients who were sent off to the 'Jobs Library' and had no idea of where to start or how to make sense of the myriad words in front of them.

Several people I interviewed for this chapter spoke of the influence of their family over early career choices. Because of this mix of family influence, lack of life and work experience and a not yet fully formed pre-frontal cortex (that part of the brain responsible for planning, organising and decision making), it is hardly surprising that this age group is likely to experience what Oliver Robinson[1] calls a developmental or quarter-life crisis at any stage in their twenties.

Such a crisis is not necessarily at the beginning or end of something, but can occur at any time during an extended period. People in their twenties, probably more than previous generations at that age, are still experimenting with roles and identity, and are going through the phase of 'Emerging Adulthood'. They may adopt what is called a 'Planned Happenstance'[4] to their career (and life) decision making, having a vague notion of the direction they wish to go, but not wanting yet to commit completely, and thus staying open to experience and experimentation.

Problems arise when this strategy is not working, or there are other factors at play, such as the continuing need to pay off loans, the wish to move away from the parental home, but the inability to afford to buy a property. Robinson defined it as a turning point or a time of transition. It is a time of instability and can last at least a year. People going through a developmental crisis can feel overwhelmed, have trouble coping and struggle with negative emotion. It can be a period of intensive questioning about life.

His research asked this question: *What is the most prevalent feature of your quarter-life crisis?* The answers revealed some interesting gender differentials:

Men:

1 Being trapped in a job you don't want to be in any more
2 Stress and pressure in work
3 An unwanted period of unemployment
4 Financial factors

Women:

1 Relationship break-up
2 Financial factors
3 Being locked in a relationship you don't want
4 Family conflict or crisis

Robinson suggested these factors could be seen as 'locked in' or 'locked out'. Someone can be either trapped in a career, role or relationship, which he described as a search for authenticity and autonomy. Or the individual can't get what they want, which tends to lower self-esteem. Robbins and Wilner[5] suggested that individuals in the throes of a quarter-life crisis may experience insecurity, confusion, loneliness and, most importantly, isolation, driven in part from the realisation that something is missing from their lives, namely a meaningful career or relationship.

Both men and women have financial concerns in their top four choices. Men cite reasons mostly associated with their work while women comment on the importance of personal and family relationships.

Are There Differences Between Early and Late Twenties?

People in their early twenties are kick-starting their careers and may be fresh out of college, university or an apprenticeship. My interviews suggested that even people in their late twenties look on their junior partners as being very much more tech savvy. This 'older' group have also had 2–3 jobs by then, and a few will have entered the property ladder, with all the financial responsibilities that entails. They may have made career decisions which reflected their need for financial security and stability rather than choosing an ideal role. Manjit experienced a big change in corporate culture, which was not to his liking:

> The organisation is quite corporate now. The company I worked for was bought out three years ago. It used to be 25 people and it was personal and I enjoyed being there. Now we have 3,000 people. It is more soulless. I am paid more, but I have no passion at all. Then you felt your contribution was more valuable. Now I have an employee number. I don't get proper feedback from my manager.
> I'm getting to the point where I am thinking is it really what I want to be doing.
> I still think about my dream job but have to pay the bills. When I first started this job it took two years to get used to it.
> It's important to find out what you're good at and it's a balance between enjoyment and stability. It's what you are contributing towards. Right now I don't feel a part of it.

Drew, 28, was also affected by an organisation restructure, and also reflected on his enjoyment of smaller work environments:

> I don't have a sense of purpose. I want to bring my best self to work but currently feel stifled. I would want more support from a manager. After being promised at interview they would bring in a new consultancy-type culture, there was a big restructure and the managers who recruited me left. It feels unproductive . . . no one is really achieving their potential. This is the culture of really large or old companies. I preferred working in smaller environments where I could see the connection between what I did and the purpose overall.

> I always want to know about the bigger picture and how I can add value. It feels that I am being unproductive. After graduating in Industrial Design, I worked for a tiny employer and loved it: I could see how everything connected. I could see how information trickled down and how everything operated. I could connect the dots. I want to work for someone I could learn from and be inspired by. Where I am now is very slow. If you don't have your work recognised you lose your passion.
>
> Now, when I make suggestions about new ways of doing things, I come up against constant blocks: 'It doesn't matter, safety concerns, budgetary constraints, this is not a team or a strategic priority'.
>
> If I was a manager, I would protect the younger ones – I miss the opportunity to excel in design. I need time to understand corporate structures. I lack a clear vision and strategy from leaders who are not good at taking ambiguity and turning into opportunity. Managers should increase their understanding of the motivations of individuals – and individuals need to understand the managers above them. I'd love to succeed in my role.

Francesca, age 30, works for a large organisation in asset management, and reflected on how some of her core needs are not being met at work:

> I'm not able to develop my skills or bring a creativity to work. There is not enough work–life balance. There have been huge changes in the organisation in the leadership team. Before, the manager was much more hands-on. Now my manager is somewhat at a loss. In terms of developing my skills I was working on an exciting new AI-driven project which has now been put on hold.

Although there is some disappointment about lack of personal needs or ideals being met at work, she acknowledged the value of security and focus on well-being:

> We have a great policy on well-being and have access to CBT, doctors, physio, massage. Although we are encouraged to take time for work–life balance, there has been more pressure and the workload has gone up because we are leaner. The company was very good to me when I had to take time off for ill health.

But Francesca was understanding of her manager's predicament:

> My manager is a people pleasing person and goes above and beyond. Recognition is key, which is more difficult when you're working hybrid, when your time is not really appreciated. Recognition as 'awesome' is better than 'thanks'.

At 30, she talked about 'young people':

> Younger people: they very much want to move quickly and job titles are important. They ask 'what are *you* going to give *me*'? And all the questions tend to be on bonuses and money. Waiting two years is too long. They are more tolerant and aware of mental health and well-being. They're not going to kill themselves for seven years and the loyalty is not the same.

One positive offering by this employer is to encourage employees to network with the most senior and influential people. Francesca continued:

> They have lots of opportunities given to them for example, coffee with the CEO, special lunch and learn, voluntary opportunities, meeting senior people, projects abroad.

From these cases, it seems that when an organisation grows, and when the economic climate is supportive, employers may offer a great deal of the 'comfort' or extrinsic factors such as pay, good working conditions and a focus on the well-being of employees, but may neglect the intrinsic motivation and aspirations of the individual in favour of targets and performance.

Why This Age Group Matters to Employers

While any generalisation is at best misguided and at worst can lead to stereotyping and overt bias, there are some trends and truths which are evident that distinguish people born after 1995:

- They are 'digital natives': they are the first generation to have grown up with the internet.
- They can connect online and get knowledge instantly.

- They are more aware than previous generations about what is going on in the world.
- They expect tech processes to be seamless and efficient.
- They hold employers to a high standard regarding their ESG (environmental, social and governance) standpoint.
- They have a proclivity for digital collaboration but also value face-to-face connection.
- They want work that is meaningful, aligned to their values and where they can connect to the wider purpose of the organisation.
- If their strong need for flexibility is not met, they are likely to move on.
- They want their work to be meaningful and see the connection between their input and the overall purpose of the role.
- They have grown up with tech platforms where they have shared their feelings with a wide variety of individuals and groups (although some young people have now 'contracted out' of using social media).
- They have a strong need for financial and job security.

Consider the case of Patrick who found out what meaningful work meant for him by his own experience:

> After my Masters in Art History and Philosophy I dreamed of becoming a museum curator, but they wanted office experience which I didn't have. My mum worked for the NHS and she suggested I try there. I worked initially in radiology doing patient experience, and having generic office jobs. I then saw a job advertised in Organisation Development, which I knew nothing about. I thought it was an admin job. It involved working with the leadership team and I discovered that my values aligned which were around compassion, helping and kindness. People had often spoken about their dreams, but did not know how they would get there. We were enabling people to create those dreams by helping them to develop.

Patrick also linked a thirst for learning and experimentation with a fear of being 'told off':

> Young people bring new perspective, hunger, and want to learn and prove themselves but weaknesses may include anxiety about

> being wrong – they are not experienced enough in how to use their voice. Personally, I have this terrible fear of being told off. And feel that if I don't complete a piece of work well I'll be pulled up for it.
>
> Weaknesses may also be around attention span and interest. Older colleagues will work 9 to 1230 and have a lunch break going to be back at their computer. For me, I will work a little bit, look around, and get a cup of tea and then carry on. It's important that we ensure that the work stays engaging. When I write reports I don't just sit there and do it, I do a little bit, I use PowerPoint, different visual software programs and try and make it fun. I guess looking at TikTok and many different videos has contributed to my attention span.

Patrick followed his values and was fortunate to find an area that aligned with what mattered to him. He acknowledged a lack of confidence about 'using his voice' and a fear of making mistakes. And he also was aware that his approach to work was very different from older generations.

Patrick did not fit many, if any, of the stereotypes often levied at Millennials and Generation Z.

Myths Associated with the Twenties

One Human Resources Director of a Global employer I spoke to challenged some of the stereotypes about Millennials and Generation Z:

> I have pushback on the generalities about Millennials and Generation Z. They are not from another planet! What they want is typical: to progress by working hard for similar reasons to others. Blocks can be affordability of property and significant debt. A lot of young people stay with us for ten years or more, starting as apprentices and graduates. So some of those generalisations are rubbish. We had a speaker recently who said that Generation Z is not as resilient and has mental health issues. This is nonsense – what about the young people in the war in Ukraine. Hardly wishy-washy and overemotional.

But he did make some collective comments himself:

> On an individual basis, I do see some evidence that they like to work a bit differently – flexibly, and with technology this facilitates their ability to work flexibly. Younger people have a greater sense of inclusivity and diversity and are more tolerant and open minded.

I have heard various comments in my interviews:

> They are entitled.
> They lack loyalty.
> They job hop.
> They are lazy and don't want to work hard.

These generalisations are not just unhelpful, they are untrue, If managers and others jump to these false conclusions based on stereotyping, they will not be open to developing the contribution and potential of the younger members of their teams.

How Can Managers and Organisations Respond

Employees matter to employers, but they do not always act as if that was the case. Enabling people in their twenties to see their development within the organisation will evidently contribute to retention. They bring fresh ideas, energy, a willingness to learn and a strong desire to contribute to the purpose of the organisation. Plus a questioning and sometimes critical approach, but also (as in the case of Patrick above) an anxiety about making mistakes and a reluctance to speak out. A 'one-size-fits-all' approach will thus never work. This does not make the job of the manager easy, as they need to take the time to get to know and really listen to and understand each member of their team. Managers too can be nervous about initiating career and developmental conversations.

Use the cases and the questions below to stimulate your thinking about effective ways of responding with empathy to these different people in very different situations. Use the tips below to guide your responses. And do make use of some of the Career Tools available in Chapter 11.

Case Questions

For each of the cases below, answer the following questions:

- What are this person's key concerns?
- What might this person be feeling (but not saying)?
- What are the influences outside of work which impact on work motivation and engagement?
- In what ways could you respond in a supportive and useful way?

Samual

Samual is 30, and a committed and talented member of the team. He joined the organisation in this role two years ago. He is a professional in his field and was pleased to find an employer that aligned with his personal values. He likes the role and the organisation.

The team rely heavily on his expertise and knowledge and his performance has always been high. He is keen to take on a new and exciting challenge, but isn't sure what that might be or what is possible.

While Samual would want to stay within the organisation, there are a lack of obvious career options and, in the past, conversations with his manager have focused on performance rather than aspirations. He does not overtly share his career ambitions at work but talks about this at length with his partner and friends, who are other young professionals. They suggest he should leave the organisation if still in his current role nine months from now as his skills are well sought after in the market.

Samual's manager sees him as a great asset, but her focus thus far been on growth and development of other team members.

Bilal

Bilal really enjoyed all the opportunities the graduate programme has offered, taking advantage of the various rotations.

Two years on having passed a variety of qualifications, he is attached to a department which he ended up in, partly by default. He is a bit disappointed that he is only assisting others in research and analysis rather than taking more responsibility.

Bilal believes he doesn't have the same support as others in terms of development opportunities being flagged to him. He would like to know more about learning and role opportunities, and the experiences of others who have had a long career with the company. He wants to build a clear career plan.

He knows he still has a great deal to learn about the different sectors and products but is not really sure how to go about developing the skills and knowledge needed.

Bilal found taking on a permanent role a bit of a 'shock to the system', after the placements and training and mentoring offered on the graduate programme. He feels a bit 'left in the lurch' now and has no idea how to progress his career and have a plan for the future.

Ellen

Ellen, aged 28, has been with the organisation as an administrative assistant since graduating from university. She has received consistently good feedback. Ellen is married with two children and has recently returned to work following maternity leave following the birth of her second child. She is the main breadwinner as her husband's work as a freelance photographer is somewhat erratic.

Ellen is very committed to her work and has put in more than her fair share of long hours. She has recently received feedback that she is a potential Team Leader and her Department Head would like her to attend the Management Development Programme.

Ellen is ambivalent about putting herself forward for the programme. On the one hand, there is pressure from her husband to 'go for it'; since her potential higher earnings would mean that they could educate their children privately, which he would like. On the other hand, Ellen has always lacked self-belief in spite of her career progressing well. There is also the issue of her children – she is concerned about the increased demands an upward move would place on her time.

She is also anxious about the implication of turning down the opportunity offered by the Management Development Programme. Would she be seen as a failure? What would be the alternative career moves within and outside the organisation?

Maria

Maria, now aged 23, attended a local girls' school. Her father was a construction worker and her mother served in the local bakers, and they lived in social housing. Although Maria did well at school and stayed on to study for A levels, she never thought about applying for university, as no one in her family had ever been. After leaving school, she was unemployed for several months before finding work as a receptionist in the organisation, where she has also been able to use her computer skills.

> She has always been told how well she has been doing by her manager. She was therefore very upset to be unsuccessful in her application for a more senior role, following a recent re-organisation.
>
> Meanwhile, a friend has been encouraging her to leave work and apply for university, to study Law. On the other hand her father couldn't understand why she wanted to do the course, saying 'you've got a good job already'. Maria was in fact offered a place at university, but, at the last minute, found she was unable to bring herself to accept. She is uncertain about her future direction, in or out of the organisation.

Tips for Managers to Have Holistic Career Conversations

A holistic approach:

- Show an interest in the person's whole life: what are the influences outside of work which might impact on work motivation and engagement?
- Show flexibility towards whole life needs (mental and physical health, well-being, work–life balance) but be clear about what is expected in terms of delivery.
- If your team member expresses anxiety or emotion, listen without judging or trying to solve the problem. Be aware of professional well-being supports within your organisation or in the community.

Listening with a positive intent:

- Listen properly to the needs of every member of your team, and allow new members to feel important in sharing ways they might approach a project, especially in the use of tech.

- Focus on the positive, not just the gaps. Look for the strengths of the person's experience, in or out of work, that can be transferred to the team and the work.
- Enable your team members to feel psychologically safe – not fussing or mollycoddling, but providing a space where they can air their concerns, aspirations and be honest.
- Use open questions such as 'what's currently going well / what are you learning / what are you struggling with'?

The work itself:

- Recognise that people in their twenties are learning and exploring. They have not yet decided on 'the right career'.
- Help your team members to understand the work, its overall purpose and connection to the wider mission of the organisation.
- Give as much responsibility as soon as possible.
- Give genuine appreciation and recognition of work well done.
- Encourage job crafting: this is the process of making changes to a job inch by inch to make it more fulfilling.

Growth, development and confidence building:

- Provide opportunities for stretch and growth but alongside support.
- Provide opportunities for young people to try out new roles or at least be involved in a variety of projects, if they wish.
- Build confidence by helping them to build their 'psychological capital' – see the Chapter 11 Career Tools 'Work Values' and 'When I'm at My Best'.

Regular communication:

- Provide opportunities for team members to learn from each other.
- Have regular catch ups and opportunities for two-way feedback.
- Consider reverse mentoring.
- Focus on organisation, department and individual common goals.

Notes

1 Robinson O, Wright GRT, Smith, JA. The holistic phase model of early adult crisis. *Journal of Adult Development*. 2013;20(1):27–37. doi:10.1007/s10804-013-9153-y.
2 Herzberg F. *One More Time: How Do You Motivate Employees?* 2003. https://hbr.org/2003/01/one-more-time-how-do-you-motivate-employees
3 Toffler A. *Future Shock*. Turtleback Books, Bound for Schools & Libraries; 1999.
4 Mitchell, KE, Levin, AS, Krumboltz, JD. Planned happenstance: Constructing unexpected career opportunities. *Journal of Counseling & Development*. 1999;77(2):115–24. https://doi.org/10.1002/j.1556-6676.1999.tb02431.x
5 Robbins, A, Wilner, A. *Quarterlife Crisis: The Unique Challenges of Life in Your Twenties*. Penguin Putnam; 2001.

Chapter 3

Mid-Career

The Impact of Experience

Rob Nathan

I had a client who, at 21, told me 'I feel really old'.

Rather than label people as mid-life or mid-career, what I notice is the many ways in which life experiences affect energy and engagement with work. Those experiences of course may be in or out of work, and managers and coaches need to be open to how such cumulative experiences, as well as ways in which current work and non-work responsibilities, impact the person in front of them.

Does the Mid-Life Crisis Exist?

This chapter focuses on people's life experience which may be in 'mid-career' or mid-life. This varies as individuals may feel they are in mid-career/life from 35 upwards. It will illustrate, through extracts from relevant research, my own client experience, real cases, and the lived experience of this group, their vulnerabilities and strengths. The aim is to enable anyone supporting people in these 'middle years', including managers, coaches and mentors, to be able to appreciate how their life and work experience might impact engagement at work and, thereby, to be more likely to identify and utilise their strengths.

A lot has been written about the so-called 'mid-life crisis' – and sometimes this has been an object of mockery. In 2019 Professor Mark Jackson told the Royal Society that men in mid-life need support, not derision. *Many people can reach 40 and suddenly realise that all the success they had once hoped for in relationships and jobs has not happened*. His tenet, and I agree with him, is that this is a neglected group.

Brene Brown suggests that the word 'crisis' is inaccurate, as that word implies an intense and time-limited experience that can be controlled and managed'[1]. She prefers to use 'unravelling', which describes a chronic condition rather than an acute episode. It is thus something which creeps up gradually, and refers to a burgeoning awareness of the finite. It comes with the challenge of reviewing relationships and achievements, along with the responsibilities of caring for family.

> The truth is that the midlife unravelling is a series of painful nudges strung together by low-grade anxiety and depression, quiet desperation, and an insidious loss of control . . . seldom enough for people on the outside to validate the struggle or offer you help and respite. It's the dangerous kind of suffering – the kind that allows you to pretend that everything is OK.

At some point during this 'unravelling', it may be that people begin to reflect on their life experiences to date. Bill Gothard[2] drew on Levinson's[3] dated but seminal work where he described several polarities that indicate the kind of changes going on for someone reflecting on their life. These include:

- **Young–old:** Where we may be observing younger generations entering the world of work and begin to feel older (despite still feeling youthful inside) or 'left behind'.
- **Destruction–creation:** Where we may begin to face our own mortality whilst having an increasing desire to express our own creativity and autonomy.
- **Attachment–separateness:** Attaching to the world of work through our desire to adapt and evolve, whilst developing a greater sense of separateness through developing our internal world through reflection.

I have worked with many clients who present with a conflict in terms of what they really want. They may feel frustrated with their lack of progression but also have a developing need to express their autonomy. An understanding and empathic manager can make a huge difference to someone experiencing these conflicts and perhaps enable that person to become clearer. Often I find that clients are wanting to do something more meaningful. And, with age and experience, that need may become more urgent, as their external world matches less and less their internal reflections. This is what 39-year-old Layla said:

> Although I enjoy a lot of what I do, I don't want to do it forever. And I had a burnout two years ago. I feel like I'm firefighting all day. There's more and more pressure that I am holding. There are 200 emails in my inbox almost every day. There are deadlines – clients who are being demanding. I need more time to train new people properly.
> I went through a divorce eight years ago. My employer was incredibly supportive and gave me as much time as I needed. I decided to change things after my burnout and my employer agreed to give me a three-month sabbatical.
> I am a different person now – I am more aware of my values and how I want to work. Now, I lead much more by intuition and empathy. I have a curiosity for people, I want to support people and help them to avoid burnout. At 29 I wanted to be recognised and be seen. This is not so important today. I realise that I have an empathic side. I'm good at holding the space for people.

After her burnout, Layla evaluated what mattered to her, and resolved to realise more her creative and autonomous self. She also was becoming less 'attached' to the need to strive and be recognised by her employer. She was going through an inner transition towards matching her inner self with her outer actions.

There are many other experiences which can contribute to a reflection about self and what really matters. It is not uncommon to experience a bereavement of a friend or family member, or to receive a significant health diagnosis. One colleague I spoke to described the impact of receiving a late diagnosis of neurodiversity:

> Having a late diagnosis for neurodiversity can be a big challenge. Am I the same or different person? How do other people see me? Will my manager assume that I was the person I was before? Will they continue to see the more superficial work focus side of me rather than the whole person?

Chapter 5 explores in some detail the impact of neurodiversity in the workplace. The above example demonstrates starkly the distinction between what a person might be experiencing on the inside and the outer projected side which, like the proverbial tip of the iceberg, is the only visible part, but which hides a maelstrom of deeper activity. The question is – how relevant is all this to the world of work, and how can the people responsible for supporting, engaging, coaching and managing individuals respond appropriately?

Before I move on to how managers and coaches can effectively support people going through this middle or reflective period, I want to delve a little deeper into what might be contributing to this mid-life 'unravelling'.

Why Does Happiness Get Harder in Your Forties?

In his book *The Happiness Curve*[4] Jonathan Rauch says:

> I was not comparing my forty-year-old self to my twenty-year-old self, as the twenty-year-old version of me had assumed I would. I was comparing myself to other forty somethings in my peer group, many of whom also had sustained relationships (often longer), accumulated wealth (often more), and achieved professional status (often higher). True, I was better off than most of humanity, but most of humanity was not my comparison group.

Rauch draws on repeated research indicating that happiness is U-shaped. The younger and older years are characterised by greater happiness, while the middle years more by turbulence, uncertainly and questioning.

I can only pose some questions here, through examples and my experience of career coaching, as life experiences as well as any biological or physiological changes are experienced differently at an individual level. Yet it is known that unhappiness can lead to anxiety and depression, and that the highest suicide rates occur at around age 50, with men being three times more likely to commit suicide than women[5]. This would imply that the forties are a challenge for many people.

Perhaps, with the middle years, comes a period of greater work demands, maybe elderly relatives require more time, care and attention, and it could be that teenage or older children are making financial or emotional demands.

Life expectancy is significantly higher than for previous generations. *The Hundred Year Life*[6] suggests that the traditional three stages of education, working and retirement are neither true nor relevant to today's world. There is more of a blurred boundary and a fluidity to our life experiences. We don't, indeed cannot, stop learning when we leave school or university. We may well have several careers in our lifetime. Living longer comes with benefits, but also numerous potential burdens. Enough money is needed to pay for a longer life, which impacts on pension contributions as well as current outgoings.

The authors say that, at a time when needed skills for work are changing rapidly, learning, up-skilling and personal and professional development are becoming increasingly important. They describe the skills and qualities that will stand us in good stead, emphasising the usefulness of having a 'juvenescene' mind-set (carrying youthfulness, plasticity and playfulness forward throughout our adult lives) and a sense of efficacy (believing I am competent) and agency (believing I have the control).

This is all going on at a time when a person in their forties may have experienced periods of unemployment or may be fearful they could be in line for redundancy. In his book *Healing the Wounds*[7]

David Noer writes about the complacency that many employers have demonstrated in assuming that employees left behind after major layoffs would be grateful and thus be utterly engaged and focused. They were wrong, as those same people became far less engaged and focused.

Of course, it is impossible to ignore the biggest external event that has impacted so many people in generations – Covid-19.

Ronan explained his response to work post-pandemic:

> Since Covid, I have been less motivated and am realising that I use work to value myself. Today I am doing things, many things – I don't see the purpose. I nearly had burnout. Work is just a means, not my identity. I had one and a half years really struggling with purpose. At 50, you suddenly must balance what is required with what is important. I was so committed and spent so much time on the computer. I didn't pay attention to my physical needs.

Ronan described how attached he became to his work. Work can merge with a person's identity, sometimes so much so that it becomes increasingly difficult to notice the impact of external demands, until those demands overwhelm, and the energy output is greater than energy input. Ronan neglected himself, even his physical well-being, until burnout beckoned, and he was forced to take corrective action.

Career Needs of People in Mid-Life

One person I interviewed for this chapter, a senior manager responsible for career development in a global organisation, told me:

> As people progress in their career they may start to need more from their employer, as the cost of changing jobs increases. For example, they may need more support in terms of work–life balance. Job security becomes more important as outgoings are possibly at their height, as well as responsibilities for adolescent children and elderly relatives.

This time of life is often one of greatest stress, and one of deep reflection. It may also be a time of wanting to learn and grow. A question for managers and employers is how to position themselves to best respond to their team members in consideration of their life circumstances, and to reduce or eliminate the inclination to see the more superficial side of a person.

Another person I interviewed put it as follows:

> They just see the most superficial work focus side of me rather than the whole person. This person might be peri-menopausal as well as neurodiverse and therefore suffering from brain fog. You may have built a reputation from the past but now things are different, and both the manager and you put pressure on yourself.

Carole Carlson[8] agrees that this time of life can be challenging and emotionally demanding, citing some common questions that people in mid-life can raise:

- How do I continue to have impact in my professional life?
- How do I get my changing interests and values met at work?
- What can I do that really adds value?
- How do I transition to a new area where I could be successful?
- How can I contribute?

She suggests that some people may have invested in the success of their work ambitions at the expense of maintaining quality relationships with family and friends. Often, I see people for career coaching in mid-life who are in somewhat of a hurry to transition to something new. They may have been successful and become competent in their particular area, but cannot see themselves remaining in that career or sector for the rest of their working lives. People in their mid-forties are today contemplating another 20–25 years of work. They want to spend time examining and making sense of their interests, their values, so they can move forward to what Avivah Wittenberg-Cox calls 'Q3' – the third quarter of their lives.

There seems to be some tendency among mid-lifers to cling on to their jobs for fear of not gaining re-employment. Ageism and concern about ageism may have something to do with this.

Biases Against People in Mid-Life

One BBC Worklife article states: 'Gen X workers are being passed over for roles of all kinds, especially as employers see young people as more malleable'[9].

Mid-life workers may be caught in the middle between the younger digital natives and the older, steadier and less ambitious workers (see Chapter 4: Later Career). Managers may thus be faced with someone desperate to hang on to their job but who no longer gains any joy from it, and who has lost any sense of ambition or clarity about ways in which they can develop.

Women in mid-life face particular challenges, many of which are explored in Chapters 7, 8 and 10 on Career Returners, supporting parents and talking about the menopause. Ammerman and Groysberg[10] asked a group of 100 senior women at what stage in their careers they had experienced the most gender bias or discrimination, and half of their respondents reported that this has been in mid-career – between their middle thirties and late forties. They found three major challenges:

- Unfair assumptions

One assumption was that women who are parenting and in mid-career are not committed to leadership. Another was that women are less suitable for leadership than men and coping with 'high pressure' jobs.

- Unhelpful attention

The women they talked to mentioned hyper-scrutiny and scepticism in mid-career and the dilemma of the 'competency-likeability' double-bind, where you are seen as either ruthless or motherly.

- Unequal access

The authors reported that networks become highly gendered at mid-career level with 'men having superior access to senior leaders'.

They purport that leaders can aim to introduce objective measures of performance, but these too can contain bias.

A study by Encompass Equality[11] suggested the following to be the most important factors in convincing women to stay or leave their job:

1. Support from line manager
2. The day-to-day work
3. Team
4. Organisational culture

What leaders and managers could do is to show vulnerability, admit that they are sometimes wrong, and devote enough time getting to know all their people, to understand their lives as a whole and their aspirations. They may then be less likely to lose some very good and talented employees if more widely supported by the organisation's culture.

Many of the biases experienced by mid-lifers also apply to older workers. But, since mid-lifers are on the way to becoming older workers, that is not surprising.

One bias is the view that 'older people' are not as flexible or creative as their younger counterparts: research by Grabmeier[12], based on a study of Nobel laureates in economics, suggests that there are two cycles of creativity: one that some demonstrate early in their career (conceptual) and another that occurs later in life (experimental). The study found evidence that the most conceptual laureate delivered their single best work at age 25, while for the most experimental laureate this happened in their early or mid-fifties (see Chapter 4 for a deeper discussion on the over-55s). While conceptual innovators tend to challenge conventional wisdom and come up with new ideas suddenly, experimental innovators acquire knowledge throughout their careers and then analyse, interpret and synthesise that data into new ways of understanding.

Another bias is the view that younger people think (and thus learn) more quickly than older people. Interestingly, Raymond Cattell[13] described two types of intelligence: fluid and crystallised. Fluid intelligence is 'the ability to perceive relationships independent of previous specific practice or instruction concerning those relationships'. Fluid intelligence involves being able to think and reason abstractly and solve problems. This ability is considered independent of learning, experience and education. Crystallised intelligence is the accumulation of knowledge, facts and skills that are acquired throughout life (otherwise defined as wisdom). Fluid intelligence begins to decline after adolescence, but crystallised intelligence continues to increase throughout adulthood.

There is plenty of evidence to suggest that brain training can improve both fluid and crystallised intelligence. Suggestions to develop fluid and crystallised intelligence include:

- Learn a language
- Develop a skill
- Socialise with different people
- Think of new ways to do things
- Introduce variety into the day
- Take on tasks which stretch and challenge
- Take aerobic exercise

Ladders or Development?

Avivah Wittenberg-Cox represents mid-life (Q2–Q3) as a time of turmoil and uncertainty about the present and the future. On one episode of her podcast 4 Quarter Lives[14] she interviewed Helen Tupper, Co-Founder and CEO of Amazing If. Helen said that people get stuck on thinking about ladders, not development. My view is that they have been taught, by experience, that ascending through grades is the only way that progress is truly recognised. There is a tendency to see only opportunities similar and more senior to their current role.

This is too narrow a view. So, we need to broaden perspective and move from a planned and linear way of thinking towards possibility thinking. One exercise in Chapter 11 on the Career Tools, 'Planned Happenstance', can help to develop such a broader view of the future.

Mid-Career Dilemmas and How to Support

Below I list some questions that may be posed in a mid-career coaching conversation. The four-stage framework outlined in Chapter 9 can provide a structure to respond with empathy and pragmatism to these questions. The key is to remember that the manager or coach is an enabler, not a problem solver or provider of solutions. The statements and questions listed below are examples of what I call 'empathic statements'. Such statements start with a reflection on the current felt status quo and what the person would like to be different. The question is then phrased in a way that makes a collaborative career conversation realistic. You may like to make a list of the kinds of statements mid-life employees might want to address.

- I want to boost my visibility with the leadership team; how can I do this?
- My personal circumstances have changed and I want to get the right work–life balance, but still want to be achieving and adding value at work. Can we explore options together as to how I can get this to work?
- I want to work on more challenging and fulfilling projects. How can I secure these opportunities?
- How can I align my career with the department's goals for the next few years?
- How can I grow and develop in my current role?
- Are there any opportunities for collaborating with other departments?
- Are there are any current or future promotional opportunities for me?

- I'm feeling disillusioned with the lack of impact my role is having. I don't feel I am making a difference and I want to. How can I change this?
- I'm exhausted. My elderly parents have become very ill/needy/dependent, and I have to spend more time seeing them. Can we talk about how I could work more days virtually?
- Since returning from secondment, I have been unable to get a permanent internal role. I did a one-year maternity leave cover, a four months manager cover of an overseas team, and I am now in a temporary role. I am not working to my potential and am not demonstrating my strengths. Can we talk about what roles I could work towards, as I don't want to leave?

The Strengths of Mid-Life Experience

Employers do not want to risk losing valued skills, knowledge and experience. One organisation I work with found the following results from their annual Employee Engagement Survey: 50% cited 'lack of opportunity for career advancement' as their main reason for leaving the company; 32% said that career growth was the principal reason for staying. I imagine this does not tell the whole story, and that there is a build-up to perhaps a final straw which convinces a person to leave.

People mostly want to stay in their work role, unless it becomes untenable for a range of reasons. One of the employers I interviewed for this chapter highlighted:

> I'd say people in mid-career are certainly more interested in pursuing meaningful and purpose driven careers that feel authentic and fulfilling as well as providing a work/life balance.

One public sector employer said:

> People within this age bracket may have repeatedly experienced the impact of austerity within the public sector and so are experiencing change fatigue.

Another emphasised the importance of being valued for their skills. Many employers don't have plans for people who have progressed as far as they can but don't see any opportunities for themselves. These people may feel overlooked or forgotten. They may have a desire to change but are locked in financially.

People who are exhausted, locked in or uncertain of their future direction are not well placed to value their own skills, strengths, knowledge and experience, let alone be able to imagine how they could be used better or differently in the future. But strengths or 'assets' they do have, as Gratton and Scott point out.

They refer to groups of 'intangible assets', those resources we acquire throughout life:

1 Productive assets such as skills and knowledge (expertise)
2 Vitality assets: mental, physical health and well-being (energy and drive)
3 Transformational assets: self-knowledge, support networks and openness to new experiences

Even if these assets are either present or developing, they may not always be visible, and thus not recognised or utilised by the employer or the individual. For example, some experienced employees may want to support or mentor their colleagues. When I have set up training programmes for career mentor volunteers in organisations, there is often a long waiting list of people who want to be involved.

As people gain in experience and self-knowledge, they want increasingly to have work that matches their values. Many may also want to be challenged. As one employer put it, they give:

> Support by providing opportunities to constantly develop and evolve within and beyond their current role. Inclusion in visible projects which offer stretch and challenge and the chance to acquire new skills.

Career workshops, career coaching and regular career conversations which focus on aspirations and not performance can also tap into these dormant but vital assets. Another employer told me what they provide:

> Specific mid-career workshops, regular career development conversations with all, career coaching and mentoring, staff apprenticeships, career mobility schemes.

So how can employers, managers and coaches enable these assets not only to be identified, but also to be valued, recognised and utilised?

Recognising and Utilising Age-Diverse Team Strengths

The CIPD's *Managing an Age-Diverse Workforce: What Employers Need to Know*[15] highlighted the following perceived benefits of age diverse teams:

- Knowledge-sharing, different perspectives and enhanced customer experience were identified as key benefits of age diversity.
- There is widespread appreciation that both younger and older colleagues can add value in these areas.
- Younger colleagues feel that older age groups can share practical experience and expertise, while older colleagues look to younger groups for skills training and new working methods.

In his book *Managing the Gap*[16] Steve Butler reinforces the importance of knowledge sharing:

> As our workforce ages, transferring knowledge from one generation to another will become a key activity.

He also suggests that younger workers can help their more mature colleagues keep up to date with the latest in tech.

Butler continues:

> To help businesses function smoothly in a time of rapid change, it's important to have people around who have longstanding client relationships, who can remember best practices developed over years and who can provide some continuity with the past.

In Butler's own organisation, systems are in place to encourage everyone to speak up if they wish. Some younger people's voices are not heard. In Chapter 2, we saw that Patrick experienced that very challenge:

> Young people bring new perspective, hunger, and want to learn and prove themselves but weaknesses may include anxiety about being wrong – they are not experienced enough in how to use their voice. Personally, I have this terrible fear of being told off.

Butler is clearly committed to creating effective age diverse teams. He cites Wegge's research[17]. When teams mix older and younger workers, productivity goes up and complex problems find more novel solutions because the strengths and weaknesses of both groups are balanced.

The Behavioural Insights team[18] suggests going right back to the recruitment stage, and challenging age bias in recruitment practices.

Work Engagement

Given the evidence that mid-lifers may experience several challenges and conflicts, I often find that this can surface in the form of a lack of engagement with the work and the workplace. So, what can employers and managers do to increase engagement at a time of possible disengagement?

Research by Deloitte[19] and McKinsey[20] suggests the several key elements which contribute to work engagement. These are three of them:

- **Create a culture of recognition:** This varies from person to person, industry to industry, but without it, people will lose motivation and not feel valued.
- **Balance five pieces of praise to one area of criticism or development:** Positive psychology research suggests we remember more easily any negative comments than positive ones. So we need to work harder at the positive ones!
- **Build trust:** If your team members feel their judgement, character and autonomy are respected and trusted, they will deliver much more.

The above points of course apply for any age group, but at a time when mid-lifers may be questioning their commitment to the work or the organisation, when they may be feeling overlooked, and that their future is uncertain, managers who build trust, recognition and an inclination to praise rather than criticise will go some way to re-generating engagement.

The 'CCS Work Engagement Wheel' (see Career Tools in Chapter 11) can be used by managers to gain a sense of the areas that need to be addressed with their team to build engagement. The following factors are included:

Stable, Secure Work Experience
Job and financial security
Physical and mental health

Trusting Relationships
Work with people I trust
Being recognised for my work

Social Cohesion and Inclusion
Being treated fairly
Having supportive co-workers

Individual Purpose and Contribution
Achieving work goals
Fulfilling my personal purpose
Bringing my best self to work
Balancing work and personal life

Building on the value of focusing on strengths, Seligman's PERMA Model[21] outlines five factors characteristic of a flourishing individual:

P: Increasing positive emotion, which can come from appreciation and praise.
E: Engagement or 'flow' are more likely to occur when people use their top strengths.
R: Relationships in the PERMA model refers to feeling supported and valued by others. There is evidence of this everywhere, but social connections become particularly important as we age.
M: Meaning is defined as serving something greater than ourselves. Having a purpose helps individuals focus on what is important in the face of significant challenges or adversity.
A: A sense of accomplishment and well-being results from achievements and working towards goals.

There is a plethora of research studies which suggest that praise should outweigh criticism by a 4/5/6:1 ratio, but there is little data that suggests a clear improvement in work performance. I prefer the voice of experience from Hughie, an ex-Olympian, and now a manager and coach:

> I've so far come up with about 16 areas that should be met by managers to ensure they get the most out of their teams. They include: Acceptance, Achievement, Appreciation, Attention, Encouragement, Fairness, Inclusion, Praise, Respect, Security, I've learnt that when core needs are met, the following are all high, including motivation, staff retention, performance and morale! I've also been looking into positive communication which I also use when I coach my athletes and I find it to be very effective and motivating! This includes being more selective with the use of certain words, for example: 'No, But, Not, Unfortunately, Error' And words ending with 'n't' e.g.: 'Can't Don't Won't'. I've found that the combination of positive communication plus meeting of core needs maximises staff morale and motivation!

Guidelines for Managers

The operational side of work is important, and tasks need to be completed on time, to budget and to a certain standard. This means that your people need to be in good enough shape to deliver. Here are a few tips to support the engagement of mid-life employees:

Using strengths:

- Optimise the general and individual strengths of the team.
- Strengths spot: use the Skills and Strengths Grid (see Chapter 9) to notice any strengths or skills your team member demonstrates and give them this positive feedback.
- Use the 6:1 ratio for positive–negative comments.
- Allow each person's voice to be heard and feel validated, and that they matter.
- Make use of the person's accumulated institutional knowledge and experience.
- Consider pairing up team members, with people having complementary strengths, and who can balance and support one another.

Development:

- Use the four-stage Career Conversations framework described in Chapter 9 to enable your team members to consider a variety of ways to develop, other than by focusing on the 'next level up'.
- Encourage your direct reports to focus on incremental steps towards a range of goals, rather than just considering the 'big prize' (which may be management in your organisation).

Well-being and meaning:

- Enable team members to find more meaning in their current role (one study found that doctors who devote at least 20% of their time to meaningful tasks have less chance of burnout).
- Find ways for the individual to coach or mentor younger colleagues.

- Have regular catch-ups to keep people informed about how their work connects to the bigger purpose of the department/function/business.

Balance and burnout:

- Keep a watch out for signs of potential burnout. This might be a change in usual behaviour, such as a poor work–life balance, lack of concentration, habitual tiredness, irritability, increased emotional response, overwhelm and working too hard.
- Help your team member set clear boundaries about time devoted to work and other activities.
- Encourage team members to take regular breaks.
- Provide a regular, non-threatening space to have confidential discussions.

Job Crafting[22]

Valuing skills and experience was mentioned in my primary research as a key element influencing retention. Many jobs can be adapted to suit the job holder. Just look at the same job being done by different people – it is never done in the same way. Job crafting can be a way of reinforcing a person's autonomy and individuality whilst increasing work engagement and enhancing performance.

Start by allowing your team member to voice their view of how they could improve the way the job is done, and how they could apply their unique skills or knowledge to it. Might there be ways in which your team member could build relationships in or outside the team to improve the quality of the work?

Do refer to the Strengths and Skills Grid in Chapter 9 as a basis for exploring with your team member which skills and strengths they could apply to the role.

Job Crafting Cases

How would you go about job crafting with Tom, who appears to have a self-limiting belief of only being able to do what he knows?

> Tom aged 48, has been working in the same department and job function for 15 years. He has however had a wide range of assignments during this period. But, since the arrival of a new department head two years ago, he feels that his good performance is never recognised. Despite finding work dispiriting, he believes that changing his job is not a realistic option.
>
> 'What else could I do?' he thinks. 'I'm no longer capable of performing any other duties'. He is convinced that younger staff members have a better skill set and hence his applications would not even be considered. He is also wary of jumping into yet another poor working environment.
>
> He cannot see a way out. His wife has just taken early retirement to set up a small antiques business. They have two children at university.

In Helen's story below, she 'crafted' her own approach to her job, and was able to use and develop skills and confidence that stood her in good stead over the long term.

> One of my early jobs, in underwriting and payment collection, gave me skills I use today. We used analytical skills to assess risk about customers. We had to ask them questions about their background. We had targets on how much we had to reduce the debt. We had to be very disciplined. A lot of people absconded when they were in arrears. You had to think about the situation you are in and what you can do to find out about the borrower. I continuously had to think around the problem. Despite being one of the few females, I was one of the top performers. I treated customers with respect. Of course, there were some people who never intended to pay the money back – but an awful lot more had lost their job or their relationship.
>
> I learned a lot from this job: persistence, thinking about tactics and, most importantly, using your own style to get results.

Marcus was able to put his life experience to good use in his role as a Human Resources manager:

> Marcus's wife passed away around eight years ago which resulted in him becoming a single dad to their two children. The key challenges he faced included what he should prioritise in and out of work. Work was a good place for him to escape from his challenging personal situation. He was grateful for good friendships at work, and it helped that he has a strong sense of purpose towards his role and the impact he makes. He was encouraged by his own manager to find ways to bring his many strengths and skills to the role, for example, his emotional intelligence, leadership, empathy, resilience, his technical HR skills and knowledge. In particular he thought he could bring his understanding of life as a single parent to demonstrate understanding for others in a similar situation. As a result, Marcus set up a support group for single parents – the organisation already had a number of other support groups in place.

Malik's work engagement could benefit from adapting the work to play to his strengths. How might you go about this, as his manager?

> Malik is 49 and works as a senior IT consultant for the UK division of an American IT consultancy, managing a team of six. He has worked in sales IT for 20 years, the last five being for his current employer.
>
> He has met or surpassed his targets annually, is well remunerated and is considered a valuable member of the talent cohort. However, he feels he is not sufficiently recognised for his team-leading and relationship-building skills.
>
> He is beginning to feel jaded and disillusioned and sees the culture prioritising short-term profit before longer-term relationship building and the work no longer feels meaningful.

> Above all, he feels he is 'duping' some clients into buying software solutions they don't really need. He never minded this previously but recently he has found himself wondering about the point of what he is doing.
>
> Recently divorced with three children from a previous marriage, he has a new partner, and he is seeking a better work–life balance. He doesn't know what to do to alleviate his increasing unhappiness at work.

Dina's concern revolves around how to maintain her work–life balance while still progressing in her career. How could you go about enabling her to develop her job role and to stay engaged?

> Dina has worked for the same employer for 11 years. She feels very lucky, as they have supported her during two maternity leaves, and she has been able to gain promotion to a senior role while keeping her 3.5 days a week. At 39, she feels she has been successful by managing expectations and having clear boundaries. But her current concern is that she feels tied to her employer, and that no-one outside will be interested in employing her for 3.5 days. And she is still ambitious. Her partner has recently been made redundant and, while he helps more with childcare, she is still the main home manager.

Summary
- People in mid-life may be reflecting deeply about different aspects of their lives – their relationships, their work, their achievements – and their values.
- It can be a time of great responsibility, with adolescent children, caring for elderly parents and the need to keep up 'a front' of holding things together, when it can feel like anything but.

- People in mid-life may feel that time is passing them by, and they are not as quick or tech-savvy as their younger colleagues.
- Mid-lifers are individuals and generalisations are fraught with potential bias.
- Managers can recognise the individual needs of their mid-life team member while still fulfilling the requirements of the business. This can be done by 'job crafting' – tailoring the way the team member conducts their job in accordance with their preferred way of working, and perhaps any identified development.
- A holistic career coaching approach involves providing the time, space and empathy to really listen to a team member – listening to learn, not to respond.

Notes

1. https://brenebrown.com/articles/2018/05/24/the-midlife-unraveling/
2. Gothard B. The mid life transition and career counseling in Britain. *Journal of Career Development*. 1996;23(2), 167–74.
3. Levinson DL et al. *The Seasons of a Man's Life*. Knopf; 1978.
4. Rauch J. *The Happiness Curve: Life Gets Better After 50*. Thomas Dunne; 2018.
5. www.samaritans.org/about-samaritans/research-policy/suicide-facts-and-figures/
6. Gratton L, Scott A. *The Hundred Year Life: Living and Ageing in a World of Longevity*. Bloomsbury; 2016.
7. Noer D. *Healing the Wounds: Overcoming the Trauma of Layoffs and Revitalizing Downsized Organizations*. Jossey-Bass; 2009.
8. Carlson, C. *Carole Carlson: Coaching Midlifers Through Their 3rd Quarter Transitions*. 4 Quarter Lives Podcast; 16 November 2022.
9. www.bbc.com/worklife/article/20240320-gen-x-workplace-ageism
10. https://hbr.org/2022/09/3-workplace-biases-that-derail-mid-career-women
11. Encompass Equality. *Why Women Leave*. July 2023. www.encompassequality.com/reports
12. Grabmeier J. Creativity is not just for the young. *Ohio State News*; 2019. https://news.osu.edu/creativity-is-not-just-for-the-young-study-finds
13. Horn JL, Cattell RB. Age differences in fluid and crystallized intelligence. *Acta Psychologica*. 1967;26:107–29. doi:10.1016/0001–6918(67)90011-x
14. Wittenburg-Cox, A. *Democratising Career Development*. 4 Quarter Lives Podcast; 14 February 2024.

15 www.cipd.org/globalassets/media/knowledge/knowledge-hub/reports/managing-an-age-diverse-workforce_2015-what-employers-need-to-know_tcm18–10832.pdf
16 Butler S. *Manage the Gap: Achieving Success with Intergenerational Teams*. Rethink Press; 2019.
17 Wegge J, Jungmann F, Liebermann S, Shemla M, Ries BC, Diestel S, Schmidt KH. What makes age-diverse teams effective? Results from a six-year research program. *Work*. 2012;41:5145–51. doi:10.3233/WOR-2012–0084-5145.
18 www.bi.team/blogs/bridging-the-generation-gap-promoting-age-diversity-in-the-workplace
19 www2.deloitte.com/mt/en/pages/human-capital/articles/mt-employee-engagement-and-covid-19.html
20 www.mckinsey.com/business-functions/people-and-organizational-performance/our-insights/covid-19-and-the-employee-experience-how-leaders-can-seize-the-moment
21 https://positivepsychology.com/perma-model/
22 Wrzesniewski, A, Dutton, JE. Crafting a job: Revisioning employees as active crafters of their work. *Academy of Management Review*. 2001;26(2):179–201. doi.org/10.5465/amr.2001.4378011

Chapter 4

Later Career
Opportunities and Challenges Faced by Older Workers

Gilly Freedman

Introduction

This client, Clara, came to see me for some career coaching feeling thoroughly disillusioned:

> I've worked in this organisation for a few years now and I'm the oldest in the team by far. It's easy to be invisible and overlooked here as an older worker. I've never had a career discussion with my manager and formal training isn't offered to me. I could work longer but I'm thinking of retiring as I don't really feel valued.

Longevity is something to celebrate for us all caused by improved medical treatments and tailored personalised medicine, better public health provision, improved nutrition and enhanced economic conditions overall compared to the early 20th century. With the legal retirement age removed people are working longer with the potential to continue contributing from their store of knowledge and skills as well as offering well-honed interpersonal skills and broader perspectives based on experience.

However, the changing needs and motivation of workers as they age are in danger of being neglected or assumed through bias and stereotyping, leading to a possible waste of talent and for some organisations, a reluctance to employ older workers looking for new roles.

In this chapter I begin by defining what is meant here by an older worker before giving a rationale for focusing on this group (abbreviated to OW throughout the chapter). I emphasise the importance of taking a holistic approach to nurture and retain this cohort, providing benefits both for the organisation and the individual.

Through analysing the 'lived' experience of OW based on 30 questionnaire responses and ten interviews, I identify what are the most important factors for work engagement with some clear themes emerging, although of course there are individual differences.

I also analyse *what is happening* with this group and, together with the powerful reflections from case studies of previous clients, see what happens when managers take a holistic approach and are listened to and respected as opposed to management practices based on stereotyping and bias.

Finally, I identify some organisationally relevant examples of longevity strategies and offer advice and tips for what managers and coaches can do to provide a nurturing and empathic environment and bring out the best in OW.

What Is an Older Worker?

OW is defined as 55 plus.

Although some studies pinpoint 50 plus as the defining age for OW, I have chosen two particularly influential surveys which identify 55 plus as where trends begin to really appear.

James Root et al.[1] have found that workers in the Western world over 60, apart from USA, cite interesting work and autonomy generally as more important than salary and promotion. They identified six archetypes and, although some people fall into the categories of *Artisan* (a desire for mastery over your work) and *Giver* (a desire to give back) for all their working life, after age 55 the trend for these two archetypes became particularly prominent (see section below on 'What Do Older Workers Want and How Do Managers Respond?' for the model and more detail).

The second survey, carried out by the OECD[2], categorises older workers as 55 to 64, as distinct from mid-career workers categorised as 45 to 54.

For my primary research, the age range started from 55, however it was left open-ended as people inevitably work into their sixties and seventies and even eighties[3].

Demographic Need for Older Workers

In the Western world we are nearly at a tipping point with a shortage of skills and reduced numbers of younger workers.

The World Economic Forum has found that 'In countries like USA, UK and Germany, natural population growth is slowing and is projected to become negative in parts of Europe'[4].

Younger people are having fewer children and fertility rates are declining across the industrialised world. This is in part due to women delaying or avoiding childbirth for career and educational reasons, economic uncertainties and the cost-of-living increases coupled with the expense of childcare provision.

In parallel with a decreasing number of younger workers to fill skills shortages in OECD countries, the number of older people is increasing, with the over 65s expected to reach 27% of the population by 2050[5].

To truly attract and retain this cohort, employers and managers must aim to make workplaces accommodating, motivating and attractive places for OW to work where their aspirations, experience, feelings and thoughts are invited and welcomed.

People Over 55 Want to Work

According to the Centre for Ageing better[6] one million people in their fifties and sixties would like to work now, and a Gallup poll reveals that of those employed, 30 to 40% intend to work beyond the traditional retirement age of 65[7].

Although the rate of economic activity amongst the over fifties was increasing before the pandemic, the rate of employment since then has declined in the 50 to 64 age group more than in any other age group.

Several reasons have been cited for this decline, amongst which are health reasons (15%) and caring responsibilities (11%) as well as 46% taking early retirement through dissatisfaction at work[8].

There is now no legal age for retiring in most European countries, and the legal age for retirement in the UK was phased out in 2011, except in the case of physically demanding professions such as the Fire Service, The Police and the Army. When unemployment was high, OW were encouraged to take early retirement and make way for the employment of the younger generation; however, now OW are a much needed cohort and should be encouraged to continue working, without any age cut-off, given they wish to do so.

Perhaps 'retirement' is an outmoded concept. Chris Farrell[9] in his book, *Unretirement: How Baby Boomers are Changing the Way We Think About Work*, coined the phrase 'pro-retirement' emphasising continued productivity and engagement beyond the traditional retirement age. Jonathan Collie[10] in an interview also challenged the notion of retirement more recently, replacing it with 'all-age working'.

There certainly seems to be a contradiction here between, on the one hand, a decline in economic activity for the OW and, on the other hand, an unfulfilled desire to work, given the right circumstances.

The answer to this contradiction lies partly in the ageism and stereotyping OW are facing and in some cases subscribe to themselves (see section below on stereotyping and bias against OW) and this finding is endorsed by several reports, surveys and articles including by The Centre for Ageing Better[11] and the OECD[12].

What Organisations Are Doing

The CMI (Chartered Management Institute)[13] carried out a series of polls in 2022 and found that:

> 20% of respondents thought older workers were under-represented in their organisation. Of those who thought older workers were under-represented, 95% either said the organisation was not proactively trying to recruit older workers to diversify their workforce or did not know if their organisation was taking any action.

It seems that organisations are only just beginning to catch on to this new reality of the necessity for actively recruiting older workers, retaining them and motivating them by discovering what they really want.

According to Ann Francke, CEO of the CMI[14], whilst much needed culture change to focus on longevity is slow in coming, she claims that managers themselves can create the changes needed by adapting their mindset and behaviour to include and embrace OW. Of course, the culture and policies set by the organisation will have a major impact on how OW overall are embraced.

Clients from one organisation, not known for its inclusive culture, told me that OW in a particular department were revered by the manager, canvassed for their views on upcoming changes and encouraged to mentor younger staff with the outcome that the department had a higher ratio of OW than other departments and they felt listened to and supported.

One behaviour that is key for managers to engage in, and is universally agreed by longevity pioneers, is to give time for one-to-one meetings on a regular basis, to all staff, but particularly to OW who tend to get forgotten. This involves asking questions about their motivation, showing genuine interest in them and listening. This may seem obvious but according to James Root[15] (see above) and Michael Fossat[16] at Schneider Electric, and my primary research, this does not often happen and OW are often a neglected group.

What Are the Organisational Benefits of Employing Older People?

Once people reach the age of 55 self-report studies show they are generally happier, more accepting of life and work and have 'let go' of unattainable goals and put more emphasis on present relationships and finding meaning in life and work. Rauch[17] puts forward various explanations for why we feel happier in our fifties and beyond. 'Research shows that older people feel less stress and regret, dwell less on negative information and are better able to regulate their emotions. Nor is status or competition as important'.

The following positive attributes of OW are well known and endorsed by many managers I have worked with. These are:

Reliability: OW are known to be typically more loyal, have less time off for sickness and to have lower turnover rates. Time off for sickness should, however, be qualified as inevitable in some industries that require physical resilience, e.g. the retail industry. OW need more time for recovery from surgery or musculoskeletal issues.

Interpersonal skills and emotional maturity: Their interpersonal skills are often highly developed, and they can be more tuned into the needs of older clientele.

Wisdom: Their experience and knowledge, gained over many years, can enable them to see the bigger picture and be less short-term in their approach and better able to predict what comes next.

Outputs: In an experiment to measure typing speed between older and younger typists, although younger workers' tapping speed was faster, OW were not slower in terms of overall typing because they were more aware of what characters came next[18].

Performance standards: Furthermore, when employers are asked about the performance of OW they admit that they not only measure up to younger workers but 89% say they are likely to outperform them[19].

Interestingly, positive images of older workers occur more often amongst managers who are themselves older. A 2017 study of 905 managers found a connection between managers' own desires to continue working past age 66 and their view of other older workers[20]. Those not planning to retire were more motivated to retain older workers and held positive attitudes about older workers' valuable contributions and experience in the workplace, particularly valuing their mentorship. Managers who intended to retire at age 66 subscribed more to negative stereotypical views about older workers.

Overall, with age diversity in the workplace, and inter-generational team-working, evidence shows that a broader range of different perspectives can lead to increased innovation and improved decision making.

An OECD report[21] showed that productivity is enhanced with an inter-generational workforce. Most importantly, teams with team members of varying age ranges working collaboratively seem to be most effective.

These acquired qualities could give 55 plus workers a positive advantage in the workplace, in whatever capacity they choose to continue.

However, not only is it advantageous to employ OW for their age-related qualities, but there is a business case for employing OW to address the older clientele and consumers who are aging fast[22].

The Economic and Business Case for Employing OW

Given the demographic situation which will increasingly see the need for OW to work and given the real qualities and attributes OW bring, as well as financial needs and a desire to work for many in this age range, it makes sense on many counts to recruit and retain OW. The following reasons summarise the business and economic reasons for hiring OW:

- There are labour shortages across many industries partly caused by these demographic shifts.
- The pension age is rising, currently at 67 for men and women in the UK, on average in 19 European countries the age is 65 but set to rise, and in the USA either 66 or 67 depending on when you were born, thus necessitating some OW to continue working longer than previously.
- OW contribute to the economy, earning, spending and paying taxes thereby reducing the burden on pensions.
- OW are more motivated and in better psychological health than if they weren't working, therefore are less likely to need to access GPs and the NHS.
- OW enhance the skills of others through mentoring and sharing their skills and knowledge.
- OW can relate more to the needs of an ageing consumer population.
- OW themselves can bring a wealth of skills, experience and wisdom and can help to increase productivity.
- Organisations who can brand themselves as successfully demonstrating age inclusivity are more likely to attract and keep talent across multiple generations.
- Finally, by retaining OW, organisations can reduce recruitment costs of new employees.

What Are the Potential Benefits to Older Workers Themselves?

Whilst OW motivation for working will vary depending on personal circumstances, health, well-being and financial situation, clear benefits pertain for those OW who want to continue working beyond traditional retirement age, given the right circumstances for them to thrive.

The 21st century has seen a transformation from the linear three stage pattern of education, work and retirement to much more nuanced cycles of development, as mentioned in Chapter 1. These cycles of development include phased retirement, career changes, flexible working sabbaticals and continuous learning, making it, in theory, easier and more desirable for OW to remain in the workforce[23].

Based on primary and secondary research studies, benefits to continued working show:

- **Financial security** and continued earning capacity, especially important for some in the face of delayed pensions.
- **Cognitive confirmation** that OW are still able to up-skill and re-skill if required and motivated to do so.
- **Personal satisfaction** of authenticity and finding meaning and purpose as well as giving back to society.
- **Social aspects** including rewards from mentoring younger workers, enjoyment of being in mixed teams with younger workers and maintaining social connections.
- **Health gains** including evidence to show that keeping the brain active with adequate rest in between can help to stave off dementia.
- **Psychological well-being** such as increased self-esteem from being able to draw on expertise and experience where it is valued.
- **Structure and routine** which work can provide.
- **Career opportunities** including maintaining, pivoting, accelerating or retiring depending on motivation and organisational need[21]. There is also in some organisations, notably the NHS, the chance to reduce previous responsibilities and return after retirement, taking on new and different roles.
- The possibility of leaving a positive **legacy**.

In my experience of working with numerous OW, the idea of retirement is often attractive initially, however, as it approaches and the realisation dawns that suddenly their identity, routine and daily social interactions will be removed, fear and disorientation can set in.

One client came to see me after six months of retirement feeling lost and finding life lacking in purpose. She had plenty of interests and even involvement in a small charity, but she had no overall goals and focus and felt increasingly isolated. This example supports the need for organisations to introduce phased-retirement as a bridge to full retirement both for the benefit of the organisation and the individual. However, this was not the case for my client who realised she missed many of the benefits of her previous work. She eventually took on a part-time role whilst also being able to focus on one or two key interests.

What Do Older Workers Want and How Do Managers Respond?

Many OW I have worked with complain that their needs and wants are often ignored which can result in less motivation, low self-esteem, jadedness and potentially less productivity.

What is apparent from the research studies and my primary research is that OW in organisations are often bypassed when it comes to career discussions about the present and the future. It is assumed too frequently that their intention is to stay in the same role, doing the same type of work until retirement, with no career aspirations for the future. This assumption can also lead to a 'sitting it out' by managers, waiting for an unspecified retirement date, and as well as being demotivating for OW, it can also allow for not addressing key performance issues (see also section on stereotyping/bias).

Michael Fossat[24] set up 'Future Ready' at Schneider Electric based on a company survey that indicated that at the cut-off point of 51 plus, workers weren't as motivated and engaged as other employees. Compared to younger workers, they were having either no discussions about their careers or basic career conversations that tended to focus only on the present or short term. They were asked simply 'what do you need to do the job now?' rather than 'how do you see your next ten years, and how can you make them as fulfilling as possible and what support do you need from the company?'

After questioning 4,000 employees of this age range who left the company in 2021 to 2023 about what they wanted, their much broader desires were neatly summarised within four 'personas':

- **Continue or pivot sideways:** Continue in the same role or make a lateral move that draws on transferable skills
- **Transmit knowledge:** Give back to the younger generation and be recognised for their expertise
- **Accelerate:** Move to a more senior position
- **Retire:** Leave or semi-retire

So the question for OW within organisations of 'What do you want from your work now and what are your aspirations and plans for the future?' is all too rare.

James Root[25] asked the pertinent question: 'Why do you go to work?' of 40,000 workers, of all ages, across all sectors and job types within 19 countries.

From a brief quiz[26] he discovered that there was no such thing as the average worker, and he identified six archetypes across all workers.

Intriguingly there was a growing trend of older workers of 55 plus who, rather than citing pay as the most important factor, consistently related to the two archetypes of *Artisan* and *Giver* (as mentioned above).

The other four archetypes identified are Explorer; Pioneer; Striver; and Operator. The diagram consists of four images: one for Explorer with a hot air balloon and clouds symbolising freedom and adventure; one for Pioneer with an arrow wrapped around the earth's circumference symbolising a vision to change the world; one for Striver with a medal dangling from a ribbon symbolising drive to compete and make something of their life and one for Operator with three hands connected symbolising a person who seeks safety rather than looking outwards and sees colleagues as friends.

Later Career 73

Operator

Looks for meaning outside work

Does not seek to stand out at work

Tends to shy away from risk

Often views colleagues as friends

Artisan

Seeks out work that fascinates them

Motivated by pursuit of mastery

Desires autonomy

Places lower emphasis on camaraderie

Striver

Wants to make something of their life

Motivated by status and compensation

Forward planner, and often risk-averse

More competitive and transactional

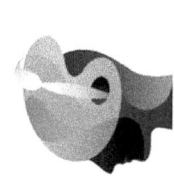

Giver

Finds meaning in helping others

Least motivated by money

Strong team spirit

Values personal growth and learning

Explorer

Values freedom and experiences

Craves variety and autonomy

Willing to trade security for flexibility

Less motivated by status

Pioneer

On a mission to change the world

Autonomous and risk-tolerant

Identify profoundly with their work

Vision is often at least partially altruistic

Figure 4.1[1] The six archetypes
Source: Bain & Company

This research highlights the changing motivation of people beyond 55, and whilst there are always exceptions it can gives clues as to how managers might provide a workplace that is more engaging for this age group. Opportunities for 'giving back' such as formal or informal mentoring schemes could be encouraged (see 'Opportunity to Mentor' section below) as well as opportunities for 55 plus workers to focus on areas of work that give them meaning and where they can build on their expertise and feel they are contributing.

The rest of this section looks at the categories of *Artisan* and *Giver* in more detail. The results reflect, with some variations, my independent primary research (see above), however it is crucial to treat people of any age group as unique individuals within these broad general categories and to be aware of individual differences.

For the *Artisan* category, in interviews with OW, I encountered a strong desire to focus on the parts of work that were interesting and to have a sense of purpose and leave behind other parts of the role. Some interviewees had found this possible through doing part-time work or job share, or simply communicating to their managers what they felt they could do best at this stage in their careers.

Although some interviewees appeared jaded by seeing the same changes come round on a regular basis throughout their long career, for one or two others it was an opportunity to 'speak out' about what they felt was not working in the team or department without fear of consequences for their career progression.

The word 'authentic' was used several times to describe doing work that could give opportunities to show-case OW's expertise and draw on their skills and strengths, whilst 'being themselves' rather than having to play a role to move up the career ladder.

Some respondent comments that fitted well with this archetype from the interviews and questionnaires were:

'What attracts me now is being able to choose aspects of work that play to my strengths and leave out less interesting work'

'I have the ability now to choose the assignments I want to do using my experience'
'I can be authentic in this organisation at my stage and say what I genuinely feel is wrong with our department'
'They redesigned a job to suit my perceived top skills'

For the *Giver* category, some comments that fitted well with this archetype and with Michael Fossat's 'Persona' of 'Transmit' were:

'Sharing the wealth of knowledge I have gained with younger staff and students'
'Feeling measurably useful'
'I want to be acknowledged for my contribution to others'
'Making a difference to others'
'Feeling I am making a difference to other peoples' lives'
'Helping make a difference to clients and their organisations using my interpersonal skills'

My primary research based on extensive and detailed questioning revealed a wide range of areas that matter for this cohort. The questions, on the questionnaire and in the interviews, were devised based on other secondary research pertaining to this group including reports, podcasts and career management theories. The respondent comments reflect some good as well as some less helpful ways of engaging and attending to the needs of this age group.

The key categories considered for the questionnaire were:

Flexibility
Opportunity to mentor
Respected for experience and expertise
Social inclusion
Doing meaningful work
Learning and personal growth
Cognitive skills

Those that came out as the strongest areas and where OW most want managers to focus were: 'Respected for experience and expertise' – the number one category – followed by 'Flexibility', 'Opportunity to mentor', 'Doing meaningful work' and 'Learning and personal growth'.

Respected for Experience and Expertise

There is a universal need for all workers to feel respected and valued, however it appears particularly pronounced for this cohort as they have typically amassed several years of experience and developed expertise. They also feel 'more sensitive to the possibility of being side-lined' as one older worker phrased it. This came out as the *most important factor* by far, valued as the top factor for 23 out of the 30 respondents, from a list of ten factors.

There was also the *biggest gap* between how important this factor was, and how well it was being practised in organisations.

Positive comments were:

'People value my continuing commitment and mentorship role in recent years'
'I am valued for being fair, balanced and humane and people now know that I will complete work to the highest level of excellence'
'The invitation to attend conferences and write articles shows that I am valued'

However, there were also some comments from OW who had felt hurt, disregarded and unappreciated for what they could still offer:

'over the years your work and level of effort becomes taken for granted'
'I don't feel as valued as in the past. I don't feel visible now'
'I feel my work is a young man's game and don't feel valued as I was before'
'I feel I've had my day in some areas now'

Two case studies based on clients I have worked with illustrate the importance of respect for expertise and experience. The first shows missed opportunities for finding out what really motivated the case of John and showing him that he was valued.

> John, as Head of Operations, was tasked with a project of bringing sponsorship support and money into the organisation for an upcoming international conference. He was told that he would earn a good percentage commission on every major sponsor he won over.
>
> He still cared deeply about doing a good job and, despite constant worry about an aged, unwell mother, worked hard to achieve quality work based on thorough research. Money had never been a prime motivator for him.
>
> Early in his career, he had received positive recognition for his work. However, he was now beginning to feel unmotivated by this project to the point of thinking about early retirement.
>
> He was often uncertain as to what was expected of him, and he had an uneasy sense of not being particularly valued or even noticed by his boss for his good work and vast experience. It was very difficult to get a meeting with her and when he did ask for feedback he was told that he and his team needed to get more involved in the restructuring of Ops but he was not told in what way.
>
> He had also heard rumours that a consultant from outside might be brought in to be temporarily overhaul the department. Neither John nor his team were invited to a major meeting to discuss the content of the conference.

Questions for reflection:
- How might John have been feeling?
- How much did his manager know about what motivated John now?

- What was the impact on John?
- What might you do in this situation, as a manager or a coach or head of the project?

The case of Aisha illustrates excellent practice in treating an OW, who was Head of Department, with respect, dignity and sensitivity as they began to step down from current responsibility.

> Aisha had been Head of Maths at Shorley School for 15 years and taught in the school for five years before that. She was 66 and aware that her energy was not what it had been, but she was still passionate about the job of teaching. She was now a widow, and she claimed her life was the school and the pupils.
>
> The manager in conjunction with the headmistress was keen to bring in a fresh young person to head up the department but she still valued Aisha's skills and knowledge and wanted to retain her in some capacity. She realised that Aisha could be demotivated and hurt if this situation was not handled with sensitivity.
>
> With the deputy head, she devised a plan to enable Aisha to reduce her responsibilities whilst still contributing to the school and feeling she had a part to play.
>
> Firstly, Aisha was asked which aspects of her role she felt she would like to cut down on and together they agreed she should partly relinquish the Head of Department role, continuing teaching and being supported by a new younger person to deputise as Head of Department whilst she mentored this person. She was given a small pay increase to recognise her contribution in this new position.
>
> After a year, because she knew the exam system inside out, she was invited to completely relinquish the teaching and Head

of Department role and to take over management of all the online exam data admin, and to liaise with the Head of Internal Exams. Not only did this reduce the burden for her as teaching became increasingly tiring but it also gave her the opportunity to do something new, based on her previous knowledge. Again, she was given a small pay increase.

She had originally decided to retire at 70, two years from now, however she was asked if she would consider, as a part-time role, if she would like to take on the role of managing the external exam team of freelancers which she accepted.

At 70 there was still a role offered to her which was to manage the mandatory training of external examiners, bringing the examiners into the school three times a year for refresher courses in invigilating and health and safety.

Questions for reflection:
- How did Aisha know she was valued?
- What aspects of the manager's behaviour could you incorporate into your approach with older workers?

Given the importance of respect and being valued for this age group, and considering the wisdom, perspective, experience and expertise that OW can still bring, it is disappointing that this does not always happen.

OW are often considered to be less relevant to the workplace as they near what used to be the typical retirement age. The assumption is that they will not need any career discussion about the future at this stage and therefore they typically don't receive positive feedback and discussion on their current contribution as well as future career plans (see section below on stereotyping and biases against OW).

Another reason for lack of career conversations for this group which emphasises their sense of being disregarded could hinge on the difficulties a younger manager might feel in initiating conversations with OW. This could be related to their sense of 'imposter syndrome' in that a younger manager might be aware they are far less experienced than the OW and might feel embarrassed or uncomfortable in discussing their career. Alternatively a younger manager aware of the 2010 Equality Act could fear their approach might instigate a complaint of age discrimination by the 'litigious cynic' (see tips for managers and coaches at the end of this chapter).

Related to being *respected and valued for experience and expertise* is the notion of *legacy* – how an OW has contributed to and made a difference to their team/department/organisation and what reputation follows them after they have retired from the organisation. Through interviews with senior managers, legacy came out as an important factor as they move into the latter part of their career. Particularly if an OW has been in an organisation for some time it becomes more important for them to be valued for what they have contributed and how they might have shaped their team or their department. Legacy is not always under the control of the OW if the current economic context or departmental changes impact negatively on their prior contributions.

Many clients I have seen of this age group have left or been 'let go' with no acknowledgement of the value they have brought and the difference they have made. As well as being hurtful, lack of recognition for the contribution an OW has made, who has had a successful career history to date and is approaching the latter years of their career, can negatively impact their desire to continue in any new role offered in an organisation and may influence taking early retirement and their willingness to look for another role.

Flexibility

The Covid pandemic demonstrated the unthinkable – much good productive work could be achieved from anywhere, not necessarily from a single organisational site, and that flexibility made a huge impact on job satisfaction for employees in all age groups.

Hays[27] has done considerable research into this area for older workers. For their third report, they surveyed 9,000 workers and found that 65% of workers over 55 value flexibility and 50% want to work four days a week and 50% remotely.

Flexibility seems to be universally important as younger workers also rated it as very high in importance (see Chapter 2). It seems that partly because of experiencing home-working there is more appetite for it. Surveys such as those by Gallup[28], McKinsey[29] and FlexJobs[30] have identified flexibility as desired across all age ranges.

However, only 45% of employers offer flexibility and there is some evidence that older workers are more hesitant about asking for flexibility as, until recently, they have often not experienced flexibility in their working lives and fear that it might prejudice how they are viewed by their employer.

Timewise[31] and Centre for Ageing Better[32] teamed up with six large employers to do research on the over fifties and flexibility. They found that, whilst flexibility is desirable across the ages, 'It is what happens round the edges that is different for over fifties'. Such issues as planning for retirement, older care responsibilities, physical health issues and work–life balance all matter a great deal to OW.

Comments from my primary research reinforced the desire for flexibility. Whilst both men and women in my survey valued flexibility highly, there was even more demand from women. Perhaps women are still tasked with more of the caring roles, such as caring for elderly relatives or grandchildren. There were mixed results in terms of how much flexibility was available to this cohort; on the positive side:

> 'Since moving from a 100% contract to 60% I have complete freedom two days a week and have quality leisure time, and as a result I work better in the three days at work'

'I now have control and flexibility and more free time which makes me all round happier and more productive'

'All of my working relationships are based on mutual flexibility: if I need to miss a regular meeting or move it, there is usually no issue and vice versa'

'My mum (86) lives with me and my employer has always accommodated me when I have needed to take her to appointments and work from home to look after her'

'Allows me to support charities by taking time for trustee work. Flexitime is available'

'Very flexible, on the whole well supported. Work has menopause help, mental health, book club, games club etc.'

Offering flexibility to valuable OW, who might have caring responsibilities or have less energy to do a full-time role but still have an important contribution to make, seems an 'easy win' for managers where the role is possible to be carried out part-time or as a job share, but unfortunately this does not always happen. Some of the negative comments from the questionnaire were:

'Not given opportunity for job-share prior to retirement, causes me frustration'

'Expects me to be available at any time'

'Important meetings often arranged on my NWD and I'm still expected to be there'

'Ironically job sharing is harder than I imagined as it is effectively a long handover letting go prior to retirement and I don't feel supported in this'

'Working with an all younger than me male Board – toxic environment'

'The organisation should allow more choice for hybrid working'

'Coming up to retirement I was very keen to do my role part-time but unfortunately I wasn't given the opportunity, so I decided to take holiday one day a week in order to do a four day week. . . I felt some resentment about this . . . the role was easily manageable four days a week'

Opportunity to Mentor

This category relates to the archetype *Giver* but specifically relates to mentoring younger workers. Chip Connelly[33] claims, 'Elders reflect on what they've learnt and incorporate it into the legacy they offer younger generations'.

Mentoring others is attractive to many older workers and can increase self-esteem and remind them of what they have to offer both in terms of soft skills such as life and social experience as well as more technical knowledge and skills. They can also learn from younger workers through reverse mentoring.

However, Hays[34] found in their survey that whilst older workers said they want to mentor, only 7% were taking up the opportunities whilst 16% said they had structured mentoring opportunities. They identified a gap in clear communication for older workers as to what is available to them.

These figures, however, based on primary research, do not perhaps consider that older workers often *informally* assume the mentor role and gain much from giving as well as receiving in the work context. There is also the possibility that OW are offering mentoring through ad hoc support without realising they are doing so. Nevertheless it seems important that managers encourage their OW employees to offer mentoring on a formal basis wherever possible as this does seem to fulfil a strong need to 'give back' for this age group and can also greatly benefit the younger worker.

Positive comments were:

'Being a mentor to doctoral students where I now feel I can make a real difference to their success, probably because they really appreciate it'
'Feeling measurably useful when younger members of the team ask my advice'
'I like dealing with difficult colleagues when they come to me, bringing wisdom to bear and mentoring'

> 'Valued as a source of wisdom in team discussions'
> 'Inspiring students in the field of male infertility'

This older worker was particularly enthusiastic about the mentoring role:

> I relish the younger members of the team and enjoy their energy and enthusiasm. They often come to me as a sounding board and we can each learn from the other. I've seen a lot of changes in my time in other organisations and I can bring different perspectives to the current transformation. But you must show interest in the younger members and make an effort to join in. For example, they were having a softball game and, whilst I'm not going to play(!) I showed interest by going along. I could easily be side-lined if I don't join in and show interest in them as people.

It takes a positive mindset and self-belief for older workers to think they *do* have something to offer younger team members. This is where the manager can encourage and remind the OW of their valuable contribution based on their experience and expertise.

> Negative comments were:

> 'I want to mentor younger workers but I'm not sure I have much to offer them; they seem so smart and switched on'
> 'Opportunities are not there in the organisation and I don't think others are interested in my opinions'

The two senior older workers below demonstrated some cynicism in the face of resistance to their suggestions for managing a change and retreated into half-hearted acquiescence:

> 'I have seen the idea of an international strategy to take account of different sub-cultures and language within the organisation pop up again and again but I know it doesn't work. We need to change the vision, but the younger workers are determined to pursue the original idea and don't want to learn from me'

'I am not listened to by younger people when it is out of line with current fashionable groupthink. Now I feel neither the drive nor motivation to perform at my peak and stretch myself. I am coasting'

The comment above demonstrates a gap in perceived value of an OW by younger workers and the cynicism that can ensue.

One way for managers to try to tackle this is to encourage reverse mentoring where OW can learn the more contemporary IT and social media skills that the younger worker might be more versed in as well as promoting inter-generational working to bridge the perceived gap between different age groups (see section at the end of the chapter on tips for managers and coaches).

'Doing Meaningful Work'

As people age, what they need and want from work typically changes. Instead of being about promotion, financial compensation and job title, it is more about what matters to them, whether that be 'giving back' or 'gaining mastery over their work', corroborating James Root's research.

Psychologist Shalom Schwartz[35] with over 220 articles and studies across 80 countries looked at values and showed that there was a clear connection between age and our personal values: generally, as people get older, they can become 'less preoccupied with their own strivings and more concerned with the welfare of others' and doing meaningful work.

From my primary research and interviews, *finding meaning in their work* was the second most important motivator for this cohort together with *having autonomy and flexibility.*

The case of Marina illustrates the meaning an older worker had been finding in her approach to mergers and acquisitions in a travel organisation – an approach which she felt was no longer valued.

Marina, aged 65, was considering retiring in a couple of years having worked in the travel industry doing mergers and acquisitions for the last 15 years. She prided herself on being self-sufficient and not making a fuss and never taking a day of sickness.

However, although she still had interest in the role, she was beginning to feel less useful and that the company valued 'younger brighter things' who appeared to 'clinch deals' and get more companies 'onto the books'.

She was also trying to help her daughter, who had developed Lupus, with her new baby.

She saw three much younger employees being brought on board and one in particular, Gerard, was being given transactions to manage that would previously have been given to her, as she saw it.

He seemed to get through them quickly but not care how well matched buyer and seller were.

Marina additionally felt hurt that she had not been formally put forward for training on the new software system for the department.

Marina's manager assumed Marina would carry on for several more years and relied on her. He was relieved she would just get on with the job as he had his hands full managing the business, and he valued, but took for granted, her ethical stance and ability to form long-term client relationships.

He had given a small transaction to Gerard to test him but was disappointed by his approach and felt Gerard should be taking a longer-term view of deal-making. He had wondered if

> Gerard could do with some mentoring but he had as yet done nothing to implement this.
>
> He was shocked when Marina came to hand in her resignation.

Questions for reflection:
- What value did Marina bring to the organisation?
- How did she feel?
- What could the manager have done to forestall her resignation?

The lesson here for managers is to ask the question of OW as to what aspects of their work does give meaning and purpose at this stage in their life and where possible to enable them to focus on those areas. In doing so, OW are likely to be far more motivated and productive and bring their experience and wisdom to bear.

Learning and Personal Growth

There is an assumption that OW are no longer interested in learning and developing (see section on bias and stereotyping), however this is not borne out by either primary or secondary research. OW appear to be open to up-skilling in particular and some re-skilling, although it is important at this stage that they can see the relevance of the training to their life and career and that the training methods suit their learning styles.

Positive comments were:

'I have opportunities for formal training but choose not to take these; there is opportunity for informal training with shadowing if I want it'

'In this organisation everyone is encouraged to take up training whatever their age and everyone has career conversations about what would suit them best'

Data analysis by Restless.co.uk[36] identified that the least likely group to have workplace training were OW, with only 23% of 55–65-year-olds being trained, whilst for younger workers it was 33% of 16–24-year-olds, between 2004 and 2017

Hays[37] found that whilst older workers say 'we are all for training', it is however reported that 'training falls off a cliff for over sixties'.

They found several reasons for the training not happening:

- They are not given time for the training by their managers and the training is seen as a priority for younger workers.
- They are directed to unsuitable training, e.g. e-learning or classroom settings which can be alienating when they have been out of those settings for many years.
- The training offered is not effectively marketed to older workers so that they don't see the value of it.
- Older workers could fear re-skilling in technology, imagining they won't be able to adapt to new technology.
- Older workers have not been brought up with social media and IT and it is not typically second nature to them as it is for the younger generation.

There can certainly be resistance to IT and AI for some individuals in this group. Another factor here is that younger workers can sometimes demonstrate a sense of superiority due to their natural familiarity with social media and speed of implementing IT skills and this can inhibit OW motivation to acquire these skills even though they may well have the capacity. This is an area that will need addressing more in the future as the requirement for these skills increases. Since there is no evidence to suggest that OWs can't learn new skills, there is a place here for managers to support and encourage the uptake of IT skills at any age if they are relevant to the role.

For IT re-skilling negative comments were:

'I am definitely slower and more reluctant with new IT skills; they have to be shown to me I do not naturally understand what needs to be done'

'I probably have the ability to learn new skills, including IT, but I don't prioritise it as much. There is a bigger team around me who pick up what I previously had to do myself'

'Appetite, time as well ability to learn additional skills is reducing'

'I have less patience with IT systems and procedures which don't help me do the job which I have always done in a certain way'

There is also evidence that whilst some OW put a premium on their own experience in particular, recruiters and managers often value formal qualifications and skills even more highly. This could have implications for older workers if they do resist re-skilling and are thinking of transitioning to new roles[38].

This is particularly so when there is a need to counter misconceptions about their suitability for any particular role and any genuine gaps in their skillset.

With AI becoming a viable alternative for many data-driven roles, employers increasingly want workers who can work fast to increase productivity. It is therefore important that OW can demonstrate that they are up to speed with IT and relevant AI skills and can demonstrate this through certification.

However, in some professions, it is not always necessary for older workers to be up-skilled in IT and AI:

> The Head of Legal in a large engineering company manages 30 people and six are over 60, four having been more than 15 years in the company. The company's ethos is for everyone to have a growth mindset and adapt to AI. However, four of the over sixties in the team are not interested in developing AI skills and all are nearing retirement.
>
> The Head of Legal is happy for these older workers to continue doing an excellent job and use their expertise and experience, whilst AI training is provided for the rest of the team.

In this example, older workers fit the *Artisan* image of being motivated by mastery of their current work as they near retirement and the manager is appreciative of their position.

What Are the Blocks to Valuing and Retaining This Cohort: Stereotyping and Bias Against OW

Many employers hold the view that OW are: 'less productive, more resistant to change, less open to training, less open to training and development opportunities, less competent, more costly and more prone to illness'[39].

The 2010 Equality Act was brought in to protect diversity although it appears that age is often a neglected factor.

According to the CMI 75th Anniversary report[40] multiple studies suggest that OW (over 55) feel pigeonholed for having too much experience, showing lower levels of commitment and being less cognitively and physically fit.

Though these stereotypical images are largely unfounded, through secondary and my primary research (see above) they clearly persist. Hence, OW are less likely to be short-listed for interviews – employers apparently are no more likely to interview people with 25 years' experience than people with five years' experience possibly because they see them as over-qualified or expecting to be paid more[41]. They are also less likely to be hired and less likely to be put forward for training or offered other opportunities, and when they lose their job they are likely to be unemployed for longer and to gain roles that are less skilled than previously[42].

Another apparent issue with the 2010 Equality Act is that managers are sometimes reluctant to implement career discussions for OW as it might appear that they are singling them out because of age, and they fear contravening the law[43].

Additionally, if managers have not been trained in conducting career conversations and are not aware of the different needs and values of OW compared to younger workers, they will typically avoid having these discussions and make assumptions about OW's lack of aspirations for developing themselves in their careers.

Equally problematic is that OW can 'buy into' these stereotypes in two ways[44]: externally they can be so fearful of fitting the stereotype that it can inhibit their ability to focus and thus performance suffers, and it becomes a self-fulfilling prophecy. Internally, if OW have been continuously exposed to negative predictions of what they are capable of later in their careers, they can impose self-constraints and believe and take on board that they are cognitively weaker and less capable. Paradoxically weaker memory and cognitive deterioration can occur as a result of this[45].

A recent client told me that, as a senior manager on a Board with several younger colleagues, she felt undermined and 'talked over' when the question of bringing in technology to improve the data collection procedures came up, to the point that she resigned. She initially subscribed to the idea that she wasn't fast enough to contribute, but through discussion and looking at what had happened through a different lens she realised that she had been bullied and that she was perfectly capable of and interested in contributing ideas on the technology front.

Some organisations, for example the NHS, don't subscribe to the notion of weaker cognitive abilities, and, out of necessity, actively seek to retain retirees by inviting them back with the opportunity for less responsibility and seniority if they prefer, as much support as they need and more flexibility in terms of working hours.

But this can backfire as the case below illustrates.

> Yasmin, a clinician, aged 58, returned to a part-time role in the NHS after taking retirement. She had been a highly successful senior nurse and her previous boss had encouraged her to take up a new, part-time post, training junior nurses in anatomy and orthopaedics.

> Her partner was less keen for her to take up the role, citing her age as a potential problem.
>
> She had been hired on a temporary basis through an online interview and she had only had a two-hour induction and a ten-minute one-to-one meeting with her new supervisor who seemed a bit concerned about her taking the role and kept asking her how she would manage, even though she had shared that she enjoyed the little teaching she had done and received excellent feedback.
>
> Yasmin would have liked to discuss current resources suitable for these participants but was hesitant to ask as she felt it might confirm that she was 'not up to speed'.
>
> Her supervisor was overheard talking to a younger member of the team about how stressed Yasmin appeared and how she had forgotten the name of one of the participants on the course she was running.
>
> Although Yasmin had felt enthusiastic to begin with, she began to lose confidence and claimed she was suffering with imposter syndrome to such an extent that she resigned.

Questions for reflection:
- How might Yasmin have been feeling when she took the new role?
- What stereotypes might people around Yasmin have been imposing on her?
- What could her supervisor have done to reassure and retain Yasmin?

Intersectionality

Age barriers around feeling valued and respected at work can be compounded when they interface with gender, race and disability biases. Research shows that women over 55 are far more likely to feel disregarded, invisible and excluded[46].

This contrasts with older men who stereotypically can be seen as grey-haired, wise and knowledgeable[47]. It's important to note that women worldwide 55 plus still earn less than their male counterparts and have less participation in the marketplace[48]. An annual survey of hours and earnings[49] showed that women in their fifties earned over a quarter less than their male peers. This should be viewed in the context of men holding more positions of power. Fewer than 10% of the UK CEOs of FTSE 100 companies are currently female[50].

Research also shows that the biggest gap in employment for those with a disability are for the ages 45 to 59[51].

The nature of work will also impact OW's ability to work longer, with those who can flex their working pattern, spending some time at home with a computer, perhaps being able to extend their retirement age.

Finally, socioeconomic variations mean that some OW have no choice as to whether they work, for financial reasons, and the idea of finding meaning and purpose can feel somewhat of a luxury to this group.

Whilst there has been a scarcity of organisations focusing on longevity with policies and programmes, there are some notable exceptions. Below are three best practice examples of organisations set up to encourage other employers to focus on longevity in implementing policies and plans.

Three Best Practice Organisations Set Up to Focus on Longevity

Three age-focused organisations amongst a few others are taking the subject of longevity so seriously that one, *Centre for Ageing Better in the UK*[52], has set up a pledge and over 300 employers have joined.

Another is a French organisation, *Club Landoy*[53], with a longevity charter produced by 47 CEOs of major companies with a ten-point plan for companies to adhere to.

A third is 55 Redefined[54], offering 'Age Inclusive Accreditation for Organisations to become 50 plus employers of choice'.

There are also some flagship organisations now that are leading the way in introducing imaginative policies and processes as well as some who are fore-fronting the recruitment of OW, including insurance companies, some retail companies, IT and car manufacturers (see below: 'Other Organisational Initiatives'), however much more is needed.

A Flagship Organisation

An example of a flagship organisation in terms of implementing longevity policies is Schneider Electric, a French multinational that specialises in digital automation and energy management with 150,000 employees. Michael Fossat at the company has created a global programme called 'Future Ready'[55].

The programme involves career development workshops and a series of one-to-one discussions with line managers. Other aspects of the programme are:

- Line managers must be trained to conduct effective career discussions.
- OW can fit any of the persona and might move from one to another or fit two personas simultaneously, e.g. maintaining the current role but adding mentoring and new skills.
- The organisation must provide practical initiatives for the different persona, e.g. a financial platform for retirees; a leadership programme for those who want to accelerate; a mentoring programme for those who want to transmit their knowledge; a re-skilling for those who want to pivot.
- Role models of OW who have successfully navigated different pathways should be shared.
- The language used to communicate the workshops should be carefully chosen. Initially when this programme was announced, OW were fearful that they would just be planning for retirement and would be asked to leave, and as a result more attention was paid to broadcasting the purpose of the workshops.

The results so far show that there has been far more diversification in what this cohort choose to do next. It was clear that not only was the organisation making assumptions about the readiness for retirement of all OW over 50 but that the OW themselves were subscribing to this notion.

Motivation and morale amongst this group has increased and Schneider Electric are now retaining some much valued talent.

Other Organisational Initiatives

Atos[56] (global player in digital transformation): Has an age-based diversity group, 'Aeon', to discover and eliminate age-discrimination practices and behaviours. It also prioritises flexibility, realising how important this is to OW in particular. On offer are: flexitime arrangements, sabbaticals, career breaks as well as part-time and job-share working. Additionally, they offer a wide range of training programmes, and ingeniously *OW are trained up to be the trainers*, very desirable for the *Giver* archetype (see James Root, Bain Futures).

Aviva[57] (multinational Insurance company): Similarly offers flexible working as well as apprenticeship schemes for OW to re-skill, mid-life MOTs for over fifties for check-ups on well-being, finance, and plans for their future, and what they name as 'part-tirement' – options for gradual transition into retirement with part-time work.

Barclays[58] (multinational universal bank): Have introduced a 'Barclays Bolder Apprenticeship' scheme which is aimed exclusively at the over fifties, with the purpose of creating new jobs for OW through re-training, as well as implementing skills development programmes for attracting and retaining OW. Additionally, reverse mentoring and inter-generational working are part of their longevity policy.

BMW[59] (German manufacturer of luxury vehicles and motorcycles): As part of their diversity charter have developed a mentorship programme which includes reverse mentoring. OW who have retired are specifically invited back as mentors and this particularly appeals to the OW with a *Giver* archetype (see James Root as above).

Cisco[60] (multinational digital communications technology company): Has introduced an innovative scheme – which they name 'Grandternity' – allowing OW who have recently become grandparents to take two paid weeks off, as part of their broader focus on longevity to retain valued OW. (**Mercer**[61], **HireVue**[62] and **Saga**[63] are now following suit and, interestingly, the country Denmark[64] is now offering 'senior days' or one paid day off a month to workers over 62.)

EY[65] (multinational professional services company): Has a programme called 'Life Reimagined' offering employees with ten years' service or more, who are 50 plus, to reduce their working week by 20%, two years before retirement, whilst receiving 80% of their pay.

Sanofi[66] (French pharmaceutical and healthcare multinational): has set up 'Global ERGs' (Employee Resource Groups) and one of its five divisions is 'EveryGen' which provides a network and opportunity for employees at all life stages to meet and learn from each other. The aim of this group is to share learning and challenges across the generations, promoting deeper understanding, as Pedro Pitella[67], Head of People and Culture and Head of ERG on Longevity explains.

Swissray[68] (global digital radiography solutions) has developed separate 'affinity' groups for different age groups, and for OW the design team have developed '12 ways to talk about retirement', including flexible working, health and well-being programmes, and lifelong learning and social engagement. They also have an affinity group for all ages for best ways of working together.

Unilever[69] (British multinational fast-moving consumer goods company) has paid attention to their advertising, particularly debunking age and gender stereotyping regarding their Dove campaigns. These campaigns feature women of all ages taking on non-traditional roles from CEOs to women entrepreneurs.

What follows is a selection of consultancies that advise and provide resources to some key companies that have set up platforms for the over 55s with resources and job opportunities:

Lucy Standing[70] is the founder of Brave Starts CIC, a social enterprise dedicated to helping individuals transition into new careers particularly focusing on older workers. She is a pioneer in the field and passionate about skilling up older workers and enabling them to contribute. She runs a series of four workshops dedicated to this group which includes psychological understanding of the benefits older aged-people bring to the workforce as well as the practical skills of self-advocating for gaining roles in the face of the age-related barriers to employment.

Jonathan Collie[71] (see above) created the 'Age of No Retirement' initiative: based on evidence that people do different types of work at all ages. He says, 'we need to stop sensationalising the fact that people might carry on working or start a business in their sixties. There are six core strands to the initiative:

1 Language: dispensing with clichés such as: 'golden age' and 'silver surfers'
2 Storytelling: older people talking about what they are doing productively
3 Design: people from all backgrounds and ages doing innovative projects
4 Age-thinking: people start early and keep learning new skills
5 Inter-generational working: he says for effective working we need: 'the combination of youthful exuberance and older wisdom, of tech savviness and life experience'
6 Work and employment being available to all ages eliminating the barriers for people over 50

Martin Frolander: Junoverse[72] has developed retirement platforms for older workers including *Ready*, *Go* and *Connect*, which are all integrated platforms:

1 '*Ready*: helps mid to late career employees 50 to 80. It includes assessments, personalised plans, algorithms, mentoring, and suggestions'
2 '*Go*: helps employees in retirement assisting them in finding post-work life productively with resources and tools'
3 '*Connect*: creates age-focused friendly communities assisting better integration of communities of different ages'

An innovative organisation, **Multiverse**[73] has identified many older workers who are keen to re-skill in AI and digital skills. They have recently (2024) started apprenticeships aimed specifically at older workers who either want to enhance their current roles or move into a different area such as data analytics or software engineering, and Multiverse see no difference in interest or aptitude between older and younger workers. However, it is worth noting that those who attend the programme might be a self-selecting group, either having been put forward by their organisations or having been recruited on the basis that they chose to take up the apprenticeship.

Summary of Tips for Organisations

- *Ensure sponsorship*: It is critical to have a sponsor: Sibylle Le Marie, founder of Club Landoy[74] and CEO of Media group Bayard in France suggests that organisations now should be thinking about building a business case, engaging leaders and appointing *Chief Longevity Officers*.
- *Collect and measure age data*: Measure and track age balance to help to address lack of diversity.
- *Have a longevity strategy*: Take advantage of diversity and inclusion to focus on a longevity strategy.
- *Avoid clichés and discriminatory language*: Focus on eliminating discriminatory language throughout the organisation, including internal and external job adverts, social media and intranet platforms and training opportunities.
- *Mixed networks*: Set up inter-generational working and networking across all ages for deeper understanding and shared learning.
- *Mentoring schemes*: Introduce formal mentoring and encourage informal mentoring and reverse mentoring.
- *Ensure benefits packages meet the needs of OW*: Tailor health benefits to age and gender needs.
- *Proactively design/re-design appropriate jobs*: Craft jobs based on the skills OW can offer as well as those needed and be imaginative in how flexible these jobs can be carried out.
- *Training and development*: Offer career development workshops and one-to-one discussions and match organisational initiatives to the different needs within this cohort.
- *Retirement planning*: For retirees, offer phased retirement initiatives to ease the transition.

- *Post-retirement return to work policy*: Have a policy for OW to return to the workplace, after retirement, for example on a part-time basis focusing on aspects of the role or in new roles or as consultants or mentors.
- *Continuous development*: Encourage lifelong learning and up-skilling and re-skilling opportunities for OW as well as for all other employees.

Tips for Managers and Coaches

The following advice and tips are drawn from my coaching and consultancy experience of best practice together with current best practice in organisations, some of which are mentioned above.

The purpose is to recommend ways for managers and coaches to retain OW by treating them holistically and providing an environment for OW to thrive and contribute to the organisation. Whilst some managers may already be implementing many of these suggestions, for others there are hopefully new tips and ideas for creating or enhancing best practice.

Career Tools can be integrated into one-to-one discussions and workshops where appropriate (see Chapter 11).

Holistic Career Discussions

Since apparently only 1 in 5 respondents to a poll carried out by the CMI[75] claimed their organisation offered diversity training for managers managing OW, and since one-to-one career discussions happen too rarely or not at all for this age group, the recommendations here are for ensuring holistic career conversations.

It is worth noting that, as a younger manger managing older workers, there can be concerns about seeming to patronise and this can be a potential block to having discussions in the first place. One manager commented: 'I fear getting it wrong or causing unintentional offence'. Perhaps one way round this is to present the career discussions in a positive frame, explaining the purpose and, importantly, asking OW to evaluate the outcomes so that the organisation and managers know they are addressing matters appropriately as well as providing training.

- *Training for line managers*: Ideally line managers receive training in conducting career discussions with a focus on the potentially diverse needs of OW.
- *Career one-to-ones*: Ensure that all employees have career discussions regardless of age and stage of career and make these ongoing (rather than once a year).
- *Initiating the career discussion*: Younger managers can sometimes feel some awkwardness, embarrassment or 'imposter syndrome' in initiating a career discussion with an OW, feeling that the OW has more experience and wisdom and imagining that they may not take the career conversation seriously or that they might feel patronised. It's important for the younger manager to be very clear as to the purpose of the meeting and to clarify what their role is and that they are here to explore and ask questions rather than to advise or 'tell', whilst respecting the experience the OW brings.
- *Take a holistic approach*: Remember that personal events outside work can evoke strong emotions and impact behaviour at work for all individuals. Show compassion and care for OW's whole life and support them through work and out-of-work difficulties.
- *Motivate each individual*: Take time to treat everyone as different and understand what would motivate them at this age and stage of their life. Extrinsic factors such as money, promotion and status are likely to motivate less.
- *Match individuals to roles*: If their responsibilities are changing or reducing, collaborate with OW on what suits them and the organisation best at this stage, and engage in conversations showing empathy and understanding of their needs.
- *Keep a non-judgemental and respectful mindset*: Challenge stereotypes as to what an OW might want (see stereotypes section above).
- *Ensure exemplary communications skills*: Use skills of active listening, open questions and summarising.

Creating a Culture of Valuing and Respecting Experience and Expertise

Feeling valued and respected at work came out as one of the most important factors for OW and without this sense of feeling recognised for their contribution and appreciated for their experience and expertise the benefits they can bring an employer may surface less and the individual OW can feel disregarded.

- *Elicit and reinforce the valuable experience and expertise* the OW can offer.
- *Reinforce the value* the OW brings to the wider team/department.
- *Seek OW views*: Show you value their experience by eliciting their perspectives on new initiatives – they might have learnt lessons from previous ventures and can help to bypass potential mistakes this time around.

Training and Learning

OW are generally less likely to be interested in promotion and status at this stage in their life and providing and communicating appropriate training opportunities as well as encouraging a growth mindset, as Carole Dweck's[76] pivotal research showed, could help employees in this age group to enrich their current role or alternatively equip them for a new role.

- *Encourage training*: Ensure OW are invited and encouraged to take up training that is available to younger workers.
- *Ensure training reflects OW needs*: Make the training appropriate to learning style, e.g. OW who have been out of the classroom situation for many years might prefer to learn on the job or through shadowing.
- *Encourage take-up of re-skilling on IT and AI skills* if relevant, reminding OW that they are just as capable cognitively as younger workers although they might need more support initially. This is in keeping with Multiverse's[77] experience with their apprenticeship scheme for OW.
- *Communicate the value of the training* to OW so that they can see the relevance to their current role or future development.

- *Creative thinking*: Provide opportunities for learning for the sake of learning as OW are less likely to be interested in promotion and status, and a growth mindset[78] could help prepare them for a new role or for retirement.

Pre-Retirement Preparation

Experience of working with clients coming up to retirement in this age group points to the clear value of helping them prepare a gradual retirement plan, often offering semi-retirement as an initial step.

As Giselle Cory[79] (2012) says:

> Over half of working age adults (56 per cent) want to continue working once they reach pensionable age. When they do come to retire, many older people would like their retirement to be phased in rather than a single event. Four out of five would find it appealing to combine part-time work with taking a partial pension.

- *Pre-retirement planning*: Help OW to plan for retirement by providing workshops where individuals can share ideas and support each other.
- *Ensure OW skills/job matching*: Don't assume that OW are not interested in doing challenging, meaningful work even if they plan to retire in the next couple of years.
- *Open possibilities of role variation*: Discuss the possibility of their returning to a less demanding role if that fits with the company culture.

Social Inclusion

- *Ensure OW are part of the team* and included in social events even if they are not directly participating, e.g. physical games and late night socials.
- *Proactive conversations*: Invite all members of the team to have a 'voice' and to share experience, knowledge and skills.
- *Create inter-generational teams* wherever possible. These are proven to increase productivity in the organisation and to foster understanding between older and younger employees.
- *Positivity*: Try to counter self-limiting beliefs about not belonging.

Ensuring Flexibility

Legislation passed[80] recently lays down that employees will have the right to request flexibility from day one of their employment, and managers will have to consult with employees before rejecting their requests. They will now also have to reply within two months instead of the previous timescale of three months. Specific advice, written before the recent legislation, comes from the Centre for Ageing Better[81] in conjunction with the Timewise-Flex-Working-Over-50s-Toolkit[82], and still applies.

> Offer information about how flexibility affects pensions and retirement options.
> Reinforce the validity of all reasons for wanting to work flexibly (it's not just for parents).
> Offer a range of informal and formal flexible working options, which can be combined and varied according to personal and business needs.

Echoing this advice it is helpful for managers to:

- *Identify ways that flexibility could be offered*: Offer different ways of working as flexibility is valued particularly by this age group. Working in flexible ways could involve homeworking, part-time work, job-sharing, offering consultancy and working freelance. There might be formal and informal flexibility on offer.
- *Enable OW to ask for the flexibility they need*: For example for caring responsibilities or health reasons.
- *Do a flex audit*: Assess the current level of flexibility by holding focus groups of OW and managers to ascertain current practice and assess different individual needs.
- *Ensure clear and consistent communication of policies to all employees* pre-empting misunderstandings, for example that the organisation wishes to reduce remuneration or prepare OW for redundancies or retirement.

There is evidence that valuable workers are not taking up positions because of lack of flexibility[22]:

- *Innovative flex best practice*: Use imagination to offer innovative attractive flexible initiatives. It's sometimes forgotten that,

like parents, those who are grandparents might also have caring responsibilities. An example is Cisco offering two week 's leave for 'Granternity! (see above).Others may also need to care for elderly parents or they may be suffering health issues themselves.
- *Allowing flexibility*: OWs who are reluctant or unable to work full-time, but have no choice, could retire early with the resulting loss of work for themselves and loss of contribution for the organisation.

Meaning

Finding out what gives meaning and purpose to OW was the second most important factor from my research, and fore-fronting what matters to an individual in this age group could make a big difference to performance and a sense of well-being.

- *Flex job design/re-design*: If possible, enable older workers to focus more on what they are good at and have developed expertise in; that might mean eliminating certain parts of their role and focusing more on those aspects that give them a sense of meaning.

Providing Mentoring

'Giving back' is one of the top two archetypes for the 55 plus age group as identified by James Root[1], and there is great satisfaction for OW in capitalising on their experience and expertise as well as bringing value to younger workers. OW can also benefit from reverse mentoring, gaining digital skills they may not have.

- *Mentoring schemes*: If there is a formal mentoring scheme communicate it and ensure older workers are encouraged to take up mentor roles if they wish to.
- *Encourage mentoring pairs*: Encourage OW to identify the skills and knowledge they could impart.
- *Arrange reverse-mentoring* so that both older and younger workers can benefit: older workers can impart their wisdom and experience of seeing the typical cycle of new initiatives and lessons learnt, and younger workers can share technology and social media skills.

Provide for Legacy

Managers can a do a great deal here to enable OW to leave the organisation with pride for what they have achieved and a sense of being recognised for their contribution.

If an OW is planning to retire, support them in leaving the legacy that they feel genuinely reflects their achievements and contribution to the organisation.

Tips for OW

Whilst this chapter focuses on what organisations, managers and coaches can do to attract and retain and provide a nurturing environment for OW, perhaps OW can go some way to helping themselves by using the checklist of tips in Table 4.1.

Table 4.1 Tips for OW

Try to notice your own stereotyping, and notice how it inhibits or prevents you from realising your potential	See section above on stereotyping and bias
Consider what matters to you and what you really want	For example: being valued, flexibility, and finding meaning Focus on the three most desired attributes of your work (See research results in section 'Doing Meaningful Work' above) What might that look like?
Make a business case for what you want in the context of the organisational priorities	Be clear and professional in aligning your needs and goals to the organisational context
Focusing on your future – how would you like it to look?	Consider options, e.g. whether you want to retire, work towards phased retirement, semi-retire, work part-time or work as a consultant
Ensure productive two-way conversations with your manager	Be open and transparent with your manager in the knowledge that you need
Develop a 'growth mindset	Try to be open to learning, including acquiring IT skills if appropriate to your role

Notes

1 www.bain.com/insights/better-with-age-the-rising-importance-of-older-workers/
2 www.oecd.org/en/publications/the-midcareer-opportunity
3 www.ons.gov.uk/employmentandlabourmarket/peopleinwork

4. www.weforum.org/publications/the-future-of-jobs-report
5. www.oecd.org/en/publications/pensions-at-a-glance
6. https://ageing-better.org.uk/summary-state-ageing-
7. www.gallup.com/workplace/285674/improve-employee-engagement-workplace.aspx
8. https://blog.ons.gov.uk/2022/03/14/the-over-50s-and-the-world-of-work-whats-happening-and-why
9. Farrell, C. *Unretirement: How Baby Boomers are Changing the Way We Think about Work, the Community and the Good Life*. Bloomsbury Publishing USA; 2014.
10. Collie, J. The age of no retirement. *Working with Older People*. 2015;19(4): 159–64 https://doi.org/10.1108/WWOP-09-2015-0020
11. https://ageing-better.org.uk/summary-state-ageing-
12. www.oecd.org/en/publications/the-midcareer-opportunity
13. www.managers.org.uk/knowledge-and-insights/professional-practice/age/
14. https://elderberries.substack.com/p/ann-francke-the-management-skill
15. www.bain.com/insights/better-with-age-the-rising-importance-of-olderworkers
16. https://elderberries.substack.com/p/michael-fossat-getting-global-companies
17. Rauch, J. *'The Happiness Curve': Life Gets Better After 50*. Bloomsbury Publishing; 2018.
18. Salthouse, T. Effects of age and skill in typing. *Journal of Experimental Psychology: General*. 1984;113(3): 345–71. https://doi.org/10.1037/0096-3445.113.3.345
19. www.generation.org/news/2023-global-impact-report
20. www.researchgate.net/publication/318570623_Do_Stereotypes_about_Older_Workers_Change_Evidence_from_a_Panel_Study_among_Employers
21. OECD. *Promoting an Age-Inclusive Workforce: Living, Learning and Earning Longer*. OECD; 2020. https://doi.org/10.1787/59752153-en.
22. https://elderberries.substack.com/p/pedro-pitella-why-and-how-sanofi
23. Gratton, L, Scott, A. *The Hundred Year Life: Living and Ageing in a World of Longevity*. Bloomsbury; 2016.
24. https://elderberries.substack.com/p/michael-fossat-gettingglobal-companies
25. www.bain.com/insights/better-with-age-the-rising-importance-of-olderworkers/
26. www.bain.com/insights/what-type-of-worker-are-you-future-of-work-report-interactive/
27. www.hays.co.uk/market-insights/what-workers-want
28. www.gallup.com/workplace/544775/front-line-workers-flexibility.aspx

29 www.mckinsey.com/industries/real-estate/our-insights/is-your-workplace-ready-for-flexible-work
30 www.flexjobs.com/remote-jobs
31 https://timewise.co.uk/
32 https://ageing-better.org.uk/summary-state-ageing-2023
33 Connelly, C. *Wisdom of Work: The Making of a Modern Elder*. Currency; 2018.
34 www.hays.co.uk/market-insights/what-workers-want
35 Schwartz, S. A proposal for measuring value orientations across nations. In: *Towards Refining the Theory of Basic Human Values*. Springer; 2003. pp. 259–319.
36 https://restless.co.uk/jobs
37 www.hays.co.uk/market-insights/what-workers-want
38 www.oecd.org/en/publications/the-midcareer-opportunity
39 Conway, E, Monks, K. Designing an HR system for managing an age-diverse workforce: Challenges and opportunities. In: Parry, E, McCarthy, J, editors. *The Palgrave Handbook of Age Diversity and Work*. Palgrave Macmillan; 2017. pp. 586–606.
40 https://www.managers.org.uk/knowledge-and-insights/professional-practice/age/
41 https://podcasts.apple.com/za/podcast/dr-mona-mourshed-confronting-corporate-ageism/id1648152043?i=1000634900374
42 Posthuma, R, Campion, M. Age stereotypes in the workplace: Common stereotypes, moderators, and future research directions. *Journal of Management*. 2009;35(1): 158–88. https://doi.org/10.1177/0149206308318617
43 www.hays.co.uk/market-insights/what-workers-want
44 Weber, J, Angerer, P, Müller, A. Individual consequences of age stereotypes on older workers: A systematic review. *Zeitschrift für Gerontologie und Geriatrie*. 2019;52:188. https://doi.org/10.1007/s00391-019-01506-6
45 Dionigi, R. Stereotypes of aging: Their effects on the health of older adults. *Journal of Geriatrics*. 2015. https://doi.org/10.1155/2015/954027
46 https://ageing-better.org.uk/resources/boom-and-bustCentre
47 https://elderberries.substack.com/p/ann-francke-the-management-skill
48 https://elderberries.substack.com/p/julie-miller-women-50-drivers-of
49 www.ons.gov.uk/employmentandlabourmarket/peopleinwork/employmentandemployeetypes/bulletins/employeesintheukbyregion/2019
50 www.statista.com/statistics/685195/share-of-female-ceo-positions-in-ftse-companies-uk/
51 www.ons.gov.uk/peoplepopulationandcommunity/healthandsocialcare/disability/articles/outcomesfordisabledpeopleintheuk/2021
52 https://ageing-better.org.uk/age-friendly-employer-pledge
53 www.clublandoy.com/

54 https://55redefined.co/group/about-us
55 https://elderberries.substack.com/p/michael-fossat-getting-global-companies
56 www.managers.org.uk/knowledge-and-insights/article/older-employees-are-the-answer-to-a-talent-pool-crisis
57 www.aviva.co.uk/retirement/tools/mid-life-mot-app
58 https://home.barclays/news/2019/05/-i-m-proof-that-age-is-not-a-barrier-for-apprenticeships
59 www.bmwgroup.com/en/sustainability/employees
60 https://fortune.com/2023/07/14/grandparent-leave-benefit-cisco-Grandternity
61 www.linkedin.com/news/story/new-work-perk-grandternity-leave
62 www.linkedin.com/news/story/new-work-perk-grandternity-leave
63 www.linkedin.com/news/story/new-work-perk-grandternity-leave
64 www.google.com/search?q=denmark+days+off+for+seniors
65 www.ey.com/en_pt/workforce/how-to-transform-your-organization-in-turbulent-times
66 www.sanofi.com/en/our-company/social-impact/diversity-equity-and-inclusion-in-and-beyond-the-workplace
67 https://elderberries.substack.com/p/pedro-pitella-why-and-how-sanofi
68 www.google.com/search?q=swissray+affinity+group
69 https://hbr.org/2020/12/how-companies-can-meet-the-needs-of-a-changing-workforce
70 www.bravestarts.com/
71 Collie, J. The age of no retirement. Working with Older People. 2015.
72 https://junoverse.app/junoverse-ready/
73 www.multiverse.io/en-GB/blog/opening-apprenticeships-to-people-of-all-ages
74 www.clublandoy.com/
75 https://www.managers.org.uk/knowledge-and-insights/professional-practice/age/
76 www.mindsetworks.com/science/
77 https://www.multiverse.io/en-GB/blog/opening-apprenticeships-to-people-of-all-ages
78 www.mindsetworks.com/science/
79 https://www.google.com/search?q=Giselle+Cory+(2012)+says+in+Unfinished+Business
80 https://www.cipd.org/globalassets/media/knowledge/knowledge-hub/reports/understanding-older-workers-report
81 https://ageing-better.org.uk/summary-state-ageing-
82 www.gov.uk/flexible-working/applying-for-flexible-working

Chapter 5

Supporting Neurodiversity in the Workplace

Tamsin Crook and Aretha Rutherford

Introduction

Welcome to our chapter on neurodiversity in the workplace. To quote the German philosopher Soren Kierkegaard, 'life can only be understood backwards, but it must be lived forwards'. With this thought in mind, we have chosen to begin this chapter by sharing why, as career coaches, we are so passionate about supporting and celebrating neurodiversity in the workplace.

> I was diagnosed with ADHD in 2017, while I was studying for my MSc in Career Management and Coaching. I switched my planned research project to one focusing on the strengths and experience of career success in adults with ADHD[1] to build on a more positive narrative around neurodiversity. After a lifetime of struggling with focus, concentration and getting into tasks, and feeling like I had so much potential, but couldn't work out how to realise it, the diagnosis gave me a different lens to look at my life through. This self-knowledge, along with significant formal and informal learning about neurodiversity coaching, has enabled me to work effectively and purposefully with my neurodivergent (ND) coachees. (Tamsin)

> For me, it started back in 2019 when I was diagnosed with dyslexia and dyscalculia. This revelation profoundly affected how I understood my academic and career journey to date, bringing compassion and understanding to some of the more challenging experiences whilst uncovering a more precise picture of my strengths. This diagnosis changed my whole career trajectory and brought to the forefront the imperative of creating neuroinclusive

work environments. As a Black woman, understanding this through the lens of intersectionality was even more critical. (Aretha)

As career coaches, we have learned much about neurodiversity derived from our own lived experience and the insights shared by the neurodivergent coachees we have worked with over the years. Our encounters have taught us that there's no one-size-fits-all approach to supporting neurodivergent individuals. It was therefore important to us that we consulted with a diverse group of neurodivergent individuals with differing intersectional identities to integrate their experiences and insights with this work.

Managers have a difficult job and face enormous daily pressures. We hope that by illustrating the meaning, implications and benefits of neurodiversity and intersectionality, and sharing narratives of neurodivergent individuals (NDers), it might help managers understand their lived experiences a little better. In turn, we hope that it will be easier to build relationships, make career conversations less daunting and facilitate a more rewarding work experience for all. Equally, we appreciate that managers reading this could be neurodivergent themselves; in which case, we hope that what we have written resonates and supports them in their work too.

In this chapter, we explain how neuroinclusive workplaces can provide safe spaces where *everyone* can thrive and work according to their strengths. We have divided it into three different sections:

Part One will introduce the concepts of neurodiversity and intersectionality, and work through some of the associated assumptions and challenges.

Part Two will explore the myriad benefits that a neuroinclusive approach can bring to a business, and we'll go into depth with the strengths of neurodivergent individuals.

Part Three will focus on the practicalities, and what employers and managers can do directly to support NDers within their teams, to facilitate meaningful career conversations and play a core role in influencing their organisation to work towards genuine inclusivity.

Before we get started, it's important to note that while the focus of this chapter is on neurodiversity and neuroinclusion, for an organisation to be truly inclusive, there obviously needs to be a broader approach. We hope that this chapter will start a conversation, however, and we have included a range of great resources at the end, which go into greater depth than we've been able to here and relate to *all* aspects of inclusion.

Part One – Neurodiversity and Intersectionality

What Is Neurodiversity?

When we talk about neurodiversity, it is generally understood as an 'umbrella term' for a range of defined neurotypes, such as autism, ADHD, dyslexia, dyspraxia, dyscalculia and Tourette's Syndrome (or tic disorder). The term was coined initially by Judy Singer, who proposed 'that just as biodiversity is essential to ecosystem stability, so neurodiversity may be essential for cultural stability'[2]. Each of these neurotypes has a set of 'diagnostic 'traits', as well as some broadly associated strengths. We've summarised these in Table 5.1.

Although diagnostic 'labels' can be helpful in enabling access to support and gaining further understanding of neurodivergent traits, they can only capture a fraction of a person's cognitive profile. Many people will have more than one diagnosis, as co-occurrence is the norm, rather than the exception. So, if someone has a diagnosis of dyslexia, for example, there is up to a 50% chance that they will also have traits of ADHD[6]. Prevalence of ADHD among autistic people is approximately 40%[7].

Neurodivergent traits are based on multiple axes, and every individual will experience differing levels of challenge across each of the traits of their neurotype, and this can also be contextual depending on the environment, energy levels, and other associated anxieties. It is also important to note that neurodivergency is in no way related to general 'intelligence' or IQ.

Table 5.1 A summary of key neurodivergent traits and associated strengths[3,4,5]

Neurotype	Estimated Prevalence	Associated Traits	Associated Strengths	
ADHD	5%	Difficulty regulating / switching attention Impulsivity Hyperactivity or restlessness Difficulties with sleep Heightened emotional responses	Creativity and innovation Justice sensitivity Hyperfocus Curiosity Empathy Crisis management Altruism	Humour Energy Resilience Connecting ideas Connecting with people Environmental scanning/ observation
Autism	1%	Social and communication differences Sensory sensitivities Need for structure and routine Focused interests	Depth of knowledge in areas of interest Detail-oriented Analytical Strong memory	Justice sensitivity Honesty Hyperfocus
Dyscalculia	Up to 6%	Difficulties with: Numbers and calculations Times and dates Recognition of symbols (+/-, </>) Finances and data	Strong verbal communication Creative Seeing the bigger picture Strategic thinking	Intuitive Empathy Innovative
Dyslexia	10%	Difficulties with: Reading Writing Spelling	Creative Resourceful Entrepreneurial	Can be great delegators Visual/spatial skills Big picture thinking
Dyspraxia / Developmental Coordination Disorder	Up to 6%	Affects: Movement Coordination Balance	Creative Empathy Resilience Problem solving	

Given the known overlap of neurotypes and the fact that individuals will present differently despite having a shared label, there is a greater focus now on working with functional support, rather than neurotype-specific support. Prof. Amanda Kirby's work has been pivotal to some of this understanding with her work around 'spiky profiles'. This concept explains how NDers will present with more significant contrasts between the 'peaks' of functional strengths when compared to the 'dips' of certain functional challenges, whereas neurotypical profiles tend to be more even[8]. Jessica Dark has researched the interaction of 'neuro-traits'[9], which can broadly be defined as:

- Executive functions
- Attention, inattention and inertia
- Motor-coordination and hypermobility
- Maintenance of energy
- Verbal and written communication
- Sensory processing differences

Within the following sections, we'll be incorporating more of a trait-based approach to explain how neurodivergency is experienced day-to-day by NDers in the hope that what can be a 'confusing and ambiguous' topic[10] is made less so!

Understanding Neurodiversity Through an Intersectional Lens

Humans are complex, with characteristics derived from a combination of genetic predispositions, contextual influences and lived experiences. In the late 1980s, Kimberlé Crenshaw[11] coined the term 'intersectionality' to describe how individuals experience privilege or discrimination along multiple axes of differentiation. It's the interplay of how neurodiversity intersects with all other aspects of an individual's identity, such as their race, gender, socioeconomic status, sexuality or disability, that can impact their distinct life and workplace experiences. Acknowledging the convergence of these identities is essential for establishing neuroinclusive workplaces and organisational strategies, including:

Improved Systems of Support: Neurodivergent individuals are best served when their needs are understood within the context of their social identities. This will create a better understanding of the unique challenges they may face in the workplace, leading to improved working environments and support systems, and allowing NDers to work more effectively, productively and healthily.

Psychological Safety: Being seen, heard, understood and feeling safe enough to challenge ideas or advocate for one's needs without the fear of judgement within the workplace all play a vital role in ensuring a sense of security and confidence. Understanding neurodiversity through an intersectional lens can enable individuals to feel included and respected on multiple levels, because they can bring their whole selves to work.

Some of our contributors explained how their own intersectional identities have impacted their life experience:

> Intersectionalities contributed to my experience of neurodivergence as I've found a community of friendships with people who are also queer and who also have neurodivergent conditions . . . it helps me to feel more myself with having so many people around me who have similar experiences and who understand how my brain works. (Anon; autistic, non-binary, lesbian)

> I was born in China and moved to the US when I was 12. At this point, I mainly identify as an American, but my Chinese background is still a huge factor in my life. In China, you are taught as children to listen, obey, and not to draw attention to yourself. This meant no complaining, and neurodivergence and sometimes even certain types of disabilities are hushed and ignored. (Lulu; ADHD)

> Growing up I was aware of feeling 'different' and not fitting in. I didn't know about autism at the time, so my obvious 'difference' was being mixed race. People would point out differences in my

skin colour or ask: 'Where are you really from?' Because of this, I was resentful [and] dismissive towards my mother's culture and tried to distance myself from it. I feel differently now, but sometimes I still feel like I have too many "labels" and that I'm too 'different' for many people to understand'. (Tabitha; autistic, ADHD, mixed ethnic heritage, pansexual)

Assumptions and Biases of Neurodiversity: Pushing Back on the Stigma

There has been significant progress in both research and awareness in recent years, but those in minority groups, including NDers, are often subjected to 'microaggressions' in the workplace. Microaggressions can be defined as 'subtle forms of discrimination and include verbal, nonverbal, or environmental slights that convey disparaging messages to people based upon their [marginalised] group membership'[12]. Examples of microaggressions felt by neurodivergent people could include:

- 'Joking' about someone being 'so OCD' because they like to have their desk tidy
- Telling an autistic person that they 'don't look autistic'
- Telling someone with executive function challenges to 'focus more', despite concentration issues being a core part of their difficulty

Despite the term implying almost insignificant impact, these insensitive actions, statements, questions or assumptions[13] often lead to a compounding sense of social rejection[14], hurt, inadequacy and shame. As one of our contributors shared: 'I cannot help being different. Trust me, I have been trying' (Anon; Autistic, ADHD, Dyspraxic).

Neurodivergent adults have grown up with significantly more negative feedback than their neurotypical peers at school, at home, and at work. This stigma prevents NDers from accessing support that could make a huge difference to their personal and professional lives[15,16]. We tackle a few of the myths here:

'Everyone Is a Bit Autistic/ADHD . . .'

Sometimes, this is meant kindly, trying to relate to the experience of the neurodivergent person in front of them. The reality is that it can feel dismissive to those who experience these traits so intensely that it has a marked functional impact on how they live their lives day to day. Receiving a diagnosis of autism or ADHD is a complex process undertaken by a team of clinical specialists. While some people may identify with certain traits, the diagnosis is based on the persistence, the consistency and the level of impairment caused by these traits.

'Why Does Everyone Need a "Label" These Days?'

A 'label' seems to be a pejorative synonym for a 'diagnosis'. We recognise that 'labels' are complicated, particularly with the levels of overlap of neurodivergent diagnoses and co-associated conditions[17]. They can be reductive and encourage stereotyping if the 'label' becomes the 'person' – no one is only their neurotype. However, diagnoses are currently useful, or even essential, to gain access to support and accommodations at school, university and in work. A professional diagnosis can be validating for people who are seeking an explanation for lifelong challenges, and a way of becoming part of a community when community has often been hard to find. 'Labels' do matter very much for many neurodivergent people.

'It's Everywhere Now . . .'

ADHD was the second most searched-for health condition on the NHS website in 2023, after Covid[18]. There has been an exponential rise in numbers seeking an assessment, and an associated increase in diagnosis. Despite this, around 80% of adults with ADHD do not have a diagnosis[19], and possibly no understanding that there is a reason for the challenges they are likely facing. An interesting comparison is that of the prevalence of left-handedness. Before it was officially recognised as a legitimate difference, and left-handed children were forced to use their right hands, recognised cases of left-handedness were rare. In the 1930s and 40s, as it became more accepted, cases 'shot up' from about 2% to about 11% in 1950[20], leading to widespread alarm. However, the prevalence of left-handedness has stayed stable since that point. We are beginning to realise that it is the same with neurodivergence. It's always been there, we just haven't recognised or accepted it.

Misreading Intentions Based on Non-Typical Behaviours

A lack of understanding of neurodivergent behaviours leads to damaging assumptions:

- That challenges with punctuality indicate a lack of commitment, rather than an inability to perceive time in the same way as neurotypical people.
- That not making eye-contact is somehow 'shifty' rather than an avoidance of what can be a genuinely uncomfortable experience.
- That spelling and grammatical mistakes indicate a lack of care, despite the individual checking and re-checking their work, when they are just not able to identify the errors.
- That reacting negatively to certain sounds, smells and textures is being 'over-sensitive' or 'fussy', rather than the reality of genuine hypersensitivities in these areas than can cause physical discomfort and even pain.
- That choosing to sit alone for lunch is seen as 'aloof', rather than a necessary action to self-regulate after an intensely socially demanding morning.

One particularly damaging myth specifically about autistic people is that they 'lack empathy'. This is better explained as a 'double empathy problem'[21]. Just because two parties are experiencing a misunderstanding, it shouldn't be assumed that it is the autistic person who needs to change their behaviours. Autistic people also suffer due to these misunderstandings but receive little concession or acceptance from non-autistics[22].

It is so important to have a better understanding about the lived experience of *all* neurodivergent people, to start bridging these gaps in understanding. We hope that this chapter will help to do just that.

Neurodivergence as a Disability or a Superpower

The term 'neurodiversity' was coined as a 'neutral framework'[23], so this disability vs superpower binary narrative does not align with the intention of the initial concept. Both can be harmful assumptions to make and can lead to misalignment of expectations.

Some people perceive their neurodivergence as a disability due to the severity of impact it has on their daily lives, particularly those who are affected by co-associated conditions or have multiple complicating lived experiences. These NDers may benefit from higher levels of support. Others may not feel disabled by their neurodivergence and could be concerned that this assumption may lead to inaccurate expectations of their potential and achievement.

The superpower narrative, although empowering for some, can be problematic on a wider level, leading to an assumption that every autistic, ADHD, dyslexic or dyspraxic person should have some kind of exceptional talent. Framing neurodivergence in this way can be divisive; challenges can be minimised, and NDers can be 'unintentionally commodified'[24] when there are heightened expectations of performance due to their neurotype. We will talk about strengths in more detail later in the chapter, but the reality is that while NDers do have valuable and sometimes unique strengths and perspectives, these can be inconsistent, and often impacted by their context.

The reality of being ND is often more nuanced:

Most of my colleagues know that I'm autistic and it helps that other colleagues in the business are autistic too. But I often still find it hard to share I have autism because I'm scared that people will judge me and see me as incapable. (Jorun; autistic)

There's that obvious dichotomy of 'it's debilitating' vs the set of 'superpowers'. It is what it is. But I do feel like I have a very specific way in which I can move through the world, which is unique. Or at least, I'm in the minority. And I feel like I can add value to the world because of that. (David, housing sector; ADHD)

The aim of neuroinclusion is to create a compassionate working environment where *all* team members have the best possible chance of working with their strengths. If employers and managers can work towards getting this right, they are creating the conditions for NDers to reach their personal and professional potential, contribute meaningfully to business goals, and feel seen, understood and valued in their own right.

Experiences of Neurodiversity

A Complicated Journey to Where They Are Today

Some NDers in the workplace will have been 'lucky' enough to have received an early diagnosis, been well-supported in school and at home, and have a good sense of their strengths and knowledge of strategies that they need to put in place to support their challenges. They may be very used to self-advocating and be clear about what they need, and they may feel less of a stigma with their neurodivergence. Most of this cohort will be younger – a product of increased and improved access to diagnosis and support. However, this is not the story for most people, and it's still likely that most NDers entering the workforce will have had a tougher experience of education and work so far.

In this part of the chapter, we are going to consider the hurdles that many ND colleagues, including our contributors, have overcome to be in the role they currently work in. When managers show some understanding of these issues, to be compassionate about their struggles and champion their strengths, it can open the door to deeper relationships and greater productivity.

HISTORY OF DIFFICULTIES BEING DISMISSED OR MINIMISED

One of our autistic contributors explained:

> When your sensory experience, or your emotional experience is different to other people, and you say that something is too loud, or makes you feel anxious, typically the response, at best, is 'don't be silly it's fine, you're fine!' But what if it isn't fine? What

if something is painfully loud to you, or something genuinely worries or upsets you, and you're consistently told that you're wrong? What happens is that you stop telling people when you are uncomfortable or upset. You do your best to pull yourself through, going against every fibre of your being. You stop trusting your own judgement, because you've been told that you always over-react. (Anon; AuDHD)

Growing up, all these instances of being dismissed tend to be either *internalised*, potentially leading to masking, low self-esteem, anxiety or depression or other mental health difficulties, or *externalised*, or 'acting out', which in turn brings with it additional danger, punishment and shaming.

Adult diagnosis of neurodivergence has only been recognised since 2008[25], and even in children, only the most severe cases would have been recognised and diagnosed until recently. Neurodivergence is known to be highly heritable[26], and many neurodivergent adults were brought up as dismissed or minimised children, within families with generational histories of dismissal and minimisation. Many people will have had experience of being bullied by peers and shamed by teachers at school, or have found themselves in toxic relationships. It's a cycle that can be hard to shift.

MISSED OPPORTUNITIES WITHIN EDUCATION

School can be hard for some neurodivergent students and it's unsurprising that children who are undiagnosed and unsupported at school often struggle to reach their academic potential. Some children, however, particularly those defined as 'gifted', excel at school academically. Their challenges might be more about social connection with their peers, or difficulties may come later when they are expected to be much more independent in their studies at university, or making decisions for themselves when they live alone, without the guidance and reassurance of parental support.

Not succeeding in the way that is expected by others has a lifelong impact. NDers learn that things are hard for them, but they don't necessarily have an explanation for why this might be. This feeling is compounded and internalised, regardless of potential future success[27]. A participant in an earlier research study[28] explained it like this:

> Well, I'm smart, but I'm an under-achiever, you know. And it stays. It stays with you [referring to childhood experiences of being described as such]. I would just say yes, I'm successful, yes, I've achieved a lot, but I haven't lived up to my potential. And I think, if you took the ADHD factor out of my life, I would have achieved much more. (Anon; ADHD)

A FEELING OF NOT BELONGING

Many neurodivergent people will have experienced an ongoing sense of 'not belonging' without really knowing why. They might talk about a feeling of not fitting in, of 'being on the outside looking in', or 'being on the periphery of everything'. This feeling starts young – possibly due to not always recognising neurotypical social cues, finding group dynamics difficult to navigate, not sharing the interests of the peer group, being perceived as different . . . So many compounding explanations for why an ND child . . . and then an ND teenager . . . and then an ND adult and co-worker might feel excluded.

To counteract this feeling, NDers will often 'mask' or 'camouflage' their traits, using strategies (consciously or unconsciously) to hide their ND differences from other people[29]. This might include imitating others to try to fit in or generating 'scripts' to use before socialising. Those with other marginalised identities may have additional, more nuanced perspectives on these experiences. Two of our contributors shared their experiences of masking:

> I find it difficult to tell when to speak, how to speak, and what is OK to speak about. This means I have to mimic people and practice, and I am not always successful at either. (Jennie; autistic, dyspraxic)

> I've always felt on the outside, particularly because I'm a woman in a male-dominated industry, and sometimes because I'm intelligent and can unintentionally make others feel patronised

(I will quite often mask my intelligence and play it down with platitudes to fit in). I've made myself very ill at times trying to fit in, to be told I still wasn't quite good enough in performance reviews. So, I've taken in later life to be me, to try not to compare myself or allow others' judgement to derail me. I have found through being vulnerable and supporting others' vulnerability, I make the connections I had been desperate for, without needing to change who I am. (Jenny, Infrastructure Project Manager; ADHD, dyslexic)

THE IMPACT OF A LATE DIAGNOSIS

A 'late diagnosis' (referring to a diagnosis in adulthood, rather than childhood) can be a challenge to a sense of personal identity; there can often be a feeling of grief of unnecessary struggling through education and career to date; of lost potential, and an uncertainty of what it might mean for the future, particularly in the context of their career and their relationship with their manager. There may also be relief, however, in that there is a reason why some things have been so hard; and a sense of belonging within a new community as they connect with others who have shared experiences. An appropriate diagnosis can also allow access to potentially life-changing medication, treatment and/or support that may otherwise have been impossible. It cannot be underestimated.

Executive Function

'Executive function' is an umbrella term for a series of behaviours that are important for self-management, particularly in the workplace:

- Organisation
- Task initiation
- Attention and focus
- Impulse control
- Time management
- Planning and prioritising
- Self-awareness and self-monitoring
- Working memory
- Flexible thinking
- Emotional control

Most NDers will have challenges with several, if not all, of these behaviours, across multiple areas of their lives, as David explains below:

> There are just certain things I've never been able to do . . . Never been able to hold down a hobby, never been able to be consistent or have a routine. And without, sounding arrogant, I've got a Masters degree at distinction level and a bachelor's degree . . . I've got a first-class honours degree. So, by all kinds of societal measurements of intelligence, I should be able to do basic things like brush my teeth or make my lunch. And I'm woefully inept at it. (David, housing sector; ADHD)

Many will have developed some effective strategies to self-manage over time, but they will have needed to develop these intentionally and cognitively – they don't happen automatically, as they are more likely to do for others. For example, some NDers might have real working memory challenges, but to manage this, they may write notes and lists for themselves constantly (which can come in handy for the whole team sometimes!):

> I am extremely detailed in my work which means when I write briefings for meetings, everything that could possibly come up is covered. I am used to scripting myself for conversations, and briefing others for meetings is very similar. I am not good at retaining information, so I write everything down verbatim, so if someone in my team needs to check what was said by X person at Y meeting on Z date, I have that information. (Anon, Policy & External Affairs Officer, public health; AuDHD)

The key thing here isn't just the perception of how organised someone might appear to be, but how much *additional effort* goes in to managing that organisation. A conversation that we have had with many ND coachees is that the word 'just' masks a significant level of effort. Telling an NDer who is struggling to focus on a task to '*just* concentrate' or '*just* get on with it', is frustrating and counterproductive. There is *always* a reason why something is hard – they might need greater clarity on what the task is, they might need reassurance that they are on the right track, they might need a glass of water and a movement break . . . Asking team members what they need in that moment may help them to move through that feeling of discomfort or resistance, and start on the task that was frustrating them.

Balancing a Need for Structure with a Need for Autonomy

A key trait of many NDers is a need for autonomy over their own work. NDers work differently to others, developing their own systems and processes that work for them, but might seem odd to others. It's easier sometimes just to get on with work in the way that they know works best for them, without having to explain what they're doing and risk criticism. For some, it might be that their approach to time-management is a little 'different'. If given three months to complete a project, the standard expectation might be to do a little bit each week to keep on top of it. Many NDers, particularly ADHDers, will not even start the project until there is a looming sense of urgency – and then they will work in a 'hyperfocused' state, under intense dopamine-fuelled pressure, to get the work completed, often at very high quality, by the deadline. In situations like this, managers can support their ND colleagues by giving:

- clear tasks to do with specific outcome objectives
- a defined and logical deadline
- the autonomy to get it done in the timeframe that works for them, within the parameters that you define together at the beginning of the project.

It is important for managers to challenge their own assumptions about what they see as being the 'correct' way to do things, and focus on 'what' is being done, rather than 'how' it's done, as described by one of our contributors here:

> [It's really helpful for me to have] sufficient autonomy over what I work on day-to-day that I can afford to postpone big tasks until there's enough urgency for me to focus on them; but at the same

time having accountability via regular meetings with my team and line manager to discuss and update on what I'm working on. (Anon, Policy & External Affairs Officer, public health; AuDHD)

Being autonomous or a specialist can be valuable within an organisation. However, traditional career routes often rely on a team-based structure, followed by line management responsibility. This can put autonomous NDers at a disadvantage, as they may see the only route to progression as being to move up the hierarchy. Additionally, when it comes to career development, they are often less visible and may have fewer direct and influential sponsors:

> The main thing I need is autonomy. I have this, not because I've asked for it, but because I've created it for myself via the decisions I've made on roles I've taken. I often shape the role into what I need it to be, in order that I can thrive. I'm allowed to get away with this, because I am known to deliver results, but it does mean that I am often excluded from traditional succession planning. (Jenny, Infrastructure Project Manager; ADHD, dyslexic)

We'll address these issues relating to career progression in more depth in Part Three of this chapter.

Heightened Emotional Responses

While not yet part of the formal diagnostic assessment, the commonality of heightened emotional responses, particularly with ADHD and autism, mean that it is something to be aware of, and to try to understand to better support your ND team members.

Rejection sensitivity dysphoria (RSD) is an intense emotional reaction to a piece of criticism or a sense of rejection, which is interpreted as being incredibly personal[30], and it is particularly linked to the ADHD experience. It is thought to be a response to growing up receiving repeated negative messages, building intense feelings of shame and fear of judgement. RSD may be felt as a powerful reaction to a perceived criticism about a piece of work, or a personal interaction – and it results in a very real and very uncomfortable sense of rejection. For example, saying: 'you need to re-write this section of the paper', might be perceived as: 'I'm completely incompetent and I'm going to get fired'. This response might be witnessed as an 'over-reaction', or an emotional withdrawal.

Alternatively, they might experience 'anticipatory' RSD, and the fear of rejection might prevent them from putting themselves in any kind of situation where criticism or rejection might be possible. This is one reason why it can be incredibly hard to start on a task that is important to the NDer – the fear of getting it wrong prevents them from making a start. RSD can be damaging for professional development and career progression. An NDer might be seen as someone who is 'over-emotional' in response to what others might see as fair feedback, and therefore people can be wary of them. Additionally, they might avoid taking on profile-raising or career-enhancing opportunities out of fear of failure.

If a team member seems to have a reaction that is not proportionate to a situation, it can help to address it when things are calm. Ask what might help if something similar happens in the future. It might be about framing criticism carefully, for example, saying, 'We are so nearly there with this report, and I know it's going to be so well-received. Could you change this part to include . . .'. This is reassuring and focuses clearly on the specific part of the project that needs to be improved, but also emphasises the quality of the rest of the work. The brief additional time taken to frame feedback positively will save hours (or longer) of potential anguish.

As trust builds, it's likely that the NDer will feel safer in the relationship and may be better able to manage this kind of constructive criticism.

Demand avoidance (which can be part of an autistic profile) leads to anxiety-based reactions to direct requests or demands, and they may withdraw or refuse to comply with what they are being asked to do. While the assumption of most people witnessing this kind of reaction would be a sense that the individual is stubborn or difficult to work with, the reality is that some NDers can perceive these requests as a genuine 'threat', resulting in a fight/flight response.

Supporting team members in either of these scenarios is not always easy, as managers will have their own instinctive reaction to their team member's response. The following may be helpful:

- Try to understand what is going on under the surface for the NDer.
- Give some space between their immediate reaction and addressing what's happened.
- Avoid blame or direct criticism, and communicate clearly, avoiding ambiguity[31].
- Try to empower your team member to think about what might help them going forward to reduce the emotional impact in the future.

If either of these scenarios are happening regularly, then it might be beneficial for your team member to consider working with a neuroinclusive coach or counsellor to identify some helpful strategies that work for them.

Different Perspectives

An ADHDer shared an enlightening analogy in a different study of how her ability to view things differently has caused significant frustration in her role. She wrote a '9' on a piece of paper and put it between us on the table. From where I was sitting, opposite her, I saw a '6'.

> When I come into conflict, it's because the 95% see it as a '6', and I have difficulty, going 'it's a 9, it's a 9!' And the emotional difficulties I have is when people go 'you're crazy, it's a 6!

Her diagnosis allowed her to understand that the others genuinely saw a '9', so she was able to pre-empt their different perspective, rather than trying to fight it. She also spoke of focusing more on the joint solution, 'getting to an 8', rather than getting stuck on defining the problems, which has made a huge difference to her working relationships and career progression.

A Drive for Stability, Certainty and Justice

Neurodivergent people can often have a need for predictability, honesty, fairness and loyalty as core values. These are important assets for any business as powerful drivers for both improvement and social cohesion. However, while changes to day-to-day routines, role or team restructures are to be expected within any organisation, these events can have an impact on neurodivergent members of the team; over and above what might be felt by their neurotypical peers, particularly if they have a strong personal or emotional connection to the work or the organisation.

When you know that a change is imminent, it is helpful to let your ND team member know, giving them time to ask clarifying questions if they need to. It may also be helpful to empower them to build skills in this area by thinking through their response to change and potential new opportunities in more depth. The 'Planned Happenstance' exercise in the Career Tools chapter at the end of the book could be a useful exercise, although it is important to understand any assumptions and contextual information about their difficulty with change first.

Variability of Energy, Passion and Productivity

Bailey et al. (2022) undertook some important research about following passion and energy in work[32], which, while not exclusive to NDers, can be particularly applicable for those neurodivergent employees who may struggle with a particular combination of impulsivity, a desire to please others, a 'complicated relationship with time', and where there is a real emotional connection to the work. They identified that when someone is passionate about something, and a challenge comes their way, they rise to it, and they give more of their energy to meeting it. On days where people feel more passionate about their work, they work longer hours. However, because they have been so engaged in the work, they have a harder time detaching from work in the evening – they're likely to continue thinking or ruminating about problems still left to address . . . So, the next day, they are less rested and have less energy:

> I am not defined by my least productive days, or by my most productive – everybody has peaks and troughs, and you can't have one without the other. (Policy & External Affairs Officer, public health; AuDHD)

Additionally, when people feel really passionate and engaged, they tend to become over-optimistic, and maybe take on additional projects or agree to over-confident deadlines – which then become guilt-inducing and problematic when they are in a more depleted period.

Dr Claire Plumbly differentiates between healthy stress and burnout in her book on the topic:

> Essentially healthy stress is an energised experience, where we are absorbed by reaching goals or 'fixing' problems, whereas burnout is often a hollow experience of feeling we've given all we have and are now running on empty[33].

There is an evidence-based link between difficulties with executive function and job burnout[34]. The signs of burnout include physical fatigue, emotional exhaustion and cognitive weariness. All three symptoms have been linked to difficulties with time management, self-organisation and problem solving; all issues known to be challenges for many NDers. Add these difficulties to the complications of heightened emotional responsiveness and cumulative additional stresses relating to broader life experiences (as outlined earlier in the chapter), it is unsurprising that the risk of burnout is high.

It is helpful for managers to recognise the potential 'peaks and troughs' of an ND team member's energy and productivity, and to avoid appraising their performance based only on their most productive days. This helps to avoid feelings of inadequacy on the lower days. It can also be useful to gently challenge self-imposed deadlines where there may be a concern that a colleague may be being 'over-optimistic' about the reality of what can be achieved, particularly if they have a lot on their plate already.

The Impacts of Under-Utilisation of Strengths for ND Careers

UNDEREMPLOYMENT

When neurodivergent employees are struggling in their roles, they may not develop as far as their potential and ambition would otherwise take them. Sometimes, NDers might put themselves forward for internal promotion, but not be perceived as a strong candidate, possibly because they struggle with the assessment process, and don't have the internal profile or sponsor to support them. They may not be seen as 'management material' due to some of their challenges with executive function or difficulty in navigating the social dynamics of a work environment. Alternatively, if the pressures of work are too intense due to for example an overwhelming commute or working environment, NDers may make a choice to work fewer hours a week, or remain at a lower position, to have time to recover.

PUSHED INTO FREELANCE WORK, SELF-EMPLOYMENT OR ENTREPRENEURSHIP

We're saying 'pushed' here, to differentiate from the many NDers who make an active choice to go into entrepreneurship, and with the right combination of strengths, skills and context can make a fantastically successful entrepreneurial career (but this is a whole other book chapter . . .). 'Necessity entrepreneurs'[35] are those who move into the potentially more financially precarious self-employed space, not out of choice, but as a result of struggling to succeed within more formal employment.

Rob Edwards, founder of the Neurodiversity and Entrepreneurship Association, says:

> Probably half of the neurodivergent people who come to us have arrived at the idea of self-employment to break free of difficult

experiences in employment. In some cases, this can be a general feeling of never having 'fitted' into the corporate environment but, for some, the perceived lack of support from an employer (and failure to understand about neurodivergence) has left them with significant feelings of inferiority and a huge negative impact on their confidence in their work abilities. Many have needed professional help from a therapist to work through the distress that has been caused.

Classic entrepreneurial skills of creativity and innovation, opportunity-spotting, and high energy are often not utilised to best effect, due to the difficulties and restrictions experienced in many organisational roles. Creating neuroinclusive working environments within organisations of all shapes and sizes would give NDers the structure and security of formal employment that they often need to thrive in their careers. Importantly, the businesses would be able to retain these talented, motivated and ambitious staff within 'intrapreneurial roles' instead[36].

UNEMPLOYMENT

The path to unemployment may begin immediately after leaving school, particularly if a young person has struggled to engage with education and leaves school with few, if any, qualifications. However, many of the coachees we work with may have excelled academically at school, gone on to university and gained postgraduate qualifications. What holds them back isn't their lack of academic achievement, but low confidence, and difficulty jumping through all the hoops required to find and gain access to internships, placements, graduate programmes and those all-important first jobs.

> In [my] industry, many employers expect everyone to have completed internships. Someone like myself, who left home at 15 and had to work during high school and university, don't have the luxury of doing unpaid internships. Plus being autistic and thus feeling less capable when it comes to face-to-face interviews makes it very difficult to first find employment when finishing university. It's definitely something employers should be more aware of and take into consideration when reviewing applications. Thankfully,

my organisation is very forward-thinking, but understanding the journey that autistic individuals with my background are on in order to find a job is something that needs to be discussed more. (Jorun; autistic)

Further into career journeys, non-traditional career paths and potential career gaps due to burnout, mental health and difficulties in finding work can result in sometimes incoherent CVs. It takes an understanding and inclusive organisation to see beyond what is on the application form.

There are also many NDers who drop out of the employment market for long periods of time, or indefinitely, because additional caring responsibilities add layers of complication to the logistics of managing the commitment of an organisational role as well (see Chapter 7 on supporting parents).

The challenges that neurodivergent people face in their careers, whether it is due to burnout, underemployment, 'necessity entrepreneurship', or unemployment can be highly detrimental, if not catastrophic, for the individual. Financial precarity is common for NDers, partly due to lower average salaries[37,38], leading to housing insecurity, lack of pension provision, and in some countries, a lack of access to appropriate healthcare. In addition to the financial impact, there is significant loss of career potential, shame and damage to self-confidence, resulting in anxiety, depression and a negative spiral of health and life circumstances.

Crucially, there is a huge opportunity cost at the organisational and societal level; neurodivergent people have skills, strengths and talents in abundance, and they deserve to be able to play their part. By making it so hard for NDers to connect, engage and contribute, we are all losing out.

The next part of the chapter will focus on what these ND strengths might look like, and how they can contribute to organisational success.

Questions for Reflection

- Consider a time when you have felt the strongest sense of 'belonging' within an organisation.
  - What was happening around you in terms of social connection, engagement with task and affiliation with the organisation?
  - Consider how these elements of belonging aligned with your personal needs and values. How might 'belonging' mean something different to someone else?
  - How can you work towards facilitating a sense of belonging for each of your team members? How would your team benefit if all felt like they belonged there?
- How have your own different intersecting identities helped or hindered you in your career to date?
- How can you deepen your own understanding of neurodiversity and how could you share those insights with colleagues?

Consider your initial responses to the reflections above and make a note of your thoughts and any questions that arise – are there any changes that you'd like to make as a result?

Part Two – The Strengths and Benefits of Neuroinclusion and Neurodivergence

The Organisational Benefits of Neuroinclusion

There is significant momentum building around the business advantage for creating neuroinclusion at work. The professional services organisation, EY, now has 23 Neuro-Diverse Centres of Excellence globally, and highlights the 'diversity of thought and creativity' brought by ND staff as a key 'differentiator'[39,40]. AstraZeneca, the global pharmaceutical company has a dedicated global Employee Resource Group called TH!NK, which is tasked with building the relationship between neurodiversity and the workplace[41]. In the UK, the Neurodiversity in Business industry forum (see Resources section at the end of the chapter) is a key force in supporting ND employees and working with businesses to share best practice. These examples represent a tiny proportion of the work going on in this area.

There is also considerable evidence-backed research highlighting the benefits of cognitive diversity in the workplace, including the following:

- Neurodiverse teams tend to be more innovative and creative because of the unconventional problem-solving approaches of neurodivergent individuals[42].
- A neurodiverse workforce enhances individual contributions and boosts team performance, leading to higher engagement, commitment and better group dynamics[43].
- Organisations that embrace neurodiversity have lower turnover rates, fewer employees on sick leave and higher retention rates, which can lead to improved operational continuity[44,45].
- A strengths-focused approach helps to unlock skills and talents that may have been suppressed in the past. When neurodivergent individuals thrive in their roles, they contribute to increased productivity and profitability within an organisation[46,47].

Using a Strengths-Focused Approach for ND Careers

NDers sometimes find it hard to identify their own strengths. This could be because they may have low self-esteem resulting from previous bad experiences; others undervalue their own strengths because they seem unimpressive ('surely everyone can do this?'). Some NDers have a form of 'success amnesia', which describes how it can be difficult to remember how they got to where they are because of poor memory, or an assumption that any success was due to luck rather than their own abilities[48].

Formal strengths profiling tools and questionnaires are sometimes difficult for NDers to complete, partly because the standardised statements used can be ambiguous, partly because there will generally be a lot of contextual factors that are needed for them to qualify their responses, and partly because, to be honest, the questionnaires tend to be long and repetitive and boring to work through – so responses can be 'impulsive and incomplete'[49]. This might be important to consider if there is an organisation or team-wide initiative to use psychometric tools to measure strengths.

Strengths-based coaching aims to focus on positive qualities, resources and strengths[50]. For neurodivergent people, who may well experience low self-esteem and low self-efficacy, identifying and validating strengths can be particularly beneficial[51]. There is also evidence that positive emotions that come from strengths recognition have not only short-term effects on expanding thinking and focus, but also longer-term effects in building resilience and positivity[52].

For all these reasons, it is important to work with team members to identify:

- what strengths come naturally to them
- what strengths they feel good about using in their role
- the contribution that their strengths bring to the team and the wider organisation
- the contexts which help them to capitalise on their strengths.

Later in the chapter, we'll give some ideas about helping ND colleagues to do exactly this, and also, what to do if there is a mismatch between an individual's own strengths and those that are required for the role they are currently working in.

How Are Personal Strengths Identified by NDers Themselves?

We've previously outlined some of the strengths that are commonly associated with neurodivergence. While this is helpful as an overview, it is important to be cautious about directly linking certain strengths with particular neurotypes. Everyone will have their own profile of strengths and challenges, interests and values.

In our survey, and in some follow-up discussions, we asked our contributors to tell us about their personal strengths, and how they used them in their current roles; we offer a selection of their responses here:

> Attention to detail, honesty, a desire for precision and accuracy, a strong sense of justice, a willingness to question or challenge norms, an ability to focus for long periods of time if I'm left uninterrupted and if I can get into the right mindset. I don't tend to get emotionally involved and I think this helps me to make objective decisions and stay detached from my work which can sometimes involve traumatic/difficult topics. (Anon; autistic)

> Passion and interest in my work; efficiency; amenable character; adaptable; offering alternative perspectives; team-work. I think having learnt to 'people watch' for the majority of my life has opened me up to understanding that people view things very differently. I have learned from others and developed skills in communication that I now apply in a variety of situations. (Tabitha; autistic, ADHD, mixed ethnic heritage, pansexual)

> I am good at thinking outside of the normal approach because the 'normal' approach doesn't work for me. I am very outspoken – or 'blunt' – which can sometimes be a strength, when challenging orthodox views. I don't necessarily follow the usual social rules. This means I lack an ability to be diplomatic, which can be a problem, but can also be a strength when things should be challenged but no one feels like they can do so, due to power or political dynamics. (Jennie; autistic, dyspraxic)

In discussion with Alan, who is dyslexic, and awaiting formal ADHD assessment, he described himself as a 'systems thinker' – quite a common ND strength of being able to bring different perspectives to a discussion, to connect different business functions, 'translating' and connecting disparate agendas. The depth of this strength was facilitated by another layer to his life experience – that of being a 'third culture kid'[53] – being brought up in a South American country, within an international school, with European parents.

> I feel that my contribution is bringing the additional, supplementary enablers to the table. Not necessarily knowing the solution, but actually recognising that there is someone else

in the room. I think it comes from a position of empathy, I think it comes from being the dyslexic 'third culture kid'... recognising that there's a kid over there in the playground, sitting by himself – can we include him? With that third culture thing, because you're used to being in a situation where there are different perspectives, different languages, different cultures – you absorb that knowledge, and bring it into the business world. I may not understand your language, but I know enough to recognise that it's different, and I'm able to help translate that to others round the table.

Engaging ND Strengths Within the Team

One of our contributors, a Chief Operations Officer within the technology industry, had this to say about working with strengths in a team setting:

> My biggest steer to managers of neurodivergent colleagues is to encourage them to run the team in such a way that you are playing to everyone's strengths and the things they love to do. Help them to understand and see what their strengths are, and work with them to engage with, and develop those strengths. It's like magic... It helps the whole team to understand how they can contribute best and feel great about work. It also means managers hire better across the board – because they are looking to fill specific gaps rather than having a to-do list of general work tasks for the role to complete. When strengths are balanced the whole team starts to appreciate and be grateful for one another... it's really wonderful to see.

The concept of Person/Environment fit[54] is particularly pertinent for neurodivergent team members. The theory encapsulates the importance of *context* on career success, considering the matching of individual skills and strengths to specific organisational and occupational characteristics on three different levels:

- Do the tasks that are part of an individual's role fit with their skill set?
- Is there is a fit with co-workers and the organisational social culture?
- Does the working environment fit with individual sensory needs and working style preferences?

If all three elements are in place, it can be a great basis for a successful career. If two are in place, it could be satisfactory, but stresses may begin to show. One element may not be enough to be sustainable.

Our contributors spoke enthusiastically about how they felt that the roles they were working in fitted their very different skill sets and working style preferences:

> I focus best when a task has urgency, interest and novelty, so working in a reactive public affairs role suits me very well, because it is varied, interesting and often fast-paced. When I hit hyperfocus I can do in a day what others might spend all week on. (Policy and External Affairs Officer; AuDHD)

> I feel I have a high level of empathy and emotional intelligence. My role involves supporting people's development in both their personal and professional lives, helping them feel more satisfied in their roles, which makes these strengths particularly valuable. I am also very visual and enjoy creative tasks, making the creation of presentations and internal courses energising tasks for me. (Becky, L&D Manager, marketing industry; dyslexic, dyscalculic, dyspraxic)

> One of the reasons that I've leaned towards the legal sector is that I really enjoy having and working with lots of rules, processes and procedures. A lot of my day-to-day work involves drafting similar legal documents or undertaking generally repetitive legal tasks that some people may find mundane . . . my brain likes this safety and seems to thrive in this kind of work, so I find that I am really good at it, and am more able to spot the smaller details. (Anon, legal sector; autistic)

We'll discuss how to identify and use team strengths in more depth in the final part of this chapter.

Questions for Reflection

- Who are you when you are working authentically?
    - o What strengths are you currently using in your work? What strengths would you like to be using more?

o What values drive your actions and decision making?
  o How do those strengths and values serve you in your professional goals?
- What strengths do you see already in the different members of your team? Where are you particularly strong as a group, and which strengths might be lacking? (Use the Strengths and Skills Grid in Chapter 9, Table 9.4 if it helps.)
- What can you do to help facilitate the circumstances in which neurodivergent individuals in your team can utilise and capitalise on their unique strengths?

Consider your initial responses to the reflections above and make a note of your thoughts and any questions that arise – are there any changes that you'd like to make as a result?

Part Three – How to Support and Develop Neuroinclusive Careers

Neuroinclusion at an Organisational Level

True inclusion starts at the top, creating an environment in which employees feel safe to contribute their experiences and their insights. The resulting changes are likely to be for the benefit of all, and they are essential for those who have previously been excluded or disadvantaged by traditional organisational design. This is emphasised by Maureen Dunne in her book, *The Neurodiversity Edge*:

> Research has shown that the experience of not belonging is a top reason talented employees quit (whether neurodivergent or neurotypical). . . the upside here is only available when neurodiversity is allowed to thrive under conditions of authentic inclusion, where people are embraced for who they are, where cognitive diversity is valued, and where different cognitive strengths and unique skill sets are allowed to shine through.[55]

Any work undertaken to further neuroinclusion within an organisation should be created by, or in partnership with, neurodivergent individuals. In the 1990s, disability rights activists popularised the powerful slogan, 'Nothing about us without us'. There is a balance and a responsibility in this approach, as described by one of our contributors:

> There's an additional burden on neurodivergent people, to be advocates and educators, as well as dealing with the effects of being neurodivergent in a world that's not made for us, e.g. sensory overload, masking, etc . . . While I do think it's important to listen to neurodivergent people as individuals, as we're all different, it would be great if neurotypical colleagues (particularly those in positions of management/responsibility) would also make some effort to learn about neurodiversity and start conversations about it. (Anon; autistic)

Whatever the organisational culture, being open about their neurodivergence at the very least creates a vulnerability on an NDer's part. It must be safe for them to speak, and they need to know that talking about their experience will result in support, not judgement.

Not all NDers will want to be part of any inclusivity project at work – it may be too difficult or triggering for them, they may find it too much of a commitment alongside their day-job, or it may just not appeal. Managers in charge of inclusivity projects need to be clear in their communication of the expected input, what the time requirements will be, and what the intended outcomes are of any project. This ensures that those who want to participate can make an informed decision before committing.

We spoke to a global healthcare provider who gave the following insights around training and setting up a neurodiversity Employee Resource Group as part of their neuroinclusive approach to business:

> We have brought in some highly respected expert speakers such as Prof. Amanda Kirby, and Genius Within to educate ourselves around how to support neurodiverse colleagues. We've also curated free resources from the internet and shared them via

a learning hub. We've used 'storytelling' – with some of our ND colleagues sharing their lived experience in live sessions via Teams as well as blogs for our intranet. We created a 'Guide to Neurodiversity' in collaboration with some of our ND colleagues.

We have a neurodiversity community, which has grown organically amongst our ND colleagues. We provide clear guidance on leadership roles within the network and support those boundaries to ensure the communities can be successful. Regular meetings are held, plus steering group meetings with our Executive Sponsors. Being a Community Lead gives our people exposure to different parts of our business, raises profiles and provides opportunities to build a range of skills – leadership, engagement, influencing, communication, planning and organisation, and collaboration.

By taking a neuroinclusive approach, we are unlocking skills and talents that we perhaps wouldn't typically access, and it attracts talent to the business. Importantly, it also helps us to better understand the possible needs of our customers and communities.

This is such an encouraging programme of support, because there is reciprocity in the arrangement, and clear professional benefits for NDers participating in the group. Any invitations to contribute to innovative change are backed up with budget and endorsement at a senior level to make meaningful transformation to organisational policy, procedure and culture.

Adjustments for Neuroinclusion

Here, we outline a wide range of adjustments, interventions or supports that could be made broadly available to all, but may make an exponential difference to a neurodivergent and/or disabled member of staff. Remember that a clinical diagnosis is *not* required to request reasonable adjustments if there is a clear functional difficulty that needs supporting. Suggestions offered here, many shared as examples of support from our contributors' organisations, will have differing cost, time and complexity implications, but all are worth considering.

The ideal outcome is a productive and harmonious working environment for everyone, and this means that if one person's stated adjustment needs cause harm or discomfort to someone else, or negatively impact team or organisational productivity, then it's not a 'reasonable adjustment' and an alternative option should be considered. If a new request is made:

- Consider the anticipated benefit that the adjustment would have for the individual in terms of well-being and work outcomes.
- Consider the impact on others within the team/organisation – does their need clash with someone else in the team? If so, consider how this clash could potentially be resolved.
- Consider 'trialling' the idea for a few weeks to see how it works out for everyone and then review to see whether any further tweaks are needed in any way. It is useful to revisit even the more established arrangements as needs and circumstances can evolve over time.

Neuroinclusive Policies and Broader Support

Working in an office environment can be incredibly challenging for some NDers:

> The autism 'hangover' happens after every shift. This is much worse in person than it is online. Thankfully my job does not require a lot of meetings, but previous jobs have, and the toll has been significant. I feel like I cannot speak to another human after a day of communicating at work and I feel like my brain is full of static. My body feels constantly tense. I am irritable and angry, and I cannot understand why. This impacts my home life with my children. For this reason, I try not to go into the office too often. (Jennie; autistic, dyspraxic)

Options to reduce some of this discomfort includes:

- Facilitate hybrid working, or even fully remote working for those who are more comfortable and productive at home, and where the role allows it.

- Take a flexible approach to working hours where possible. When NDers hit a level of productivity and hyperfocus, they can really enjoy the work and get more done in a matter of hours than other people may do in twice as long. It is helpful to acknowledge and normalise that the day following an intense working day may be less productive. Flexibility can also help to reduce many of the associated sensory pressures of commutes to work and social interaction on a day when energy levels are more depleted. This approach is also beneficial for team members managing long-term health challenges.
- Core working days/hours can be advantageous to balance a need to have your team in the office together, and allows flexibility for those who might struggle with the intensity of a rush hour commute. Also, this is very helpful to those with caring responsibilities.
- Review all your organisational policies to ensure that they are neuroinclusive. Policies are often, by necessity, long and complicated. Either highlight the most important bits within the policy so that they are easy to find or create a summary at the start for clarity.
- When choosing an organisational healthcare provider, ensure that provision includes screening and assessment for neurodivergent conditions.
- Set up a Neurodiversity Employee Resource Group (ERG), as part of broader diversity representation within the organisation. These groups offer a safe space for NDers to connect, share experiences, working strategies and resources, build community, as well as influence practice.
- As is clear from this chapter, there is complexity in supporting neurodivergent team members. Specific training and awareness for all line managers, run by expert internal or external providers, is fundamental. Additionally, mentoring programmes where managers who are more experienced in this area can support those who are new to it can be an effective way to ensure that this learning is embedded within the organisation.
- Review internal training programmes to ensure they are fully accessible and inclusive.

Environmental Design

A study in 2023 of 2,000 people found that 15% of neurodivergent people and 6% of neurotypical people have actually left a workplace due to the physical design of the workplace. Jennie explains how this can happen:

> When I am in meetings, or in the office, I have to spend a significant amount of 'brain time' just processing everything – how it smells, how loud it is, the glare of the lights, the different textures of the chairs, the correct etiquette for meeting someone in the kitchen, the right things to say to colleagues, the right way to listen or engage. It sometimes takes another day for me to process what happened in a meeting and so that slows everything down. (Jennie; autistic, dyspraxic)

The biggest challenges faced by neurodivergent employees in an office environment include frequent distractions, anxiety in social situations, fatigue and burnout, brain fog, and sensory overload[56]. We were able to speak to Motionspot, the inclusive design consultancy that carried out this study, to gain more of their specialist insight:

> Inclusive design instils a mindset of inclusion, and offers safety and security at both physical and psychological levels. It removes barriers and enables everyone to participate equally, confidently, and independently in spaces and places, whatever their neurotype, disability, age, gender, religion, or language.
> Not only is creating accessible and inclusive buildings the right thing to do, but there is also a solid business case for investing in it too. Neuroinclusive workplaces support businesses to recruit and retain the best talent. For example, latest data by Accenture found that inclusive businesses deliver 1.6x more revenue, 2x more profit and are 25% more productive. (Ed Warner, MBE, Motionspot CEO and Co-Founder)

- Open-plan offices can result in significant disruption to focus and productivity. It's not uncommon for those who struggle in these environments to either arrive significantly earlier than others,

or stay very late to get work done. This might be manageable if hours are flexible to allow this staggered approach, but utterly unsustainable if it just means very long days with a big chunk of deeply frustrating unproductive time during core hours. Areas for quiet work are a key provision.
- Hot-desking can cause considerable anxiety in not knowing where you will be sitting each day. Many NDers like to be able to create their own personalised working space where there is predictability, and they can feel calm and in control.
- Bookable small rooms or acoustic sound booths create a space which is helpful for those who may need privacy to make calls. Using the phone can be hard for some NDers due to the uncertainty of what the other person might say and the requirement for speedy processing of any conversation.
- Natural light, and adjustable/dimmable desk lamps to allow each person to regulate light levels as far as possible in their own space. This can help to avoid the sensory challenges of too-bright/flickering/noisy overhead lights.
- Green plants make a huge difference to a general sense of well-being all round, as well as improving the air quality of your office.
- Areas where no food is allowed to reduce the impact of overwhelming smells. If someone has real sensory sensitivities to smell, it is important to allow them to sit as far away from the office kitchen area as possible. Within the team, it may also be kind to encourage people to avoid strong perfumes/colognes.
- Separate quiet rooms in office buildings where space allows, with low lighting and comfortable seating, can be beneficial for those who need to take a sensory break or have space to stim privately, and may also be helpful for those who are breastfeeding and need an appropriate place to pump.

Assistive Technology

- An iPad or other tablet with handwriting to text functionality to support note-taking in meetings.
- An additional monitor to help to have all required information visible at once, reducing the need to switch between browser tabs/programs.

- Use of the Grammarly app to support challenges with spelling and grammar and reduce typos across the organisation.
- Speech-to-text and text-to-speech software to support those who prefer to dictate rather than write, and listen rather than read.
- Accessibility software embedded within the organisational website and internal intranet to support with modifying fonts, backgrounds and audio functionality (e.g. ReciteMe.com).
- Noise-filtering earplugs (e.g. LoopEarPlugs.com) or noise-cancelling headphones to reduce distraction and impact of noise for those with sound sensitivities, or to enable access to specific music or sounds for those who focus this way.
- Coloured screen overlays or pale coloured backgrounds for presentations can be helpful for some people with dyslexia or visual impairment.

Meeting Culture

- Arrange team meetings on days and at core times when everyone is in the office / available online.
- Provide a full agenda in advance for all planned meetings, and give people advance notice if they are going to be required to speak, so that they can prepare appropriately.
- Keep meetings as short as possible or allow breaks in longer meetings.
- Recognise that some people will find it hard to 'speak up' at meetings, due to uncertainty of when it is appropriate to do so, or anxiety about saying 'the wrong thing'. An ideal approach is using Nancy Kline's 'Time to Think' model (see Further Resources section), where all members of the team are given a chance to speak in turn, in the same order going round the real or virtual table. This ensures people know when it is their turn and gives them a chance to think about what they want to say. If they'd rather not speak, they can just 'pass' – they may appreciate the chance to share their insights by email afterwards. This strategy can be helpful for introverts as well as NDers.
- If asking for a spontaneous meeting, always clarify its purpose in the same breath. A universal nightmare for NDers is the 'can we have a quick chat?' email. It can send people into a spiral of

anxiety, fearing that they are in trouble (and yes, that may sound infantalising, but remember that this response stems from years of inadvertently getting things 'wrong' and being pulled up).
- Allowing people to use unobtrusive fidget toys and/or doodle in meetings, acknowledging that it genuinely helps people to focus better. Don't draw attention to this activity or belittle people for doing what they need to do, as long as it's not distracting others unduly.
- Consider starting meetings at five minutes past the hour, in acknowledgement that back-to-back meetings can cause stress for those trying to be on time or those who need a bit of time in between intense social contact. Better to have a short break and arrive on time and ready to start.
- Consider reducing the need to travel to meetings in different locations by encouraging virtual meetings where possible. Also good for your organisational carbon footprint, and for those with caring responsibilities for whom overnight meetings are a logistical headache.

There are many examples of straightforward and practical adjustments here that can make the difference between career success and failure within the organisation for NDers. Strategies that have a budget impact could be reviewed in the usual way, but the majority of those we have suggested are low/no cost. Schemes such as 'Access to Work' in the UK can support with advice and funding where appropriate (see Further Resources section at end of this chapter).

The Hiring Process

APPLICATION AND ASSESSMENT PROCESS

The organisation's brand and reputation are essential to attract the best talent, particularly diverse talent, who will be particularly focused on their perception of the company culture, and the wider working environment. The intention should be to begin building inclusivity, trust and mutual respect as a solid foundation for the future relationship. The hiring process represents the very start of your first conversation with a new member of the team.

One of our contributors, the Head of Talent Development in a global media firm, shared that her organisation supports ND candidates from the moment of application: 'If interviewees tell us that they require additional support due to living with neurodiversity, they are pinged to a member of the Talent Team who is also a member of the Neurodiversity & Disability ERG, who will offer support'. This allows the individual to get an immediate and reassuring insight into how NDers are welcomed and valued within the team.

Candidates can be 'shown' how inclusive the organisation is through the clarity of the application process. Some strategies that have been appreciated by our contributors include:

- Giving plenty of notice for explicitly advertised interview dates
- Ensuring clear directions to assessment venues are sent out in good time, and give an outline of what will be expected at each stage
- Having one-to-one conversations, which are less intimidating, as a first-round interview, particularly for more junior hires
- Giving the names and job titles of panel members in advance, so the candidate has a good idea of who they will be meeting
- Where possible, offer some choice at the assessment stage – a paired live exercise, a presentation with some preparation time, or an in-tray exercise – this gives each candidate the opportunity to choose what works best for them and how they can shine

This was some feedback from Victoria, an autistic Oxbridge graduate about her recent experiences as a candidate:

My best overall experiences were with three large global finance institutions. They communicated clearly what the process was and how it worked and when I would hear back. I walked away from another process because their testing centre was run out of an international call centre, and it was very hard to speak to someone to get the right adjustments.

I always asked for adjustments. I never revealed my disability, and I was never asked what it was. If a remote video screening interview was part of the process, I could record my responses

> unlimited times; but these recorded videos are the absolute worst – I found that being given unlimited recordings was unhelpful because I would keep on trying to improve it and lose my passion and confidence for an answer.
>
> Where I enjoyed the process and did well was in face-to-face interviews, whether online or in person – but where I could gauge reactions and alter my pitch and responses. I have ASD and I'm not particularly good at reading faces, but some clue – any clue – is still better than a blank screen recording.

We also spoke to Louise, a recruitment and assessment consultant with significant experience in working on a wide range of corporate organisations' hiring programmes, and asked her about current trends in organisational recruitment:

> We now see the best organisations asking candidates what they need rather than making assumptions about requirements. There has been an increase in understanding of the benefit of integrating approaches that help ND candidates access the process (laptops and questions given in advance for all, for example). Organisations are rewriting the language and style of questions or assessment exercises and resetting their scoring systems ... This has happened as Gen Z have stood up and asked for what they need way more than previous generations, and it is refreshing to see neurodivergence disclosed with an explanation of what this means for the candidate and what they need from recruiters.

APPOINTING AND ON-BOARDING NEURODIVERGENT NEW-HIRES

The time between accepting a contract and starting in an organisation is a key period to set the scene for how the rest of the organisational relationship will progress. The early days are particularly important in setting NDers up for success:

- Try to spend time with a new ND team member asking them what would be helpful for them before they start. It can also be beneficial to ask for their input into developing their induction/onboarding programme. They may appreciate the additional contact and

reassurance, especially if it's a while between appointing and starting in role.
- Check their requirements around supportive technology and ensure that it is all in place from day one.
- On their first day, introduce them to key members of the team, and potentially any ERG network within the organisation (if they have shared their neurodivergence openly, and it's been checked that they would be interested in making contact).
- Within the co-created induction programme, bear in mind the potentially overwhelming experience of new environment, new people, and new expectations. Some contributors we spoke to were offered a 'phased' induction, where they only came into the office for the mornings or afternoons of their first week and then worked from home for the remainder of the day. Another had their first day on a Friday, so they could absorb the new information, and then have a weekend to process and be ready for a fresh start on the Monday. Being open to different ideas and ways of working can result in a meaningful start to a new working relationship.
- A useful question to ask a new starter might be 'What can we do to support you, so that in three months' time, you feel that you really belong here?' Keep progress towards these 'belonging' goals on the agenda for review meetings as much as you would performance objectives.

A Manager's Role in Creating a Neuroinclusive Team

Supporting Neurodiversity as a Manager

We are grateful to Prof. Almuth McDowall, Co-Director of the Centre for Neurodiversity at Work[57] at Birkbeck College, for sharing her insights on the need to support managers in their roles:

> Because of the high likelihood of co-occurrence with mental health conditions, there is an increased level of vulnerability with neurodivergent team members. It is important for line managers to have the skills to start open and honest conversations. Rather than raising the issue of diagnosis and condition, it is imperative to

raise any observations in the context of work. 'I have noticed that you have very strong reactions to xyz / I have noticed lately that you are withdrawn and don't talk to me or your colleagues. Can we chat about how I can support you to do your best work?' Open listening conversations are a good start to making neurodivergent team members feel heard.

But line managers cannot solve every issue on their own – they are not trained mental health professionals. Thus, they need to know any referral pathways, for example to Human Resources or Occupational Health. For some people, a workplace needs assessment can be very helpful. This assesses individual needs but also takes into account business requirements, and then makes recommendations for any adjustments and support. On balance, it is better to start any conversations about health and indeed performance issues sooner rather than later. Managers need to know how to 'triage and refer' as appropriate. Good communication and feedback skills are vital. All neurotypes benefit from clear and unambiguous language without irony and sarcasm, and actions and next steps clearly summarised.

This highlights the importance of having effective training and organisational management systems in place so that managers feel confident and supported to lead inclusive teams effectively and safely.

Being neurodivergent can sometimes feel infantalising. Most NDers carry a sense of feeling judged, so avoid referring to their diagnosis unnecessarily. One of our respondents spoke of a somewhat 'overly supportive' manager: 'I found my manager almost too understanding, she seemed to over-parent when I told her and kept referring to everything with the caveat "because of your ADHD . . ."'. Maintain the adult–adult relationship as with all other colleagues. If there are difficulties (or, equally as likely, successes) with performance, focus on the issue specifically, rather than the diagnosis.

It is not always known whether a team member is neurodivergent. It's not a manager's responsibility to ask someone if they are, or to try to 'diagnose' anyone in their team, or even to suggest it as a possibility. Any assessments should be unilaterally sought by the individual concerned and undertaken by qualified clinicians, or educational psychologists where appropriate. We have tried to give a broad outline of the experience of being neurodivergent, so that should a colleague show some of the related behaviours, managers might be more aware of potential underlying explanations. This would allow them to then approach the situation with (respectful) curiosity, an assumption of good intent, and to develop some alternative strategies, together with their team member, to address any issues – with a focus on the task in question.

If there is a safe and supportive environment, a flexible approach to adjustments for all the team where appropriate, and a solid organisational approach and conversation around inclusivity, then NDers may not need to mention their condition(s) to their manager at all. The diagnosis becomes unnecessary in that regard, although they may still choose to pursue it for their own personal reasons.

Encourage Team Reflection for Mutual Understanding and Support

As indicated earlier within this chapter, only a small proportion of neurodivergent people have a diagnosis at all. Fewer still will feel safe enough to share their diagnosis or support needs with their manager or wider team, so building a culture of trust is imperative:

> My team have been very supportive, but still in some ways struggle to understand me. For example, I have explained that I find it hard to process information in verbal conversations, and I have asked them to put this information in an email instead. Sometimes they still want to have those verbal conversations if they feel it is a sensitive subject, because the social convention is that these things are better said to a person's face. In my world, though, that makes them even harder to process, because I'm trying to concentrate on making eye contact, or to read their facial expressions, or trying not to fidget or interrupt. I've had to remind

them of this a few times, but I feel like I cannot keep doing this or I will annoy them. (Jennie; autistic, dyspraxic)

The experience of this next contributor shows that if initial conversations about neurodivergence are managed well, it sets the scene for wider acceptance and support:

> When I started in my organisation, I only disclosed it to my manager at first. Her support really helped me in my role. We discussed how my brain works and what challenges I have, and she helped me to get the reasonable adjustments I need. She also built a sort of agreement between us to figure out how she could best support me day-to-day. She makes more time when I am struggling, and can let me get on with things when I need little support. She's always aware of how announcements or changes in the way we work could affect me. Over time, and getting more comfortable with people in my role and with my diagnosis, I've become quite open with talking about it to my team. They've all been quite understanding. (Anon, legal sector; autistic)

To further encourage the exploration of different ways of thinking across the team, it can be helpful to invite every member (manager included!) to create their own 'Personal Playbook' (see Chapter 11: Career Tools). This is a private reflective log that becomes a dynamic document, updated with new insights as they come to mind. Team members can be encouraged to share the elements that would be helpful for others in the team to understand – particularly around communication preferences, sensory needs and belonging. Some coachees with whom we have worked have expanded on this idea and have written extensive personal notes about their different working strategies; logging helpful habits and routines, successes, positive feedback, insightful quotes or articles and the names of people that they can turn to in different circumstances for support. 'Manual of Me' (see Further Resources section of this chapter), is a great, shareable online version of this process. While this should in no means be an expected (or shareable) deliverable, many people find both the process of writing things down immensely helpful at times when they feel stuck. The resource that they have created can also be beneficial as a basis for career planning and development.

Consider the Team Social Culture

Social culture is changing in the workplace. This is in part due to tighter organisational alcohol policies, and because of an increase in hybrid and remote working, meaning that fewer people are around for socialising or 'after work drinks' in the same way that they were five or ten years ago. It's important to recognise, however, that non-drinkers as well as those with caring responsibilities can still miss out on any continuing informal networking opportunities afforded to those who are more able to go for a 'quick drink' after work.

By looking at the team's current socialising norms through the lens of neurodiversity, it may be possible to adapt plans to be more broadly inclusive. Ideas could include:

- **'Socialising with a purpose'** – staff volunteering projects (during working hours) where everyone has a defined role, can be fun and rewarding for the individuals taking part, and a good way of building links and organisational reputation with the wider community.
- **Opportunities for one-to-one connection** – going for a walk and/or a coffee with just one team member at a time on occasion. Many NDers, particularly ADHDers, need to move to think, and 'walking and talking' is often less pressure than face-to-face discussions.
- **Organisational away days with a clear structure**, ideally within team members' usual working hours or commute time, and where the venue is fully accessible, with quiet spaces for those who might need them. Some may need to have a quiet day following intensive social contact so may benefit from being able to work from home.

It's important to ask team members how *they* like to connect with others in the organisation, and to respect the fact that some people may be more comfortable keeping boundaried relationships with their work colleagues.

A Manager's Role in Supporting ND Careers

Working with Your ND Colleagues' Strengths

Many NDers struggle to recognise their strengths for all the reasons outlined earlier in the chapter. Rather than asking a team member to list their strengths off the top of their head, here are three different approaches that may work well:

1 Using an exercise like 'When I'm at My Best' (see Chapter 11: Career Tools), may help a team member to tap into specific events, projects or pieces of work that they have enjoyed completing or felt proud to be a part of. This will allow them to tell a story, in their own words, which can then be a wonderful starting point from which to identify related strengths and values. They are much more likely to own these words as they have come from their own experiences[58].
2 The Strengths and Skills Grid, provided in Chapter 9 (Table 9.4), can be a helpful starting point for discussion too. Taking each strength or skill one at a time, team members can work through and decide whether:

- It is a core strength of theirs that they enjoy using, and might like to use more, or would like to develop further.
- It is a 'contextual' strength for them – i.e. in certain circumstances it is easier for them to access than others – if this is the case, understanding the impact of different contexts is important in helping them to define their best working environment.
- It's a non-strength for them – and it's something that needs working on to help them to reach their business objectives and/or personal goals OR this is an area where they would benefit from being paired with someone who balances their skill set.
- It's a non-strength – but it's not something they are particularly worried by or need for their role. That's fine – no one needs to be good at everything.

The Development Grid (Chapter 9, Table 9.3) might be a good framework for working out a plan to use, stretch, share and develop strengths on an ongoing basis.
3 Strengths-spotting is a way of acknowledging what specific qualities a person brings to their work and the contribution that they make to the team. It is a great way of validating team members, and at the same time helps managers to build a clear picture of their full team's attributes. Notice what they do well, over and above expectations or what is required in their role. For example: 'I just heard the way that you described the new product to the Sales Team – you have a real strength in making complicated technical information understandable to non-techies. I know it's making a positive difference to our relationship with that team'. By specifically acknowledging a team member's unique, preferred strengths and identity and appreciating the value that they bring to their role, the team and the organisation, managers can create a sense of belonging and an invitation to each person to be authentically themselves.

Coaching Approach to One-to-Ones

Regular, informal contact between a manager and their team members can allow for ongoing feedback. Building the day-to-day relationship is essential for supervising performance, understanding the motivations and engagement levels of each individual, and as a foundation for more impactful career-focused conversations.

Encourage team members to express what kind of ongoing contact is helpful. Some may appreciate a regular agenda item on a one-to-one meeting to get oversight of their current commitments and progress towards deadlines. Starting with 'What's gone well this week?' is a great way to access a positive mindset[59] which will hopefully set the tone for the meeting. Encourage them to make a note of this positive event or experience and refer them back to their growing list if they need a boost. I have a coachee who has a specific file where he adds his successful achievements, and any positive feedback he has received that week, each time we speak. (NB: Some people love this approach as a way of tracking successes that they may otherwise not recall easily; others may find it condescending and reminiscent of 'star charts' at school. Agency of the individual is essential here.)

Other questions such as: 'What's engaging you most this week?' or 'Is there anything from previous weeks that might need looking at again?' can help refocus on priorities that have dropped down the list. A simple: 'What do you need from me this week?' is an open question that gives space for the team member to lead the discussion, taking ownership for their workload and support needs. Give a couple of moments after a final: 'What else would you like to discuss?', allowing additional processing time (sometimes it can be a bit like the 'one more thing . . .' on leaving a GP appointment – often that 'one more thing' is the most important issue on their mind).

A coaching approach, helping team members to think of and work through different options to solve their own issues, is likely to be much more successful than micro-managing, which can often trigger frustration, shame and defensiveness.

Coaching Approach to Career Conversations

Career conversations differ from one-to-one catch ups. The focus is on career development planning, and progress towards longer-term career goals, rather than updating on regular day-to-day tasks and objectives. The four-stage Career Conversation framework provided in Chapter 9 focuses on four key areas, and will be helpful to work with alongside some of these more specific thoughts tailored to ND members of the team:

STAGE 1: OPENING THE CONVERSATION

Before even beginning the conversation with an ND team member, ensure that they have been given plenty of notice about when and where the meeting will be happening. A clear agenda is helpful, along with guidance around what would be helpful to think about in advance or bring along to the meeting (The Personal Playbook in the Career Tools in Chapter 11 could be a useful starting point if that is something they have engaged with). Choose a meeting location which will be comfortable and distraction-free.

STAGE 2: WHERE ARE YOU NOW?

Spend some time working through what is going well – returning to the idea of 'belonging' as a fundamental part of many people's working experience, it might be helpful to connect with them on those goals, particularly if they are still relatively new in post. Thinking about the 'Person-Environment Fit' theory mentioned earlier in this chapter – where do they see their current role matching with their preferred strengths, working style and social/environmental context?

STAGE 3: FUTURE FOCUS

It's important not to make assumptions about future goals. Some NDers might be very happy staying in a role that they enjoy and feel successful at; others might crave variety and be ready to move on to a new project. Some may struggle with visualising longer-term options. Keep open minds about career plans and encourage thinking about job crafting[60], or alternative internal career paths, where it's appropriate.

STAGE 4: RESOURCING ACTION

The Development Grid (Chapter 9, Table 9.3) is a helpful starting point for recording some concrete goals and breaking them down into manageable steps.

Consider the pace of this process: some NDers might appreciate some additional processing time to consider what has been discussed up to this point and think a bit more deeply and independently about what their future goals might be before committing in the moment. If this is the case, put a follow-up meeting in the diary and reconvene at a mutually convenient time.

ND Career Development and Progression

Career development is a shared endeavour, between the individual, their manager and the organisation. Using the CCS

Table 5.2 Career development framework for neurodivergent team members

Employee as driver	Manager as coach
• Take ownership and agency within own career development planning. • Seek to understand yourself, your strengths and how you work best. What does your ideal working environment look like? • Develop your own network of support - your manager, your organisational diversity network, coaches and/or mentors inside or outside the organisation can be very helpful. • Consider what you would like your career to look like – you don't always need to be bound by what exists currently within the organisation – where do you see opportunities that you could be a good fit for? Channel your inner 'intrapreneur' if that is a strength for you. • Use internal tools and resources – if these are not accessible, request updated versions • Develop plans and take action, accessing support as needed.	• Develop your own understanding of neuroinclusion and intersectionality. • Consider steps you can take personally within your team to create an inclusive working environment. • Coach your ND team member in taking ownership of their career, supporting when asked/appropriate. • Discuss and input into development plans, focusing on strengths and finding joint solutions for challenges. • Keep up to date with career pathways and development opportunities and discuss with your team member, using the Career Conversation Framework (outlined earlier). • Be open to considering alternative career paths and development routes for team members, such as job crafting, specialist roles or horizontal moves. • Support team members in profile-raising activities and influencing upwards. • Share your network with your team member.
Employer as enabler	**Shared responsibilities**
• Review existing organisational diversity strategy to ensure that neurodiversity and intersectionality is understood and part of the discussion. • Review all existing policies and methods of internal communication to ensure that they are accessible to all staff. • Facilitate the development of a neurodiversity ERG for neurodivergent staff and allies as part of broader inclusion.	• Co-create clear, structured employee goals, linked to business needs. • Develop employee strengths through stretch objectives, formal and informal learning, and affirmation • Track development objectives and support strategies to ensure that both parties are meeting commitments and are content with progress. Review and amend where appropriate.

(*Continued*)

Table 5.2 (Continued)

Employer as enabler	Shared responsibilities
• Develop, implement and communicate strategies that enable ND career development. • Ensure appropriate neuroinclusivity training and ongoing mentoring support is given to all managers. • Communicate your commitment to neuroinclusivity within careers pages of your website, and all hiring documentation. • If you have senior members of the team who are neurodivergent, and they are happy to be open, encourage role modelling and mentorship opportunities.	• Identify organisational opportunities – both advertised and ones that can be co-created and crafted according to individual strengths and organisational need.

Career Development Framework, as outlined in Chapter 9, we have summarised some of the key aspects of creating a neuroinclusive approach to career development for neurodivergent team members in Table 5.2. This is obviously entirely adaptable to each organisational and individual context.

Final Thoughts

Throughout this chapter, we have tried to give a balanced insight into neurodivergent strengths, and also some of the more difficult aspects of the neurodivergent lived experience. There is an opportunity in embracing neuroinclusion to challenge the status quo and push the boundaries on the traditional concepts of work, career and organisational culture. This approach is changing and encouraging the conversation around wider workplace well-being, leadership, employee engagement, inclusion and diversity. The most powerful thing about it is that everyone benefits economically, socially, personally and professionally when neuroinclusivity sits at the heart of organisations.

We've summarised some of the key take-aways for organisations and managers below:

Organisational neuroinclusion:

- Creating a neuroinclusive environment as part of a broader approach to inclusion removes structural, psychological and physical barriers, allowing all staff an equitable platform from which to perform at their best.
- Neuroinclusion within the team encourages a neuroinclusive approach to product and service development, as well as marketing and customer support. If the voices of neurodivergent people are represented in the business, the business will deliver better for the ND 15–20%[61] of their target market.
- Create a Neurodiversity Network (or ERG) as a great place to start to think about short and longer-term priorities, and a resource guide to neurodiversity which is available to all.
- The adjustments and strategies highlighted within this chapter may be helpful for everyone – particularly those who may have some functional difficulties which don't meet the threshold of a diagnosis but are mitigated by access to additional help. While adjustments need to be reasonable for both the individual *and* the organisation, not everyone needs to have a clinical diagnosis to be able to request and access these reasonable adjustments.
- Organisational trust is paramount so that all staff can be honest about their needs.
- All managers need to have specific and expert training in neuroinclusive practices, and ongoing availability of mentoring or coaching to help them best support ND team members.
- A truly inclusive approach improves the well-being and working experience for *all* your staff. Inclusion 'initiatives' without a fundamental review of policies, processes and structural systems are at best short-term, and at worst purely performative. Inclusion, belonging and well-being are the *outcomes* of a well-managed organisation, not a bolt-on policy.

Key guidance for managers:

- Managers won't always know if team members are neurodivergent (and isn't something that should be suggested at any stage), but understanding some of the common neurodivergent experiences may help in addressing a wider range of scenarios that come up within team dynamics and management of individuals.
- It is important to develop further understanding of neurodiversity and inclusion, and consider how some of the ideas in this chapter (or other resources) might influence future team management strategies.
- Seek guidance for any challenging situations and share successes and insights. Confidentiality and discretion must always be maintained.
- Every neurodivergent individual will have their own strengths, challenges, values, interests and lived experiences. Work together with all your team members, using the tools and strategies provided, to identify communication preferences, management style needs, work tracking strategies and reasonable adjustments where appropriate.
- A strengths-based, coaching approach is most effective when working with NDers. This may take additional time and patience initially but will absolutely be worth it in terms of the relationships that can be built, the engagement that will be experienced, and ultimately the improved productivity and performance of the team.
- Managers have an exciting opportunity to make a genuine long-term difference to the well-being and career success of ND team members. They have the capacity to make changes that could potentially catalyse previously underutilised skills and strengths for the benefit of the team, the organisation and most critically the NDers themselves.

We so appreciate anyone who has taken the time to read this chapter, and we hope that there have been some interesting insights and actions that will support managers in their increasingly complicated roles. We thought the best way to conclude would be to ask our contributors what their personal hopes were for the future of neuroinclusion . . .

Neurodivergence in the workplace brings unique perspectives and strengths. My neurodivergence doesn't just mean I struggle to read, write and calculate numbers. It allows me to approach problems creatively and see solutions that others might not. It means that I may process information or communicate in ways that are different to the norm, but this can lead to new ideas and approaches that benefit our team and organisation. (Becky, L&D Manager, marketing industry; dyslexic, dyscalculic, dyspraxic)

I think that systematic inclusive practices across infrastructure, technology and process will mean that we don't need to ask for accommodations, it's just part of ensuring each human is given the right environment to thrive. I see my role to continue to be a 'real model' [as opposed to 'role model'] – to continue to be vulnerable with what I struggle with and find ways to be supported, via trial and error. To seek out what skills and strengths I have to share and where/how best to share them. Creating teams that have a mixed bag of assets, and ensuring each one has the psychological safety to be open and honest so that we can support each other. (Jenny, Infrastructure Project Manager; ADHD, dyslexic)

I hope for everyone to work in a place where they feel safe to be themselves, where they will be supported rather than penalised when they share about their challenges, and where there is room for individual nuance and ongoing discussions about what people need to thrive at work. (Anon, Policy and External Affairs Officer; AuDHD)

We have all this incredible language around neurodiversity . . . we can explain ourselves in this really amazing way now. But you have to be able to hear us. (David, Housing Sector; ADHD)

True inclusivity means that all staff are trained to know and support neurodivergence. That all meetings and away days are designed with inclusivity in mind (quiet spaces, smaller groups, visual and verbal descriptors etc.). Office spaces designed to engage all staff and offer all staff the opportunity to do their best work. That neurodivergence becomes normalised. That all processes and procedures are designed with flexibility and understanding and appreciation. (Anon, Finance and Operations Director, Charity Sector; ADHD)

Further Resources

The topics of neurodiversity, intersectionality and inclusivity are broad and complex, and the scope of this chapter means it is impossible to include all the research, perspectives and insights available. We are recommending some additional books, written by some fantastic authors, as well as the details of organisations offering services and/or products that may be helpful if this chapter has made you curious to find out more . . . (NB: Other books and organisations are available!)

Books

Black, Brilliant & Dyslexic: Neurodivergent Heroes Tell Their Stories (Marcia Brissett-Bailey, 2023)
Quiet: The Power of Introverts in a World That Can't Stop Talking (Susan Cain, 2012)
Neurodiversity Coaching: A Psychological Approach to Supporting Neurodivergent Talent and Career Potential (Nancy Doyle & Almuth McDowall, 2024)
The Neurodiversity Edge: The Essential Guide to Embracing Autism, ADHD, Dyslexia and Other Neurological Differences for Any Organisation (Maureen Dunne, 2024)
Neurodiversity at Work: Drive Innovation, Performance and Productivity with a Neurodiverse Workforce (Amanda Kirby & Theo Smith, 2021)
The ADHD Guide to Career Success: Harness Your Strengths, Manage Your Challenges (Kathleen Nadeau, 2016)
Beyond Discomfort: Why Inclusive Leadership Is So Hard (Nadia Nagamootoo, 2024)
Positively Purple: Build an Inclusive World Where People with Disabilities Can Flourish (Kate Nash, 2023)
Burnout: How to Manage Your Nervous System Before It Manages You (Dr Claire Plumbly, 2024)

The Canary Code: A Guide to Neurodiversity, Dignity and Intersectional Belonging at Work (Ludmila Praslova, 2024)
Untypical: How the World Isn't Built for Autistic People and What We Should All Do About It (Pete Wharmby, 2022)

LinkedIn Newsletters for Regular, Short Updates

ND Perspective newsletter (Jessica Dark ND)
Neurodiversity 101 newsletter (Prof. Amanda Kirby)
NDnomics newsletter (Charles Freeman & Tumi Sotire)

Charitable, Government Support and Advocacy Organisations

Access to Work (gov.uk/access-to-work)
ADHD Foundation, The Neurodiversity Charity (ADHDFoundation.org.uk)
National Autistic Society (Autism.org.uk)
Dyscalculia Network (DyscalculiaNetwork.com)
British Dyslexia Association (BDADyslexia.org)
Tourettes Action (TourettesAction.org.uk)

Consultancy Services and Products

Do It Profiler (DoitProfiler.com)
Exceptional Individuals (ExceptionalIndividuals.com)
Genius Within CIC (GeniusWithin.org)
Institute of Neurodiversity (IoNeurodiversity.org/work/)
Loop Earplugs (LoopEarplugs.com)
Manual of Me (ManualOf.me)
Neurodiversity in Business (NeurodiversityInBusiness.org/)
ReciteMe (ReciteMe.com)

Notes

1 Crook T, McDowall A. Paradoxical career strengths and successes of ADHD adults: An evolving narrative. *Journal of Work-Applied Management.* 2023;16(1):112–26.

2 Singer, J. *Odd people in: The birth of a community amongst people on the autistic spectrum: A personal exploration of a new social movement based on neurological diversity*. Honours Dissertation, University of Technology, Sydney; 1998.
3 Smith T, Kirby A. *Neurodiversity at Work: Drive Innovation, Performance and Productivity with a Neurodiverse Workforce*. Kogan Page; 2021. p45.
4 Crook T, McDowall A. Paradoxical career strengths and successes of ADHD adults: An evolving narrative. *Journal of Work-Applied Management*. 2023;16(1):112–26.
5 McDowall A, Doyle N. *Neurodiversity Coaching: A Psychological Approach to Supporting Neurodivergent Talent and Career Potential*. Routledge; 2023.
6 Hirschtritt ME, Lee PC, Pauls DL, et al. Lifetime prevalence, age of risk, and genetic relationships of comorbid psychiatric disorders in Tourette syndrome. *JAMA Psychiatry*. 2015;72(4):325–333. doi:10.1001/jamapsychiatry.2014.2650
7 Rong Y, Yang C-J, Jin Y, Wang Y. Prevalence of attention-deficit/hyperactivity disorder in individuals with autism spectrum disorder: A meta-analysis. *Research in Autism Spectrum Disorders*. 2021; 83: 101759. https://doi.org/https://doi.org/10.1016/j.rasd.2021.101759
8 Smith T, Kirby A. *Neurodiversity at Work: Drive Innovation, Performance and Productivity with a Neurodiverse Workforce*. Kogan Page; 2021. p45.
9 Dark, J. *Five Problems with Diagnostic Labels*. 2024 Aug. www.ndperspective.co.uk/blog/diagnosis-vs-neurodiversity
10 McDowall A, Doyle N. *Neurodiversity Coaching: A Psychological Approach to Supporting Neurodivergent Talent and Career Potential*. Routledge; 2023.
11 Crenshaw, K. *Demarginalizing the Intersection of Race and Sex: A Black Feminist Critique of Antidiscrimination Doctrine*. University of Chicago Legal Forum; 1989. pp139–168.
12 Lee EJ, Ditchman N, Thomas J, Tsen J. Microaggressions experienced by people with multiple sclerosis in the workplace: An exploratory study using Sue's taxonomy. *Rehabilitation Psychology*. 2019;64(2):179.
13 Washington, EF. Recognizing and responding to microaggressions at work. *Harvard Business Review*; 2022. https://hbr.org/2022/05/recognizing-and-responding-to-microaggressions-at-work
14 Lee EJ, Ditchman N, Thomas J, Tsen J. Microaggressions experienced by people with multiple sclerosis in the workplace: An exploratory study using Sue's taxonomy. *Rehabilitation Psychology*. 2019;64(2):179.
15 Lauder K, McDowall A, Tenenbaum HR. A systematic review of interventions to support adults with ADHD at work – Implications from the paucity of context-specific research for theory and practice. *Frontiers in Psychology*. 2022;13:893469.

16 McIntosh CK, Hyde SA, Bell MP, Yeatts PE. Thriving at work with ADHD: Antecedents and outcomes of proactive disclosure. *Equality, Diversity and Inclusion: An International Journal*. 2023;42(2):228–47.
17 Apperly IA, Lee R, van der Kleij SW, Devine RT. A transdiagnostic approach to neurodiversity in a representative population sample. *JCPP Advances*. 2024;4(2). https://doi.org/10.1002/jcv2.12219
18 www.england.nhs.uk/2024/03/nhs-to-launch-cross-sector-adhd-taskforce-to-boost-care-for-patients-in-england/
19 https://adhduk.co.uk/adhd-diagnosis-rate-uk/
20 McManus IC. The history and geography of human handedness. *Language Lateralization and Psychosis*. 2009; 1:37–57.
21 Milton DE. On the ontological status of autism: The 'double empathy problem'. *Disability & Society*. 2012;27(6):883–7.
22 Camus L, Macmillan K, Rajendran G, Stewart M. 'I too, need to belong': Autistic adults' perspectives on misunderstandings and well-being. https://doi.org/10.31234/osf.io/5mysh
23 McDowall A, Doyle N. *Neurodiversity Coaching: A Psychological Approach to Supporting Neurodivergent Talent and Career Potential*. Routledge; 2023.
24 Silver ER, Nittrouer CL, Hebl MR. Beyond the business case: Universally designing the workplace for neurodiversity and inclusion. *Industrial and Organizational Psychology*. 2023;16(1):45–9.
25 Grant D. *That's the Way I Think: Dyslexia, Dyspraxia, ADHD and Dyscalculia Explained*. Routledge; 2017.
26 Antshel KM, Zhang-James Y, Faraone SV. The comorbidity of ADHD and autism spectrum disorder. *Expert Review of Neurotherapeutics*. 2013;13(10):1117–1128.
27 Orenstein, M. Picking up the clues: Understanding undiagnosed learning disabilities, shame, and imprisoned intelligence. Journal of College Student Psychotherapy. 2000;15(2):35–46.
28 Crook T, McDowall A. Paradoxical career strengths and successes of ADHD adults: An evolving narrative. *Journal of Work-Applied Management*. 2023;16(1):112–26.
29 Sedgewick F, Hull L, Ellis H. *Autism and Masking: How and Why People Do It, and the Impact It Can Have*. Jessica Kingsley Publishers; 2021.
30 Dodson W. New insights into rejection sensitive dysphoria. *ADDitude*; July 2024 www.additudemag.com/rejection-sensitive-dysphoria-adhd-emotional-dysregulation
31 www.pdasociety.org.uk/wp-content/uploads/2021/08/workplace-adjustments-guide-for-employers-2.pdf
32 Bailey, ER, Krautter, K, Wu, W, Galinsky, AD, Jachimowicz, JM. A potential pitfall of passion: Passion is associated with performance overconfidence. *Social Psychological and Personality Science*. https://doi.org/10.1177/19485506241252461

33 Plumbly C. *Burnout: How to Manage Your Nervous System Before It Manages You*. Yellow Kite; 2024. p3.
34 Turjeman-Levi, Y, Itzchakov, G, Engel-Yeger, B. Executive function deficits mediate the relationship between employees' ADHD and job burnout. *AIMS Public Health*. 2024;11(1):294.
35 Churchill SA, Smyth R, Trinh TA. Negative life events and entrepreneurship. *Journal of Business Research*. 2023;155:113443.
36 Neessen PC, Caniëls MC, Vos B, De Jong JP. The intrapreneurial employee: Toward an integrated model of intrapreneurship and research agenda. *International Entrepreneurship and Management Journal*. 2019;15:545–71.
37 Patel PC, Rietveld CA, Verheul I. Attention deficit hyperactivity disorder (ADHD) and earnings in later-life self-employment. *Entrepreneurship Theory and Practice*. 2021;45(1):43–63.
38 Vincent J, Ralston K. Uncovering employment outcomes for autistic university graduates in the United Kingdom: An analysis of population data. *Autism*. 2024;28(3):732–43.
39 www.ey.com/en_uk/newsroom/2021/07/ey-launches-first-neuro-diverse-centre-of-excellence-in-the-uk-to-boost-client-innovation
40 www.bbc.com/worklife/article/20240320-ey-karyn-twaronite-neurodiversity-bbc-executive-interview
41 www.astrazeneca.com/our-company/great-place-to-work/employee-resource-groups.html#!
42 Krzeminska A, Austin RD, Bruyère SM, Hedley D. The advantages and challenges of neurodiversity employment in organizations. *Journal of Management & Organization*. 2019;25(4):453–63.
43 Carrero J, Krzeminska A, Härtel CE. The DXC technology work experience program: Disability-inclusive recruitment and selection in action. *Journal of Management & Organization*. 2019;25(4):535–42.
44 Meacham H, Cavanagh J, Shaw A, Bartram T. Innovation programs at the workplace for workers with an intellectual disability: Two case studies in large Australian organisations. *Personnel Review*. 2017;46(7):1381–96.
45 Parr AD, Hunter ST, Ligon GS. Questioning universal applicability of transformational leadership: Examining employees with autism spectrum disorder. *The Leadership Quarterly*. 2013;24(4):608–22.
46 Remington A, Pellicano E. 'Sometimes you just need someone to take a chance on you': An internship programme for autistic graduates at Deutsche Bank, UK. *Journal of Management & Organization*. 2019;25(4):516–34.
47 Soeker MS, Heyns M, Kaapitirapi P, Shoko S, Modise W. Worker roles in the open labor market: The challenges faced by people with intellectual disabilities in the Western Cape, South Africa. *Work*. 2021;68(1):255–66.

48 Crook T, McDowall A. Paradoxical career strengths and successes of ADHD adults: An evolving narrative. *Journal of Work-Applied Management.* 2023;16(1):112–26.
49 Carroll CB, Ponterotto JG. Employment counseling for adults with attention-deficit/hyperactivity disorder: Issues without answers. *Journal of Employment Counseling.* 1998;35(2):79–95.
50 Seligman ME, Csikszentmihalyi M. *Positive Psychology: An Introduction.* American Psychological Association; 2000.
51 Asherson P, Akehurst R, Kooij JS, Huss M, Beusterien K, Sasané R, Gholizadeh S, Hodgkins P. Under diagnosis of adult ADHD: Cultural influences and societal burden. *Journal of Attention Disorders.* 2012;16(5_suppl):20S–38S.
52 Fredrickson BL. The broaden–and–build theory of positive emotions. *Philosophical Transactions of the Royal Society of London. Series B: Biological Sciences.* 2004;359(1449):1367–77.
53 Pollock DC, Van Reken RE, Pollock MV. *Third Culture Kids: The Experience of Growing Up Among Worlds.* Nicholas Brealey; 2017.
54 Muchinsky PM, Monahan CJ. What is person-environment congruence? Supplementary versus complementary models of fit. *Journal of Vocational Behavior.* 1987;31(3):268–77.
55 Dunne M. *The Neurodiversity Edge: The Essential Guide to Embracing Autism, ADHD, Dyslexia and Other Neurological Differences.* John Wiley & Sons; 2024. p141.
56 Motionspot. *Neurodiversity and Office Design.* n.d. https://motionspot.co.uk/blogs/neurodiversity/neurodiversity-and-office-design
57 www.bbk.ac.uk/research/centres/neurodiversity-at-work
58 McDowall A, Freeman K, Marshall S. Is feedforward the way forward? *International Coaching Psychology Review.* 2014;9(2):135–46.
59 Fredrickson BL. The broaden-and-build theory of positive emotions. *Philosophical Transactions of the Royal Society of London. Series B: Biological Sciences.* 2004;359(1449):1367–77.
60 McDowall A, Doyle N. *Neurodiversity Coaching: A Psychological Approach to Supporting Neurodivergent Talent and Career Potential.* Routledge; 2023. pp194–5.
61 Doyle N. Neurodiversity at work: a biopsychosocial model and the impact on working adults. British medical bulletin. 2020 Sep;135(1):108–25.

Chapter 6

Supporting the Transitions of Career Returners

Kate Mansfield

Introduction and Definitions

Returners represent a significant and diverse talent pool for employers, and one which remains relatively untapped, as they have until recent times been overlooked, written off as having lost key skills and experience due to time away from the workplace[1].

The term returners describes individuals with existing work experience who have taken an extended career break from formal employment. They are professionals usually with approximately 5–10 years' work experience prior to a break and most likely educated to a minimum of degree level. The extended break is typically defined as a minimum of 12 months to 2 years and can extend to 5, 10, 15 years plus. It does not include those who have been on a maternity leave or a secondment from an employer and who intend to return to their employer. This demographic may have been economically inactive or economically active during this time in lower paid ways such as running a small business, working as a freelancer or in flexible, lower-skilled roles.

Returners are all genders and career breaks might be taken for a wide variety of reasons including childcare, eldercare, health (including physical, mental health and menopause), relocation, study, bereavement, small business management or any combination of reasons.

In describing the lived experiences of returners as well as the challenges they face in returning to work, the intention is to create greater empathy, understanding and awareness amongst employers and managers of the rationale for career breaks as well as appreciation of the strengths that this group presents. This chapter will challenge some myths and assumptions typically associated with career breaks and instead offer a lens through which to acknowledge that careers come in different shapes and sizes and that time away from the workplace offers many advantages as well as skills and personal development.

The chapter recognises and describes the challenges that returners face at a macro level in society and within organisations as well as the micro challenges they face as individuals, and the interconnectedness of the two.

Both employers and returners fall foul of assumptions and biases that require some deconstruction to enable more holistic, open and creative thinking about the valuable experience, skills and strengths they offer.

The chapter draws on the pioneering return-to-work methodologies created by the social-purpose led organisation Career Returners (formerly Women Returners) and my own experience of coaching returners as part of that organisation on both a one-to-one basis and in workshop settings. I also draw on some wider research conducted by career researchers, government working groups, and employment and diversity forums.

In the last decade, Career Returners has led the way in the UK and internationally in demonstrating that there are proven solutions enabling employers to offer returners routes back into the workplace. These solutions combine ways in which individuals can overcome the challenges of returning post-career-break and that managers and employers can enable them to successfully re-integrate.

To date, a small number of employing organisations have embraced these solutions but there is still a vast way to go in breaking down barriers more widely within organisations. I hope that this chapter will convince employers and managers to think more laterally about the ways that they engage with and bring talent into their organisations, and specifically to consider the many strengths of returners in bolstering diversity of experience, thinking and approach across the organisation.

Returners require more onboarding time than other new joiners as a period of transition is needed as they adjust back to the workplace, but with the right support, the transition stage is usually a matter of months for most individuals and there will be significant benefit from this initial investment of time. This chapter emphasises the need to avoid judgement, empower the returner to acknowledge their career break positively, and look at the ways in which a returner's sense of professional identity can be restored as quickly as possible. I will share some success stories, some practical frameworks and tools that have proven to bridge the career gap successfully.

Although returners are increasingly all genders, 75% of those within Career Returners network are women whose breaks were for primary reasons of childcare or eldercare[2]. UK ONS data also suggests that 87–89% of people who are economically inactive for caring reasons are women[3].

As also mentioned in Chapter 7, the 2022 Careers After Babies report found that 85% of women leave the full-time workforce within three years of having children, and 19% leave the workforce altogether 'most often because their work cannot offer any flexibility or they cannot afford childcare[4]. PwC research found only 64% of women with pre-school children were in employment compared to 93% of men[5].

Therefore, in setting out the case for hiring returners and describing their lived experiences through cases, there is an inevitable emphasis on women's experiences. This is because it is undeniable that a key driver for organisations to consider the returner talent pool is to bolster gender diversity, particularly to bring more women into mid to senior levels in the organisation. Employers have also found hiring returners presents an opportunity to bolster ethnic diversity, with 50% of returners in Career Returners professional network from an ethnic minority background.

The chapter seeks to be balanced and inclusive overall, ultimately making the case that career breaks should be a normal and inevitable part of the longevity of careers, for all genders. The strengths section also emphasises the wider value that returners bring irrespective of gender.

Why Should Returners Matter to Employers?

Many organisations and industry sectors are facing multiple problems relating to talent shortages, with a specific shortfall in some industries such as construction, engineering and technology[6,7]. The talent shortage is compounded in some sectors which also have ageing employees reaching retirement. In addition to this, many organisations are facing pressure in relation to attracting enough women into mid- and senior-level roles[8]. There is also the issue of the gender pay gap[9], and although formally unreported, there is also an ethnicity pay gap. Taking all this into account, there are a number of challenges which need addressing and returners have the potential to tackle a number of these issues simultaneously. They benefit our businesses and the economy[10].

To date many organisations have put much time and effort into early career programmes focused on younger people. These efforts may have resulted in gender parity and better ethnic representation during early careers, but are not yet reaching the middle layer of organisations.

The negative impact of this phenomenon for organisations is powerfully illustrated by Ioannidis and Walther's Attrition Triangle model (Figure 6.1)[11]. The model highlights what they call 'gender-based brain drain' at mid-career where organisations lose the balance of female talent necessary to ensure diverse leadership and thought perspectives. This trend of losing female talent at mid-career has

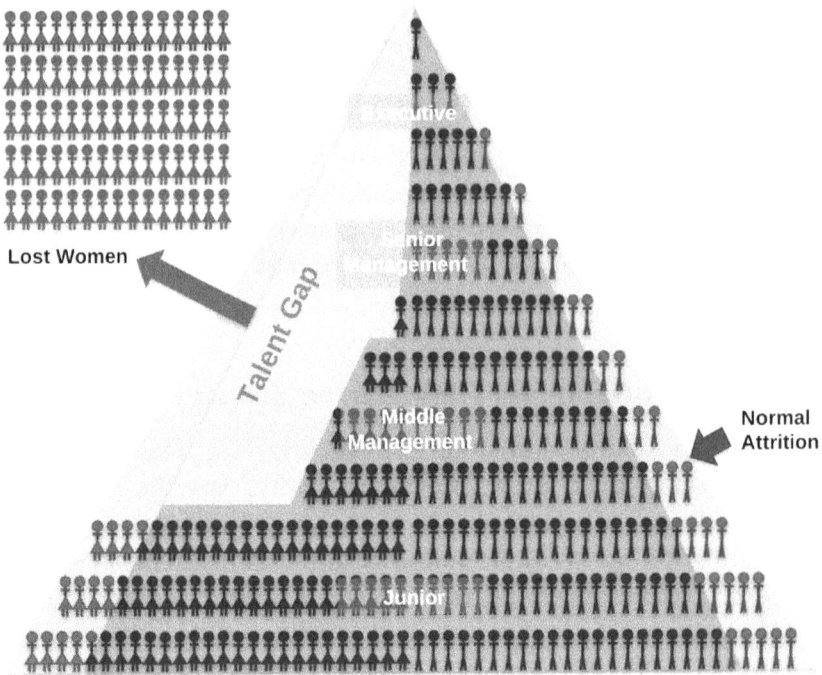

Figure 6.1 The Attrition Triangle demonstrates how organisations are investing in talented women only to lose them before they reach senior management roles

Source: Copyright Christina Ioannidis and Christina Walther 2010

also been described as the leaky pipeline[12]. McKinsey's Women in the Workplace research has time and time again made the business case for the benefits of gender diversity[13].

Many employers recognise these challenges at mid-career and are putting greater effort into retaining their women longer-term, however the focus on 'growing your own' is not often fixing challenges around gender and ethnicity quickly enough at the mid to senior levels. Returners have the potential to address all of these issues in a very short space of time.

Employers can be put off by a perception that it will take too long to get returners up to speed, but in fact most employers running returner programmes confirm that it takes less time than an early careers programme due to the levels of experience of returners. Government research also found that once employers had run one programme as a pilot, the business appetite and engagement increased significantly with the vast majority continuing to run ongoing programmes[14].

Returners are highly skilled and experienced professionals who can also boost age diversity within organisations potentially as well[15]. Employers have also highlighted the benefits relating to their employee and customer proposition, highlighting the positive feedback they have received from customers and employees on running a returner programme.

Getting the business case right upfront is probably the most important part for any employer considering how to bring returner talent on board successfully. One employer organisation highlighted the significant benefits of hiring returners below:

The Business Case for Hiring Returners

- Hiring returners strengthens the employee proposition and improves retention.
- Returners contribute to diversity goals relating to gender, age and ethnicity.
- Returners help mirror the diversity expected from clients and customers which helps revenue generation and customer retention.
- Employers can leverage returners to showcase lifetime employability.
- Returners are loyal and committed and likely to stay for long periods of time reducing further recruitment costs and re-training time.

Source: Head of Talent Acquisition, Global Professional Services Organisation

The Returner Talent Pool

The size of the global returner population is a significant talent pool for employers struggling with female skills shortages, keen to balance gender diversity and improve the gender pay gap. Global data provided by Vodafone indicated that there are an estimated 96 million skilled women aged 30–54 on career breaks worldwide, with around 55 million having experience of working at mid-manager level or above[16]. In the UK more specifically the ONS estimates that there are currently 1.7 million people economically inactive due to family and caring reasons[17].

Further data highlights the extent of this potential pool of talent across countries including the UK, Ireland and US, confirming that many have a high desire to return to work:

Data Summary: The Returner Talent Pool

- The Women's Business Council Report previously estimated that there are 2.4 million UK women who are not working and who *want* to work[18].
- Opportunity Now surveyed 25,000 UK women aged 28–40, three quarters of whom wished to return to work at some future stage[19].
- In Ireland, there are 90,000 people economically inactive and available for work. A quarter of these breaks were for caring reasons (Central Statistics Office, Q4 2023)[20]
- US research (Centre for Work Life Policy, 2009) found that 31% of highly qualified US women (and 37% of mothers) took a voluntary extended career break[21].
- The impact of the pandemic suggests that 3.5 million women additionally left the US workforce during 2020 and 2021[22,23].

Research has also estimated that increased female participation in the UK labour force could add £1.7 billion to the UK economy and boost GDP by 9%[24].

> Women are a key source of untapped potential which we need to harness to boost economic growth in the UK. (Ruby McGregor-Smith, CBE, Chair of Women's Business Council)

This topic has received government attention and funding in the UK and Scotland to enable organisations to employ parents and carers returning after long periods as well as funding to provide large-scale support to reach returners in certain geographical regions. 'Stem ReCharge', in 2023–2024, was a large-scale government-funded return to work readiness coaching programme led by Career Returners, to help enable returners based in the North and the Midlands of England to return to careers in tech and engineering[25]. The Government Equalities Office also commissioned Best Practice Guidance for Employers on Hiring Returners in 2017, co-authored by Career Returners and Timewise[26].

The rationale for hiring from a returner talent pool is a compelling one. However, the reality of doing so requires further education and understanding of this group and their needs so that employers can understand how to ensure the transition is a successful one, and to yield the benefits.

Lived Experiences: Why Do Individuals, and Women in Particular, Take Career Breaks?

In drawing out some of the reasons that individuals choose to take career breaks, I hope to create greater awareness amongst those in organisations of the vast range of reasons that individuals pause their careers and hope that it will enable those reading to recognise that these choices are decisions that everyone might need to make at some stage in their careers.

My own experience suggests that the reasons that people take career breaks are often complex and multifaceted. The role of 'choice' of course plays its part. Some readers may assume that a returner is in a fortunate financial position to be able to choose to not work for a period. However, the returner may feel that financially there is limited choice and that pre-school childcare for multiple children, for example, does not make financial sense for their family. They may also feel that the hours and the way in which they are expected to work offer them little choice but to take a break.

Jennifer's case illustrates someone who felt there was no financial choice but to pause her career when pre-school childcare was simply not a financial option for her and her family. Later Jennifer was successfully able to resume her career and become much more her authentic self when her children were older and there was time to focus on her professional role again.

Jennifer

Jennifer was a qualified social worker working for five years in a job she loved when she had her first daughter. She had hoped her parents would help her care for her child so that she could stay in employment but that fell through, and they were unable to help.

She couldn't see how she could manage a role such as social work with a young child to care for and with no family living nearby who could help. Childcare was simply too expensive. So, even though Jennifer was aware that money would be very tight for her and her husband, she decided to leave her role feeling that there really was no choice.

Ten years, two children and a relocation later, and with the youngest child now at school, Jennifer longed to return to social work. She had no contacts in the field especially as she was in a different part of the country. It seemed impossible. However, she started to complete some applications and tell friends of her wishes.

> After a year of applying for roles, a friend introduced her to a Social Worker in a local council who gave her a temporary role in their team for four weeks cover. Jennifer credits that manager for encouraging her to not to give up, who believed there was a way back for her and who said, 'let's keep in touch'. That same manager found her another post a few months later. Jennifer credits forward-thinking managers who encouraged her to train further and pursue her goals with the fact that she was ultimately able to resume a permanent and fulfilling career path culminating as an Inspector of Children's Services.

In Jennifer's case, there was a combination of factors that led to her decision to take a career break. She felt it was impossible to manage her young family and work. The decision to pause her career was complex, balancing the needs of her family, her husband's wishes, her perceived diminished value to her employer and financial reward vs increased childcare costs.

There may be biological and social reasons why more women than men choose to take career breaks. Research which has looked specifically at women's careers suggests that their career choices in comparison to men are more likely to be influenced by their relationships and the numerous 'roles' that they assume such as 'wife', 'mother', 'carer', 'friend' and 'daughter'. Women instinctively make holistic career choices and decisions that simultaneously take career and life into account[27,28,29].

A study by Gallos confirmed that some women were also willing to make career sacrifices because of the perceived negative influence on their relationships. This may be also influenced by their stage of life[30].

This is illustrated in the case of Priya who had multiple roles to play at home as both mother and carer. Despite her love for her career, she felt her only choice was to give up her career to fulfil these roles in the way she felt was expected of her as a good wife, mother and daughter-in-law.

> **Priya**
>
> Priya had a successful 15-year career in retail. She loved her work and was very successful at it and was well networked in the industry. When her first child was born, she returned to work after maternity leave, but she found the travel and having a young child challenging. By the time her second child arrived, Priya's father-in-law became unwell with dementia and he and her mother-in-law moved into the family home. As a family of Indian ethnicity, it was culturally expected for family members to take on caring duties. Priya felt constantly exhausted, stressed and guilty by the multiple demands placed upon her. She felt she was letting her family down by not being the main carer at home and did not perceive that working part-time could work in a retail environment, so she chose to resign from her role so that she could stay at home full time and focus on her roles of mother and carer. She felt for now it was more important to focus her time on others and she would focus her time on herself later in life.

O'Neil and Bilimoria (2005) described women's career and life responsibilities as 'ebbing and flowing' according to differing life stage concerns[31]. They proposed that women's careers fall into three age-related phases:

- Idealistic achievement (early career)
- Pragmatic endurance (mid-career)
- Reinventive contribution (late career)

Similarly, Mainiero and Sullivan's (2005) studies found women's 'career decisions were normally part of a larger and intricate web of interconnected issues, people and aspects that had to come together in a delicately balanced package'[32].

Kaleidoscope Career Path

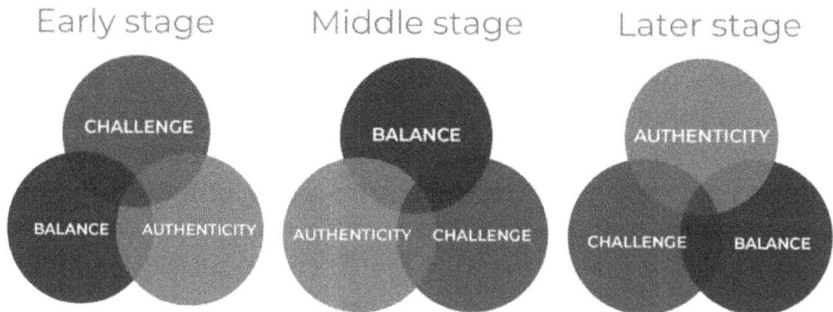

Figure 6.2 How the three aspects of career change during the beta career path (predominantly women)

Source: ECC (based on Mainiero and Sullivan's Kaleidoscope Career Model)

They proposed a three-stage model (Figure 6.2), the Kaleidoscope Career Model, defining three core elements of career – authenticity, balance and challenge – experienced in a different life sequence by men and women[33].

The model below suggests that although all three aspects are important, what features more prominently for women is challenge in early career, balance in mid-career and authenticity in late career. For men, it was typically experienced in the order of challenge, authenticity and balance.

The pursuit of balance, which features more prominently at mid-career according to the model, is a key reason in my experience that people choose to take career breaks. Women often feel anxious about how they can balance family and work, describing a rock and a hard place between competing roles and choices. Anne-Marie Slaughter (2012) described this as a double-bind faced by working mothers who feel guilty and judged if not present enough at home, and guilty and judged if they do not prioritise their professional career and work[34]. Choosing to take a career break is not an easy choice to make. A London Business School Survey found that 70% of women in business feel anxious about doing so and its consequences[35].

Balance is an often-misunderstood term with an implication there is a secret recipe to a magic balance formula. Slaughter has suggested this is just another unattainable measure or false assumption for women to fall short of. She promotes the term work–life integration alternatively which may be a much more helpful term for both women and men to think about how to balance career and family.

Of course, whilst some research is indicative of trends, theories cannot be universally applied. Whilst women may feel anxious about taking a break, it may be that they feel it is more socially acceptable to do so. However, I have come across more men taking career breaks reflecting that they also inevitably experience career patterns that 'ebb and flow' with life stages and demands. Men too struggle with issues around balance as illustrated in the case of Simon, who took a career break when he felt his family life was deteriorating due to the pressure of him and his wife having dual careers.

Simon

Simon worked in marketing in large international organisations. He decided to leave his career when his children were 4 and 2, and his wife was working as a lawyer. Both were working long hours and he felt that their family life was deteriorating. Simon admits to being unfulfilled in his role coupled with feeling burnt out with the competing demands of working and raising a young family. He says there was very little support for working parents in either his or his wife's organisation at that time and certainly no flexibility. They were both expected to be in the office five days a week and the hours that his wife worked regularly exceeded this. They had not been prepared for the reality of both being full-time working parents with a young family. Simon had no clear plan or timeline in mind as to when he would return but just knew that he needed a break. After nine months, they decided as a couple that he would take on the role of stay-at-home Dad on a longer-term basis whilst his

> wife focused on her career. He remembers feeling daunted about how he could fulfil such a parenting role well but found it incredibly rewarding and enjoyable. After years as a stay-at-home Dad, Simon did not believe any employer would consider his re-entry into the workplace.

Men may find it even more difficult than women to take a break. Simon admits that telling people that he was taking a short break felt more socially acceptable initially than saying his role would be a full-time stay-at-home parent. This changed over time however as he transitioned into his new identity and now sees the personal growth that this afforded him.

My experience confirms that the reasons for career breaks are complex, and the decision can rarely be attributed to one reason alone, although there may be an instigating factor. The individual's anticipated timeframe for their career break is also often shorter than the actual length of time taken, which also indicates some of the challenges experienced by those who take career breaks. Returners are not usually well-prepared for the psychological impact of the break, nor the barriers imposed by society and organisations when they try to return.

Typical Assumptions and Biases: What Are the Barriers Faced by Those Who Take Career Breaks?

There are several significant barriers faced by returners both systemically within society and within organisations as well as self-imposed personal and psychological barriers faced by this group.

Until the past decade, it was almost impossible for individuals who had taken extended career breaks to resume their careers at anything near to their previous professional skill or experience level, unless an ex-manager re-hired them. The structural and societal barriers have been described as the 'career break penalty' (Julianne

Miles, Co-Founder, Career Returners) meaning that professionals are penalised in terms of future opportunities to return to roles at similar levels of skill and experience simply because of the gap on their CV.

Data from the 2024 Career Returners Indicator survey (CRI 2024)[36], highlights that despite significant progress in the past decade, proving it is possible for returners to resume successful professional careers, the 'career break penalty is still alive and kicking' (Julianne Miles).

> 92% of those surveyed reporting they find it challenging to return to a professional role and 89% confirm that being on a career break has impacted their confidence negatively. (CRI 2024)

Olivia, whose case is shared below, did not anticipate how difficult it would be to resume her career, believing that her many years of experience and success in working both for employers and in running her own legal practice would mean employers would recognise she brought many skills and strengths.

Olivia

Olivia took a career break unexpectedly when her husband was offered a promotion abroad. This meant relocating the whole family from the USA to London. Olivia, a qualified lawyer, was running her own successful law firm at the time, which had enabled her to learn about business and provided her with much needed flexibility to be there for her three young children. The relocation was an unexpected career detour. It was decided that she would close her law firm and it was important for her to be available to her three young children as she settled them into new schools in London.

Olivia planned to be out of the workplace for around three years and return when her eldest started school. Her career

> break ended up being five years whilst searching for an opportunity during years 4 and 5. She initially enjoyed the time with her children, going to play groups, swimming lessons, dance and football classes as well as volunteering. She had always planned to return however, and did not anticipate that returning to work would be so challenging. With an impressive legal career including a role as General Counsel at a global bank, she was sure organisations would be interested in her skills and experience.
>
> But returning was much more challenging than she ever anticipated. Olivia managed to secure a few interviews initially but after countless rejections with no meaningful feedback she started to worry that employers could not see beyond the career break on her CV. She applied for many roles that were much more junior to her experience such as legal secretary believing that employers would find her level of experience very valuable. However, she was repeatedly told that she was 'over-qualified' for the role. Olivia began to feel frustrated and discouraged through her experience of trying to return, which then impacted her confidence.

Olivia's story is not uncommon. Many individuals with a career break on their CV have found it extremely challenging to return to their careers despite many of them reporting that their intention was always that they would return to work at some stage.

Olivia reports that her confidence was not impacted until she tried to return to work, and it was the barriers recruiters imposed that began to erode her confidence. For many others, however, the loss of their professional confidence may start way before trying to return, presenting a significant psychological barrier to returning.

The interdependent relationship between the structural and psychological barriers is perhaps inevitable, with each impacting the other.

Structural Barriers: Possible Assumptions and Biases About Returners

A study by Weisshaar distinguished between informational bias, for example, where a hiring manager or recruiter lacks information which results in false assumptions about reasons for a gap on a CV, and unconscious cognitive biases based on deeply held cultural beliefs associated with career breaks[37].

The study found that informational biases are easier to overcome by supplying positive information about career breaks. Unconscious cognitive biases however are more persistent and based on rigidly held assumptions and perceptions of ideal workers, gender-based and care-giving roles, motherhood, age and a lack of recent skills and experience.

Weisshaar found that these unconscious biases have also been found to be greater towards those who have taken breaks for caring reasons compared to those who took breaks for reasons such as redundancy and who were perceived to have less choice in the matter. These biases are often more difficult to recognise let alone challenge.

Some of the typical assumptions I came across most regularly are listed below:

Typical Assumptions and Biases Held in Relation to Returners

1. Returners are mothers who take breaks to care for children
2. Returners skills are outdated and obsolete
3. Returners don't have recent experience
4. Returners are less ambitious and committed
5. Returners only want to work part-time
6. Returners cannot learn to use new technology in the workplace

There is a lot of overlap between these assumptions, and many are linked to perceptions about care-giving roles and perceptions of what makes an ideal worker, a term originally coined by sociologist Joan Acker[38]. I have already highlighted that career breaks are not just taken by mothers for caring reasons. I want to elaborate however on some of the other biases and assumptions above.

Returners Skills Are Outdated and Obsolete

There are deeply held views ingrained in society and rooted in ideas aligned to human capital theory[39] which place great value on the accumulation of skills, knowledge and experience which in turn assumes that breaks in employment equate to skills becoming obsolete or at the very least diminished.

A 2015 US study confirmed that many managers would prefer to hire a less qualified candidate overall than one who has not been working for six months[40]. An international study by Harvard Business School also confirmed such bias with nearly half of employers in the UK, USA and Germany with automated applicant tracking systems automatically filtering out CVs with gaps of six months plus[41].

There is an inherent assumption here that skills are lost if they are not being used in the context of the workplace and a paid context.

Returners Don't Have Recent Experience

A figure of 40% of returners claim that recruiter bias in relation to a gap in experience on their CV is the biggest barrier to them returning (CRI 2024)[42]. Research also suggests that employers view those with CV gaps as inferior candidates[43].

Some studies have linked biases regarding the performance of those with non-standard work histories to concerns over performance[44]. There might be concern that the break was at least in part linked to performance issues in a former role.

During my own first career in recruitment, I was regularly asked by employers to justify a candidate's three-month gap between one role and the next, which is merely a matter of weeks. The mantra, 'hit the ground running' was used time and time again in job specifications perhaps without truly questioning what this meant and if this really was the case.

Recruiters understandably want to reduce risk as far as possible. The emphasis on recent experience rules out those who have taken career breaks and suggests that recent experience is more important than someone's overall level and length of experience and their relevant skills and wider attributes. It also discounts the very valuable transferable skills that many returners gain while on a career break through the activities they're involved in. These could include volunteering roles, pro bono work, building a 'side-hustle' home business, studying, or managing a big project such as a house renovation or family relocation.

Returners Are Less Ambitious and Committed Than Others

There seem to be some deep-rooted biases that if you have a family and chose to stay at home with them for a period that you lack ambition and commitment in comparison to others who chose to stay within their careers or indeed in comparison to those who took non-caring breaks.

Weisshaar's studies also found that those who had taken caring breaks received up to half of the requests to progress to second round interviews in comparison to those whose breaks were for redundancy[45]. The study also found that those whose breaks were for non-caring reasons still received fewer invitations to advanced interviews than those in continuous employment.

Employers may also be concerned about how ongoing caring responsibilities may impact returners' abilities to commit to their roles on an ongoing basis.

These assumptions do not take account of the complexity of the rationale for a career choice and assume that the decision to pause a career was in fact based on a lack of ambition and commitment in the first place. Returners often report that the decision to pause was partly to do with the fact that they couldn't commit to doing the work in the way they wanted to at that point in time.

Returners Only Want to Work Part-Time

Many returners have also reported experiencing assumptions that they will want to work part time because they have taken a career break and/or have a family and have found that employers express surprise if they wish to work full time. I have noticed this trend in my conversations with employers considering hiring returners, who have inadvertently and automatically excluded full-time roles from the pool that they wish to open to applications from returners. This also assumes that flexibility equates to part-time working, which is not the same. Similarly to the majority of employees, most returners would like some choice over how they manage their own time but the majority in my experience are open to working full-time hours. The Career Returners Indicator found that 69% of returners want to work full-time, although a degree of flexibility is key for 56%. The preferred working model for 82% is hybrid working (CRI, 2024)[46].

Returners Cannot Learn to Use New Technology in the Workplace

Hiring managers and recruiters have also expressed concerns over hiring returners because they believe they won't get up to speed quickly enough with new technologies that weren't being used in the workplace at the time they decided to pause their careers[47]. This assumes that age is a barrier in learning technology and that returners haven't invested in learning new technologies as part of their preparation for returning to work.

Also implicit in this is the assumption that those not in the workplace are not learning and adapting constantly to new technologies. It also misses that learning new technologies is part of life outside of the workplace and essential for almost every other aspect of modern life. In fact, many returners will take tech up-skilling courses or bootcamps to update and refresh their skills as they consider returning to work to help boost their confidence and chance of success at interview[48].

Employers and managers should be aware of these views not only in relation to the hiring of returners but during the onboarding stages when there is a risk that other colleagues and co-workers may judge them and potentially feel threatened by career paths and gaps that may seem alien to their own. One way for employers to tackle this early on is to dedicate time to IT training and up-skilling once they join, helping returners to up-skill in the key areas needed for their role so that they start feeling confident in this area.

There is no evidence to suggest that any of the assumptions above are factually correct and in fact, to the contrary, the available evidence which I will turn to shortly highlights the many strengths and advantages that returners bring to the workplace.

However, the more complicating factor is that many of these assumptions are also made by returners themselves and the resulting self-imposed psychological barriers contribute to the exaggerated perception of these structural barriers, with each one perpetuating the impact of the other.

Psychological Barriers: Self-Limiting Beliefs for Returners

My experience of coaching hundreds of returners, individually and in group workshops, surfaced some of their self-limiting beliefs stemming from some of the key biases outlined above. They often manifest for returners as an inner critic; the voice inside their heads that is often more debilitating than any external factor.

I list some of these below.

Inner Critic Voice for Returners (Limiting Beliefs)

- I am just a Mum. I don't have any skills at all anymore.
- My opinion does not count as much as those who have not taken a break.

- I don't know as much as those who have worked in the organisation for a very long time.
- I can't leave to pick up my children as others will see me as uncommitted to the role.
- That is a stupid question; everyone will think you are out of touch because you took a break.
- My family will not be able to manage without me at home. What will they do?
- I am not as quick as I used to be. How will I get up to speed?
- No employer will consider me because of the career break.

Many of these limiting beliefs combine with structural biases perpetuate a cycle where returners allow every setback and obstacle to build on the script that they tell themselves that it is too difficult or even impossible to return.

A lot of these self-limiting thoughts relate to one overarching factor experienced by returners: a loss of confidence and professional working identity. Karen Danker describes this sense of disconnect from who they were before their career break.

> 'Many people on career break experience a loss of self-confidence, in particular a loss of their 'professional identity', their sense of self as a highly competent professional. Disconnected from their working world and professional networks, they often fear that the working world has moved on without them and they just can't see their way to return'. (Karen Danker, Head of Coaching, Career Returners)

Returners lose their sense of identity as working professionals during a period away from the workplace and struggle with a loss of self-belief in their ability to become a working professional again. Greer's study found that women in comparison to men may lack self-efficacy in their ability to resume their careers, which may compound some of their anxiety and doubts[49]. Returners can feel very torn and conflicted, wanting to find that professional identity again and prove themselves, yet unsure it is possible and achievable.

Many returners I coached admitted to this loss of professional identity, regularly describing themselves using the words 'rusty' and 'out of touch'. When asked what their skills were, many would reply 'that they no longer had any skills as they were 'just a mum now'. This can also be linked to feelings of impostor syndrome in that there was a gap between their perception of who a working professional is or should be and how they saw themselves[50]. Their more recent identity as mothers had blinded them to the skills that they used to have as well as being able to identify those gained during the career break.

Many of the participants interviewed for my own postgraduate research saw a complete disconnect with who they had previously been as a working person and who they had become as a mum. They found it difficult to identify with the fact that they still had valuable skill sets even when many of them had continued with some sort of work, for example, running a fashion business or selling jewellery during their career breaks.

They saw this part of themselves as very separate from their 'career self' which they viewed as connected only to their former professional training and field they worked within such as law or financial services. They were not easily able to identify transferable skills and found it difficult to join up thinking in relation to this.

Herminia Ibarra's research into Working Identity[51], as well as Bridges' Transition model[52] (described in Chapters 1 and 8) may hold some interesting clues relating to the complexity we experience in relation to identity transition. Ibarra posits that we don't have one single working identity; instead we have many possible selves which are there to explore.

In the case of returners, they have spent valuable time exploring another self and identity and have already benefitted from the experience of transitioning out of the workplace, often a significant challenge at the time. They may need reminding of what they have gained through this transition and that they have the skills to transition back into the workplace.

In the next section, I intend to challenge further these biases and limited beliefs by describing the hidden strengths of returners and to position the career break as a positive factor that contributes to a well-rounded individual with a unique set of skills, perspectives and experience from which an employer can benefit hugely.

Strengths That Returners Offer to Employers

Every returner is a unique individual with their own set of skills, experience and attributes. However, it is important to highlight some of the key strengths of returners emphasised by employers time and time again. I hope that these will challenge the foundation of some of the myths and assumptions outlined.

> The core benefit to an organization of diversity is cognitive diversity, bringing a different perspective to a team. People who have taken career breaks bring this diversity because they have had non-linear career paths and different life experiences. (Julianne Miles, Co-Founder, Career Returners)

Returners contribute to organisations in several important ways, diversifying gender, age, ethnicity and experience. A more strategic benefit is the less visible diversity of thought perspective (cognitive diversity) which research has shown leads to more innovative problem solving in the workplace[53,54,55].

For those employers who have hired returners, many make returner hiring part of their ongoing talent attraction and management strategies which speaks for its success. It also sends important messages to other employees and prospective hires that non-linear, traditional career paths are valued, and that the organisation does not only recognise and reward linear career paths.

Some Key Strengths That Returners Offer Employers

- Highly experienced, qualified and skilled professionals
- Commitment to the organisation and to self-development

- Motivated and driven to prove themselves
- Emotional maturity and fresh perspectives (cognitive diversity)
- Focused and productive
- Role models for alternative career paths

Highly Experienced, Qualified and Skilled Professionals

Returners are typically exceptionally well-qualified with several years' professional experience under their belts prior to taking a career break. Within Career Returners' 9,500+ network of returners, 60% hold a professional or postgraduate qualification and 80% have at least five years of professional work experience[56].

Additionally, they have often spent considerable time up-skilling during their career breaks in anticipation of returning to the workplace or through volunteering. Many returners enjoy challenging voluntary work such as charity trusteeships or school governance roles to provide the intellectual challenge often missed on career break.

- Three quarters of returners spent time studying during their break, 16% at degree level and 28% with professional certifications.
- 51% have done small-scale employed work or been self-employed.
- 50% have also taken skilled volunteering roles.
- 93% of returners claim that the skills developed, and the breadth of perspective gained during their break mean they have more to offer to an employer. (CRI 2024)[57]

Many individuals also stress that there are hugely valuable skills gained during and because of caring roles that they might not have developed otherwise, particularly the skills of empathy, compassion, patience and resilience. A study by the *Harvard Business Review*, explored in more detail in Chapter 7, supports this with its findings that caregivers provide unique skills and contribute positively to organisational culture, retention and the bottom line[58].

Simon claims that his parental career break developed his interpersonal skills significantly more than if had he not taken time away:

> Taking time out to perform a caring role, whether you are a man or a woman, develops you hugely as a person. The role of raising children, guiding them, enabling them to grow without trampling on them teaches you facilitation, influencing and managerial skills in ways I simply wasn't exposed to in my 15-year career beforehand. There was no better place for me to truly learn how to empower others than doing it in the hothouse of raising children. (Simon)

Sarah Mavius, Head of Returners at FDM group, agrees and says that once her clients hire from their returner pool, these wider and transferable skills are regularly commented upon:

> Returners bring enhanced skills and strengths to the workplace. Caring or parental breaks develop and hone stakeholder management, influencing skills as well as creativity, problem-solving, patience and resilience. (Sarah Mavius, Head of Returners, FDM Group)

Karen Danker at Career Returners feels passionately that recent experience or the most up to date knowledge are not indicators of best fit for a role. Instead, employers should look to returners' underlying skills and experience gained pre-break and during their break for a better test of fit and potential.

> Highly skilled returners with years of professional experience pre-break are able to get back up to speed relatively quickly if supported – employers that discount them in favour of prioritising those with recent experience can lose out on great talent. (Karen Danker, Head of Coaching, Career Returners)

Commitment to the Organisation and Self-Development

As previously indicated, returners spend extensive time during their career breaks developing themselves in ways such as studying and high-level volunteering work. These trends tend to continue as they re-join the workforce with returners motivated to continue to learn in the workplace and keen to expose themselves to further training.

Contrary to the bias previously mentioned that returners cannot learn new technologies because of age and time out of the workplace, a study by Cisco made it very clear that older workers are fully capable of learning new technologies, but they need to be clear on the benefits of doing so and receive adequate training to do so[59].

Interestingly, Career Returners' research found that 69% of returners also said they wanted to work on a full-time basis, directly challenging assumptions about part-time working; 82% highlighted their preference for hybrid working however and in a post-Covid era, this is perhaps no surprise. Over 30% said flexible working was a key factor of consideration. This was more about the choice to deliver their work flexibly in a way that suits them personally around life commitments[60].

Motivated and Driven to Prove Themselves

In my experience, returners are highly motivated to return having spent years thinking about a return and what that might look like. Whilst money is an important motivator, particularly the idea of earning their own money, over half of the returners surveyed cited a combination of reasons including job satisfaction, intellectual stimulation and professional identity. Others also mentioned the importance of role modelling to their children that they could work and be a parent.

Cabrera (2007) points out the pros and cons of women taking a career break in the context of DeFilippo and Arthur's (1994) Intelligent Careers theory[61]. For example, they may be somewhat disadvantaged from a know-how (skills) perspective and knowing-whom (networks) because of the break. However, from a knowing-why (what they wish to do) they may be highly advantaged in being much clearer as they have had the chance to really reflect on what is important to them in life and those returning have often recognised that career is a meaningful part of their lives.

Again, in the case of Olivia, she says her period out of work really confirmed to her how much she wanted to be in work. She had never heard the word 'no' before and this made her more determined than ever to find a way back so that she could prove herself again.

Emotional Maturity and Broader Perspectives (Cognitive Diversity)

Those in the Career Returners network range from their late twenties to early sixties with an average age of early to mid-forties. Returners bring life experience enhanced by taking time away from the workplace and they often see things differently. Many organisations seek diversity of thought and approach[62].

Sarah Mavius at FDM describes the desire for 'blended teams' sought by employers. She says that cognitive diversity is a natural point of advantage that returners offer.

> Organisations say that they need 'disruptors' who challenge the status quo and 'think differently'. Returners come in with their professional and life experiences, offering unique perspectives that enhance creativity and boost business productivity. (Sarah Mavius, Head of Returner Programme, FDM)

Karen Danker, Head of Coaching at Career Returners, also highlights the breadth of lateral knowledge and life experience that returners bring:

> Returners bring broad lateral knowledge. When you've stepped off the career ladder and had different life experiences, you bring a very healthy and constructive different perspective to teams and problem solving, which employers tell us they really value. (Karen Danker)

Focused and Productive

Employers regularly remarked on returners' abilities to achieve their deliverables to high standards in a short space of time. Returners who have other responsibilities such as ongoing caring roles and responsibilities are often exceptionally talented at effective time planning and priority management.

Role Models for Alternative Career Paths

Returners serve a very important purpose of highlighting to others in the organisation that career paths do indeed come in different shapes and sizes and that it is possible to take a career break and be able to resume a professional and fulfilling career. This is important role modelling for everyone in the organisation irrespective of age or gender.

The case of Eliza below highlights a number of these strengths as well as the personal growth that a career break offers in developing leadership qualities. Eliza says that her career break makes her 'ten times the leader' she would have been without one.

> ### Eliza
>
> Eliza took a nine-year career break from management consultancy to focus on her family before returning to work. She was sceptical about the balance the sector could offer and concerned she would be doing 'half a job' on both fronts. She worried life would be a continual dilemma and pull between work and home.
>
> Eliza planned to take 2–3 years away from the workplace. But life presented a different path including more children, a house refurbishment and a dyslexia diagnosis for one of her children. As well as parenting, Eliza did a lot of voluntary work both as a Charity Director as well as for the school PTA.

> Eliza developed a huge amount of resilience and patience as a parent and says in becoming a parent, she gained much more empathy and became much more accustomed to seeing things differently. She jokes that 'having spent many hours persuading three-year-olds to put shoes on' in new and creative ways taught her so much. Eliza credits the time away from work with being now a much more emotionally intelligent leader who knows how to empower and construct high-performing teams. She absolutely credits her success now back at work with what she learnt during her time away.
>
> She also references voluntary work with helping to re-build her confidence to return when the time was right. Eliza prepared for her interviews by mapping out the skills she had gained through parenting and volunteering and practiced describing them in transferable terms to an employer.
>
> When arriving to the workplace, Eliza was reassured early on that her skills had not left her. Her skills of listening to understand, analysing, problem solving and find creative solutions were all still there. Technology had changed considerably in nine years so there was knowledge and learning to be done around this but she knew that she had the underlying core skills that enabled her to learn and get up to speed quickly.

Setting Them Up for Success: How to Integrate Returners Back into the Workplace

It can be overwhelming for individuals to return to work, especially after a long break. My experience suggests that the longer the break the more challenging this can be.

To ensure that women resume their careers at mid to senior levels, organisations need to persuade them that they can do so. Research suggests that those who take career breaks are three times more likely to return to lower-paid or lower-responsibility roles known as 'occupational downgrading'[63]. This is not usually the solution for the returner or employer in my experience, and there is a risk that they might opt-out altogether if they return to dull and unfulfilling work. More can be done by organisations to convince them that they can return to roles which enable them longer term to resume more senior leadership roles which is where they are needed.

There is significant risk involved with hiring and onboarding returners in conventional ways without putting into place the support needed to ensure a successful transition back to the workplace. Returners can't be hired and onboarded in the usual mainstream ways with an expectation that they can 'hit the ground running'. Poor onboarding experiences are potentially damaging for any new employee, but particularly so for those returning from a career break, increasing the chances they will leave the organisation.

A negative experience resulting in a returner ultimately not staying is likely to be detrimental for both the organisation and the individual, reinforcing the biases and stereotypes described above in the minds of others and significantly damaging the confidence of the individual, potentially putting them off returning to work altogether and perpetuating their own self-limiting beliefs and psychological barriers.

Greer's research looked at the training needs required by women returning to work[64]. Her study suggested that the employer focus should consider:

- Ways to increase confidence and self-esteem
- The opportunity to be part of a network of other returners
- Help with job search skills and a plan for how to re-integrate

In the past decade, there have been many employers in the UK, US and Europe who have trialled various means of attracting, engaging and supporting returners to resume their professional careers. Other organisations can now benefit from these proven approaches and models when planning to engage and integrate returning talent into their organisations.

Career Returners have worked with up to 180 leading employers since 2014, to pioneer several key models and approaches to bringing returners successfully into organisations in a supported way which makes the transition far more likely to be successful.

These return-to-work models include those shown in Table 6.1.

Table 6.1 Aspects included in return-to-work models

Returnship Programmes	A term first used by Goldman Sachs in 2008, with Career Returners first introducing the concept for employers in the UK in 2014. This programme includes a professional placement, usually for 3–6 months on a fixed-term basis, allowing both the returner and the organisation the opportunity of a trial period before a permanent role is offered. A structure is offered by the employer, which may include coaching, training, mentoring and buddying. The returner is typically part of a cohort who offer invaluable shared support to one another. Career Returners has pioneered successful UK cross-company returnship programmes in several sectors: the Investment and Savings industry (in partnership with the Diversity Project), Insurance (in partnership with the Insurance Families Network) and Fin-Tech. This is where multiple organisations collaborate on a returnship programme presenting a highly cost-effective way of bringing returners into the industry and increasing sector-wide diversity.
Supported Hiring	Option 1: Supported Hiring Jobs are ad-hoc roles usually open to any applicants, however applications are welcomed from people who have taken a long career break. If the returner is successful, they are provided with returner coaching through the transition. Option 2: A Supported Hiring Programme involves recruiting for multiple (often ringfenced) roles either starting on a fixed date, cohort basis or as part of ongoing recruitment on a rolling application basis. Returners receive a similar support structure to a returnship programme.
Returner Re-training Programmes	A form of returner programme where people who have taken a long break are re-trained into a new or related field or re-skilled to return to practice in their previous field. This can be combined with an ongoing role at the end of the training or be standalone. Return to Practice programmes are typically in the public sector, for areas such as nursing and social work.

One employer highlighted the benefits of running a return-to-work programme:

- Successful placement of candidates into permanent positions.
- External recognition of our efforts to run such a credible programme which helps our employer brand for lifetime employability.
- Sends a positive message for female talent in the marketplace.
- From a diversity perspective we are engaging in a programme that taps into a pool of people we have previously not been engaging.
- Clients have made specific comments about their delight we run such a programme, which is in line with their own diversity initiatives. (Head of Talent Acquisition, Global Professional Services organisation)

Returner Inclusive Hiring

In addition to or in lieu of a programme, some organisations are adapting their recruitment and talent acquisition strategies more widely to make them more 'returner' friendly in attempts to make returner hiring the 'norm' on a longer-term basis. This includes reviewing of job descriptions to make them more skills-based and less focused on recent experience. This needs to be reflected in the language used in role adverts and avoiding language such as 'hit the ground running' and 'recent experience'. Assessments are adapted for candidates without recent experience and recruiters and line managers are educated to understand returner applicants. Organisations may also offer 'insight' events whereby returners can attend to understand more about the organisation, its opportunities and support they will receive to resume their professional careers.

Re-Building Their Confidence and Professional Identity

The infrastructure offered via the routes outlined above include coaching, mentoring, buddy and peer support and have been proven to work with organisations, with Career Returners reporting conversion rates after returnships into longer term and permanent roles of 80% to 100%.

Olivia's case, continued below, illustrates why the creation of a supportive infrastructure matters in order to ensure returners can successfully transition back to work. Returners are often unaware themselves, as Olivia was, of what is required to help them re-build their professional identity.

> **Olivia**
>
> After two years of searching for an opportunity to return to law and feeling very discouraged, a friend told Olivia about a programme in partnership with Career Returners. This presented a lifeline. Olivia knew she had a lot to offer an organisation, having honed her skills and learnt a great amount during her career break, not least having relocated and settled a whole family from the USA to London. Nevertheless, she felt anxious: would they want her after so many other rejections? They did and Olivia was offered a place on the programme as part of a cohort.

Olivia was in denial about what she needed to help her successfully return to work:

> I was an experienced, confident professional outwardly. As were all my peers on the programme. We were mostly mid to senior level women, and two men, with lots of experience. I didn't know I needed coaching at the time and couldn't see how it would benefit. However, I now see it was the much-needed confidence boost I needed to make it work. You don't realise what five years out does to your confidence.

Olivia credits the structured coaching that she received as invaluable. She says that being part of a cohort of like-minded peers was also one of the most critical factors in making a successful transition back into the workplace as it provided a ready-made network who were all very experienced but also had empathy because they too had paused their careers for their own reasons.

Exercise: Think about your organisation and how a returner talent pool can benefit your organisation. The following questions may help:

Questions to consider:

- What is the business case for hiring returners in my organisation?
- How can this enhance our employee proposition and employer brand?
- What are the cost benefits of running a programme in the medium and long term?
- Are there any successful returner case studies that I can highlight?
- What support is realistic to offer a returner in our size/culture of organisation?
- How can I make others aware of unconscious bias issues within the organisation?
- How can we identify more roles as 'welcome to returner applicants?
- Where are line managers likely to be open to returner hires?

Are there roles where skills matter more than recent experience and there is time for returners to transition?

Not all organisations have the number of roles available to offer a returner programme. Small and medium-sized enterprises (SMEs) looking to bring in smaller numbers of returners can also benefit from the key lessons provided in these models, however. For example, you might consider one-to-one specialist coaching for the returner you are hiring, as well as considering who in your organisation could be a suitable buddy and mentor for the individual returning to your workplace.

How Long Does It Take for a Returner to Transition Successfully Back into the Workplace?

Most returnship programmes run for 3–6 months, to allow an adequate trial period before conversion to a permanent role.

Career Returners have created their own returner transition model, acknowledging the psychological transition that returners experience over the first six months, as they regain their professional identity in the workplace.

Drawing on Bridges' Transition model[65], referenced in Chapter 1, and elsewhere, the model illustrates how returners move through a sequence of stages. The transition begins with an ending of their career break life (for example, their identity as a carer; stay-at-home parent; student; small business owner) and ends with a new beginning, where they fully identify with their identity as professional worker.

The model highlights the range of emotions experienced prior to their return; during the first few weeks; in months 1–3; and in months 3–6. The range of emotions can be positive or negative throughout the transition, ranging from excitement and motivation to anxiety and overload.

Support from line managers, buddies and coaching is incredibly important in helping returners to manage the negative aspects and to navigate a smoother transition back to their professional work identity.

FDM, a global business and technology consultancy, offers a return-to-work programme where experienced professionals looking to get back to work after a career break are employed by FDM and placed in roles with their global clients[66].

Sarah Mavius, Head of the FDM Returners Programme says that they invest time and attention in ensuring that the returner is confident and 'ready' to re-join the workplace through up-skilling, coaching and mentoring before they are placed into a client organisation. In turn, this benefits the organisation, making the transition period shorter. The case below highlights how the Returners team prepared a cohort for roles at a global investment bank.

> **FDM Example Returner Case Study**
>
> One FDM returner cohort spent 13 weeks up-skilling in software engineering and were all ultimately successful in finding long-term roles at a global investment bank.
>
> In addition to updating core technical skills with assignments accredited by TechSkills and qualifications recognised by Microsoft and Cisco, returners also enhanced their transferable skills through professional development sessions.
>
> One-on-one career coaching and mentoring gave them the confidence to explore flexible working options and supported them on how to make flexible work requests. The cohort drew on the support of the other returners in the group which proved to be essential for confidence-building. Other returners offered shared empathy as well as a ready-made network of LinkedIn contacts and ongoing supporters. The FDM cohort also received an additional confidence boost from networking with other FDM cohorts such as those who are on the Ex-Forces Careers Programme.

Sarah says there is no 'cookie-cutter' approach when it comes to working with returners as they are all unique individuals with different backgrounds, skills and experiences and should be treated as such. Each conversation is personalised to their needs, but it is important that they know that support is available.

What Managers Can Do to Enable Returners to Successfully Transition Back into the Workplace

As a manager with a returner joining your team (or an HR professional looking to educate managers further), it is helpful to be aware of the key issues that might be on the minds of those returners joining your team:

- Loss of professional confidence
- Need for knowledge and skills refresh
- High pressure to prove themselves
- Concerns about managing work and family

Re-Building Professional Confidence and Skills Development

Remember that returners have not lost their skills and strengths, but they may feel 'rusty' and need some help to be able to fully recognise and utilise their skills and strengths. Specialist transition coaching can help them with this if you have the budget available but as a manager you might also think about some key things such as:

- Remind them of why you chose them in the hiring process and what particularly impressed you about their skills and experience.
- Ask them about their strengths and expertise and how they would like to use them in their new role and explore opportunities for them to do so. If they need help to articulate this, encourage them to take a strengths test such as CliftonStrengths[67].
- Work with them collaboratively for some quick and simple ways that play to their strengths, for example, some high-level research into a topic that interests them, and to provide you with a brief overview.
- Position them as an experienced professional, rather than simply as a returner. Mention their career break, but position this as a bonus and value add to the experience they bring. Your team will take their steer from you.
- Set some realistic goals for the first couple of months that enable them to gain some 'wins' and that will boost their confidence quickly. Review regularly that goals feel manageable.
- Ask them what they need from you and what areas of the role they are feeling most excited about.
- Help them to manage their workloads and check in with them on this frequently.

- Encourage them to create a stakeholder map linked to their goals and make key introductions on their behalf.
- Ask them what training they might feel interested in doing rather than you telling them what they 'need' to do.

Knowledge/Skills Refresh

Once you have established their strengths and identified some goals for the first few months, it should be easier to identify where any up-skilling or learning is needed. The following points can help further:

- Before they start, send them team acronyms so that they can begin to familiarise themselves with any key terms.
- When they start, share how to find key resources/documents.
- Signpost to how and where to access internal training courses and the process for getting these signed off.
- Help them to prioritise any mandatory training that will enable them to quickly understand processes and start delivering.
- Encourage them to stagger learning over their first three months so there's time to absorb and apply, and it's not too overwhelming. Focus first on key skills gaps.

Ensure Regular Check-In Conversations

One of the key things to be mindful of with returners links back to the limiting beliefs outlined earlier in this chapter. You may ask them what they need but they may not be completely honest with you because of that little voice in their head that is telling them they need to prove themselves to you because of that career break.

It is therefore important to ask the same questions regularly and remind them that you are fully there to support them. They will need more additional support from you in the first few weeks (and possibly up to 12 weeks) but it will pay back dividends in the months to come. One of the greatest gifts you can give is your time.

Quick daily 15-minute check-in calls in their first couple of weeks can help returners establish priorities for the day and help answer any questions they may have that might otherwise hold them back. Then ensuring regular check-in meetings weekly for the first 4–6 weeks will help you keep check of this. They only need to be 20–30 minutes, but they are important. For those returners where managers did this, their confidence came back much more quickly than those whose managers did not set this up, were not present or regularly cancelled those check-in calls.

Concerns About Work and Family

You can support with practical issues that parent returners may be worried about, such as how their families will manage without them or how they will manage their health issues, by asking how they would like to structure their working time.

- How do they need to work?
- Are there better days to be in the office?
- What office hours feel manageable to them?

Communicate non-negotiable commitments from your perspective such as the time for weekly team meetings but communicate clearly what is within their own sphere of influence. Perhaps it is fine for them to choose which days they come to the office, or you could communicate that you are more output-led, are happy for them to manage their work as they would like to. Also share examples of how other team members manage their time to take account of caring responsibilities. Sharing team norms can help put returners at ease on this front.

How to Position the Career Break and Introduce Them to Others

It is important to set up the returner from the outset by positioning them and their skills and experience in the most positive way. If you are aware of unconscious bias that occurs in relation to returners you can better manage this early on. I once coached a returner whose manager introduced her on her first day on a programme to a room of 20 people as 'the girl who had taken all that time out'. Remarkably she stayed and transitioned to a permanent role.

I would suggest you ask them to lead on introducing themselves and then they can position themselves and their career break as they would like to. But you can pre-empt their arrival with a positive email/message outlining the many skills and valuable experience they will be bringing to the team. There is no need to mention the career break at all unless you have agreed with the returner that they would like you to.

Additionally, do make sure that returners on a returnship aren't grouped with interns on your organisation's intranet as this can undermine their position/experience and hamper their progress.

Neutrality of Language

Career Returners emphasise the importance of being mindful of the language used in hiring and onboarding returners. During the interview process, for example, asking questions that focus on skills rather than asking 'for a recent example' is very important.

Similarly, when onboarding a returner, avoiding language that is steeped in acronyms and jargon is essential so that they do not feel panicked or isolated because they are too uncomfortable to ask what you mean. Incidentally this may apply to any new joiner!

Tools to Support

- You might find it useful to use the 'When I'm at my Best' template in the Career Tools (see Chapter 11) to get them to tell you about a time they have thrived.
- You might find the CCS Development Grid described in Chapter 9 useful for short-term goal setting.
- Creating a stakeholder map is a way to help your returner visually map out contacts in the organisation.
- Work–Life Balance Commandments could be a useful tool to help returners map out their boundaries around life and work and set up some good habits from the outset.

Summary Checklist for Managers to Positively Support Returners

- Empower the returner by providing the opportunity to introduce themselves and position the career break the way that they would like to or not like to. Do not assume you must take ownership for this as the manager.
- Don't over-focus or emphasise the career break. If you do mention the fact that they have had a career break, focus on presenting the positives of the skills that they have gained during their break as well as focusing on the years of experience prior to the break and what they bring without a focus on dates.
- Ask the returner what support they feel they need in returning to the workplace. What additional training would they find valuable for example?
- Set up a support system in addition to you: buddy, coaching, mentor.
- If you have other returners within your organisation, do connect them and make introductions. If you don't, contact Career Returners and connect them with their networks and resources.
- Spend time educating those in your team about the value of career breaks to offset any fears or misunderstanding from others.

Employer Checklist

Career Returners have also issued ten action steps through their #EndtheCareerBreakPenalty campaign that employers can use as a valuable guide to ensure that they are setting up successful and sustainable approaches to hiring returning talent[68]:

Employers' Call to Action from Career Returners #EndTheCareerBreakPenalty

1. **Learn About Returners:** Further stories can be found via the Career Returners podcas. Challenge your stereotypes.
2. **Remove Screening Bias:** Check that your automated or manual application process is NOT screening out candidates just because of their CV gap.

3. **Reduce Advertising Bias:** Make sure your job adverts are only asking for 'current/up-to-date knowledge' or 'recent experience' if this is essential.
4. **Reduce Interview Bias:** For competency-based interviews, adapt your questions to not ask for 'recent work examples'. Focus technical interviews on skills rather than knowledge.
5. **Promote Returners as a Strong Candidate Pool:** Put Career Returners on the radar for your recruiters and business leaders as a high-calibre and diverse talent pool. Educate on the full business case and ESG case for hiring returners.
6. **Support Returner Hires:** Provide transition support for returner hires, such as training, mentoring and (if you have the budget) Career Returners coaching to help them to re-build confidence and more rapidly re-integrate.
7. **Provide Returner Training to Line Managers:** Educate on hiring and supporting candidates returning from career breaks.
8. **Target Returner Applicants:** Consider adding to job adverts 'We welcome applications from candidates who have taken a career break'.
9. **Run a Cohort Returner Programme (if a larger organisation):** Use a proven framework to accelerate returner hiring and create a peer support network.
10. **Champion Returner Successes:** Continue to break the bias using your real-life examples of successful returner hires.

Source: Career Returners

Conclusion

Career breaks can be viewed as necessary and positive ways to develop skills and life experience which in turn can benefit careers and employers. The value as individuals is not solely derived from being continuously employed in a conventional sense; parenting, caring and doing other things that a career break allows can bring many new skills and perspectives to the workplace which brings valuable cognitive diversity to organisations.

In the *100-Year Life*, Lynda Gratton and Andrew Scott suggest that the norm for us all will be career patterns requiring constant reinvention and that look very different to traditional linear career trajectories and patterns of employment[69]. Ultimately, I hope for a world in which employers focus primarily on the skills and attributes of individuals and where career breaks do not have to be justified, challenged or require specific programmes of support but are viewed as a normal healthy and beneficial career trajectory.

Acknowledgement

This chapter has benefitted greatly from the work of the organisation Career Returners and for whom I was exceptionally proud to be Lead Coach between 2014 and 2022. Specific thanks go to Karen Danker, their Head of Coaching, for her support in writing this chapter, and to Julianne Miles, Co-Founder & CEO of Career Returners for access to updated key information and data.

Notes

1. www.careerreturners.com
2. https://careerreturners.com/returners/sign-up/
3. www.ons.gov.uk/search?q=economically+inactive+by+gender
4. www.careersafterbabies.org/careers-after-babies-report
5. www.pwc.co.uk/economic-services/women-returners/pwc-research-women-returners-nov-2016.pdf
6. https://researchbriefings.files.parliament.uk/documents/CDP-2023-0001/CDP-2023-0001.pdf
7. www.kornferry.com/insights/featured-topics/future-of-work
8. www.mckinsey.com/featured-insights/diversity-and-inclusion/women-in-the-workplace
9. www.pwc.co.uk/services/economics/insights/women-in-work-index.html
10. Ioannidis C, Walther N. *Your Loss: How to Win Back Your Female Talent*. Aquitude Press; 2010.
11. www.vodafone.co.uk/newscentre/features/people-returning-to-work-need-our-help-our-economy-depends-on-them/

12. Blickenstaff, JC. Women and science careers: Leaky pipeline or gender filter? *Gender and Education*. 2005;17(4):369–86.
13. www.mckinsey.com/featured-insights/diversity-and-inclusion/women-in-the-workplace
14. https://assets.publishing.service.gov.uk/media/5ab9179fed915d78bc2347cf/Employer_research_on_returner_programmes.pdf
15. https://assets.publishing.service.gov.uk/media/5a992dfc40f0b67aa5087d3f/Returner_Programmes_-_Best_Practice_Guidance_for_Employers.pdf
16. https://newscentre.vodafone.co.uk/app/uploads/2021/05/Lost-Connections-2021-180521-Pages-Web-1-1.pdf
17. www.ons.gov.uk/employmentandlabourmarket/peoplenotinwork/economicinactivity/datasets/economicinactivitybyreasonnotseasonallyadjustedinac01nsa
18. https://assets.publishing.service.gov.uk/media/5a7c9dde40f0b6629523aae8/DCMS_WBC_Full_Report_v1.0.pdf
19. https://wearethecity.com/wp-content/uploads/2014/04/Project-28-40-The-Report.pdf
20. www.cso.ie/en/releasesandpublications/ep/p-lfs/labourforcesurveyquarter42023/personsnotinthelabourforce/
21. www.pwc.co.uk/economic-services/women-returners/pwc-research-women-returners-nov-2016.pdf
22. www.forbes.com/councils/forbeshumanresourcescouncil/2021/11/12/took-a-career-break-why-now-is-the-best-time-ever-to-return-to-work/
23. Power K. The COVID-19 pandemic has increased the care burden of women and families. *Sustainability: Science, Practice and Policy*. 2020;16(1):67–73.
24. www.pwc.co.uk/economic-services/women-returners/pwc-research-women-returners-nov-2016.pdf
25. www.stemreturners.com/stem-recharge-return-to-work-support-programme/
26. https://assets.publishing.service.gov.uk/media/5a992dfc40f0b67aa5087d3f/Returner_Programmes_-_Best_Practice_Guidance_for_Employers.pdf
27. Gallos JV. Exploring women's development: Implications for career theory, practice. In: Arthur MB, Hall DT, Lawrence BS, editors. *Handbook of Career Theory*. Cambridge University Press; 1989. p110.
28. O'Neil DA, Bilimoria D. Women's career development phases: Idealism, endurance, and reinvention. *Career Development International*. 2005;10(3):168–89.
29. Cabrera EF. Opting out and opting in: Understanding the complexities of women's career transitions. *Career Development International*. 2007;12(3):218–37.

30 Gallos JV. Exploring women's development: Implications for career theory, practice. In: Arthur MB, Hall DT, Lawrence BS, editors. *Handbook of Career Theory*. Cambridge University Press; 1989. p110.
31 O'Neil DA, Bilimoria D. Women's career development phases: Idealism, endurance, and reinvention. *Career Development International*. 2005;10(3):168–89.
32 Mainiero LA, Sullivan SE. Kaleidoscope careers: An alternate explanation for the 'opt-out' revolution. *Academy of Management Perspectives*. 2005;19(1):106–23.
33 Mainiero LA, Sullivan SE. *The Opt Out Revolt: Why People Are Leaving Companies to Create Kaleidoscope Careers*. Davies-Black Publishing; 2006.
34 www.theatlantic.com/magazine/archive/2012/07/why-women-still-cant-have-it-all/309020/
35 www.theguardian.com/women-in-leadership/2014/mar/25/70-of-women-fear-taking-a-career-break
36 https://careerreturners.com/career-returners-indicator-2024/
37 Weisshaar K. From opt out to blocked out: The challenges for labor market re-entry after family-related employment lapses. *American Sociological Review*. 2018;83(1):34–60.
38 Acker J. Hierarchies, jobs, bodies: A theory of gendered organizations. *Gender & Society*. 1990;4(2):139–58.
39 www.investopedia.com/ask/answers/032715/what-human-capital-and-how-it-used.asp
40 www.huffingtonpost.co.uk/entry/unemployment-discrimination_n_3085686
41 www.hbs.edu/managing-the-future-of-work/Documents/research/hiddenworkers09032021.pdf
42 https://careerreturners.com/career-returners-indicator-2024/
43 Weisshaar K. From opt out to blocked out: The challenges for labor market re-entry after family-related employment lapses. *American Sociological Review*. 2018;83(1):34–60.
44 Pedulla DS. Penalized or protected? Gender and the consequences of nonstandard and mismatched employment histories. *American Sociological Review*. 2016;81(2):262–89.
45 Weisshaar K. From opt out to blocked out: The challenges for labor market re-entry after family-related employment lapses. *American Sociological Review*. 2018;83(1):34–60.
46 https://careerreturners.com/career-returners-indicator-2024/
47 https://assets.publishing.service.gov.uk/media/5ab9179fed915d78bc2347cf/Employer_research_on_returner_programmes.pdf
48 https://careerreturners.com/career-returners-indicator-2024/
49 Greer TW. Facilitating successful re-entries in the United States: Training and development for women returners. *New Horizons in Adult Education and Human Resource Development*. 2013;25(3):41–61.

50 https://careerreturners.com/building-confidence/returning-to-work-dont-let-imposter-syndrome-hold-you-back/#:~:text=Imposter%20Syndrome%20is%20most%20common,after%20a%20long%20career%20break.
51 Ibarra H. *Working Identity, Updated Edition, With a New Preface: Unconventional Strategies for Reinventing Your Career*. Harvard Business Press; 2023.
52 Bridges W, Mitchell S. Leading transition: A new model for change. *Leader to Leader*. 2000;16(3):30–6.
53 www.hrmagazine.co.uk/content/comment/promote-cognitive-diversity-to-boost-performance
54 www.cs.jhu.edu/~misha/DIReadingSeminar/Papers/Hewlett14.pdf
55 https://hbr.org/2017/03/teams-solve-problems-faster-when-theyre-more-cognitively-diverse
56 https://careerreturners.com/career-returners-indicator-2024/
57 https://careerreturners.com/career-returners-indicator-2024/
58 https://hbr.org/2023/08/research-caregiver-employees-bring-unique-value-to-companies
59 www.cisco.com/c/dam/en_us/about/ac79/docs/wp/ps/Report.pdf
60 https://careerreturners.com/career-returners-indicator-2024/
61 Cabrera EF. Opting out and opting in: Understanding the complexities of women's career transitions. *Career Development International*. 2007;12(3):218–37.
62 https://hbr.org/2017/03/teams-solve-problems-faster-when-theyre-more-cognitively-diverse
63 www.pwc.co.uk/economic-services/women-returners/pwc-research-women-returners-nov-2016.pdf
64 Greer TW. Facilitating successful re-entries in the United States: Training and development for women returners. *New Horizons in Adult Education and Human Resource Development*. 2013;25(3):41–61.
65 Bridges W, Mitchell S. Leading transition: A new model for change. *Leader to Leader*. 2000;16(3):30–6.
66 www.fdmgroup.com/
67 www.gallup.com/cliftonstrengths/en/252137/home.aspx
68 https://careerreturners.com/career-returners-indicator-2024/
69 Gratton L, Scott AJ. *The 100-Year Life: Living and Working in an Age of Longevity*. Bloomsbury Publishing; 2016.

Chapter 7

Supporting Parents in Their Careers Through Parental Leave and Beyond

Frances Cushway

Eve, Account Director, on having discovered she was going to be a mother:

> I've always wanted to have children but throughout my time at my agency I was unsure how it would be possible to continue [my career] after having children. Despite being a female heavy workforce, I rarely saw anyone choose to have children, and those that did either never returned or left not long after returning having been told to not reveal their family situation to clients.

Adam, Civil Engineer, reflected on how his organisation supports him being a dad and developing his career:

> I wouldn't say my organisation supports me being a dad. From my experience, organisations want you to do your work and to do it well and they do not really take personal circumstances into account. Sure, line managers understand if a parent has to leave work because their child is sick etc., but at the end of the day, if parental duties encroach on your ability to do your work, then your career prospects are diminished.

Becoming a parent is one of the biggest identity transitions someone can go through after adolescence and very often the most impactful to happen in their lifetime. It is also a period of enhanced brain neuroplasticity[1] that sees the brain change in ways not seen since adolescence. The arrival of a new person who is completely dependent for typically the next two decades requires a huge upheaval to the sense of self and a subsequent adjustment in identity.

DOI: 10.4324/9781003510475-8

Accompanying this is a possible change in values, motivators and goals for the next period of life.

In this chapter I will look at why it is so important to take a holistic approach to supporting parents in their careers and why nurturing parents can bring huge benefits at both a team and organisational level. I will look at what happens when employers and managers get this right, and how quickly things can begin to unravel when they get it wrong. For this chapter, I conducted original research at The Maternity Coach, and will share key findings and case studies alongside published research.

I will look at the role assumptions and biases still play in the experience of parents returning to work after parental leave and what can be done to challenge these attitudes and behaviours. I will also share some of the experiences of parents in my survey as they navigated parental leave and how this impacted their career when they returned. In particular, I will look at some of the, maybe surprising, hidden strengths parents bring to their careers, which also add huge benefit to their organisations when they return to work.

Finally, I will look at what you can do to support parents at both an individual and cultural level to enable them to thrive in their careers after parental leave and beyond.

'I Have Some Exciting News!'

Hearing the news that a friend, colleague or client is going to become a parent often elicits a wave of thoughts and emotions, unlike any other announcement. As a manager, when one of the team shares their news these emotions can be even bigger. Typically the news comes out of the blue as people rarely share that they are trying to start a family, so the feelings of joy and happiness for the colleague are often accompanied by feelings of anxiety as to how this will affect the team, their targets and goals, and the anxiety of how the team will manage without them.

The chances are that your team member will also be feeling a huge range of emotions. They are likely to be feeling joy and relief if their journey has been a long one. When the journey has involved fertility assistance or adoption, this will have added to their stress, particularly if someone is on this journey on their own.

They will also most likely be feeling a sense of anxiety around the unknown, hoping the pregnancy or adoption process will go well, and might be wondering how things will work financially for them as well as the impact on their future career. They will probably be worried about telling you and the impact their news will have on the team.

This is why I recommend that the first thing you say to anyone when they tell you their news is 'Congratulations!' Everything else can wait. Everyone involved needs time to process the news. A plan for support and managing the parental leave can be organised for another day.

Why Is It Important to Support Parents in Organisations?

Western society has been built to depend on the model that in a family set-up, one partner (historically typically the man in a heterosexual relationship) works 'office hours', usually 9am–5pm and one partner (historically typically the woman in a heterosexual relationship) manages childcare and the home.

Since the 1970s, increasing educational levels of women, the shift in women's working patterns and increases in the cost of living has meant that the number of women[2] and mothers working has increased, while there haven't been any significant changes in the number of fathers working. With 82% of women becoming mothers by the age of 45[3] and the majority of mothers now working and juggling home life, employers need to be aware of the scale of numbers of women whose needs need to be taken into account when planning employee support.

With both parents most likely to be working now, this means there is less time to manage the home and childcare and this burden is still falling primarily to mothers. In March 2022, mothers spent more time on unpaid childcare (average 84 minutes a day) and household work (average of 169 minutes a day) than fathers (55 and 106 minutes respectively)[4]. Our organisations want and need mothers in the office, but we aren't seeing fathers picking up additional work at home.

While role accumulation suggests having multiple roles in life benefits us by providing multiple opportunities for satisfaction and pleasure, and non-work roles contribute to performance at work and well-being, they can also lead to exhaustion and burnout if not properly supported.

Confidence at work is critical to performance, and the loss of confidence that comes with taking a prolonged break from work can affect the ability to make decisions, take appropriate risk, build relationships with colleagues as well as personal development – all of which can hold back both team performance as well the impact on the organisation overall. Women are almost twice as likely to experience a drop in confidence than men[5], and need support in re-building their confidence for their return to work.

The Impact of the Transition to Parenthood

As discussed in Chapter 1, the work of Bridges is hugely useful to understanding the stages people go through in response to change. This model is equally applicable in understanding the transition to parenthood, and how people feel as they adapt to the new identity of 'parent'.

The experience of this identity transition can be different for mothers and fathers due to the disparate societal assumptions and expectations of the differing needs of mothers and fathers. This can have a big impact on the support parents receive as they navigate the transition. It's important to remember that individuals differ in their ability to adapt to change with some people needing more support than others[6].

Stage 1 – Endings

The key ending in the transition to parenthood is leaving behind the 'pre-parent' identity. This can be particularly tricky if someone's identity was very tightly linked to their job/career which gave them purpose, confidence and satisfaction and they need to (temporarily) put this to one side to start the journey to parenthood.

It can be uncomfortable to realise that pre-parent life doesn't make sense anymore and values and purpose might change as a result. Expectations about being a parent might be far from reality, and the skills and experience that were invaluable in life pre-parenthood might not be so valued as a parent.

It's not uncommon for parents-to-be to feel resentment, bitterness, grief, disappointment and guilt in this stage as they come to terms with ending the pre-parent stage in life, and move into the neutral zone.

Stage 2 – Neutral Zone

The 'Neutral Zone' is a period of liminality, where new parents can feel a bit lost, disorientated or uneasy. It can be challenging and they can sometimes feel quite isolated. Their emotions can swing wildly between hope and despair, and sometimes all they can do is live day to day, or even hour to hour.

New parents need to travel quite slowly through this period to have a successful transition. It's where the key part of the transition takes place as they begin to re-align and re-orientate themselves internally with their new situation.

During this period, new parents learn about themselves as parents and how to integrate parenting into their new identity. Spending time with other new parents can be particularly supportive as they help cement parenting as part of their new identity.

Values and what is seen as success often changes during this period as new parents learn more about what they really want as an individual rather than what society or others tell them they should be as a parent. At this stage, new parents might start to question whether their role still fits with what they value and want from life, and if they want to return to it or find a role that fits better with their revised values.

This stage in the transition to parenthood typically happens during parental leave. The longer statutory leave provided to mothers can help ease the journey through this stage, giving them time to understand their new identity. Conversely, the brief break afforded for statutory paternity leave makes it harder for fathers to spend the time required to successfully navigate this stage. In Norway, fathers are entitled to 15 weeks parental leave, and here being a good father and a good employee are compatible identities[7].

This might help partly explain the anecdotal evidence from my clients that their partners' lives have returned to how they lived before becoming a parent – they may not have fully integrated the role of father into their identity which is still very tightly linked to their career. A study of US stay-at-home fathers found that when fathers stayed at home to care for their children, they had time for the emotional caring aspects of parenting to become part of their masculine identity rather than being opposed to it[8].

Stage 3 – New Beginnings

This stage often brings an acceptance that parenting goes through phases and that parenthood is about learning how to deal with new situations and challenges.

Parents start this stage with revised values and outlook on life as they understand their purpose and how they want to participate and contribute in life as well as at work. It can be helpful at this stage to redefine the meaning of success to something that reflects their new identity and what they want to achieve now. Giving themselves credit for what they can achieve at both work and home can make the transition to their new identity much easier.

Returning to work during this stage, new parents might feel excited to pick up and develop their career and return with renewed energy and enthusiasm. If their values have changed and they no longer feel aligned with their role or organisation, they might consider taking more time off work to think further about what they want, or they might decide to leave their role and pursue other options.

The Importance of Supporting New Mothers

While women are entering the workforce at similar rates to men, their representation at leadership roles declines with each step up[9] – this is known as the 'leaky talent pipeline'. Motherhood is known to be one of the major 'leaks' in the talent pipeline, with 84% of mothers facing difficulties returning to work after maternity leave[10]. The 2022 Careers After Babies report found that 85% of women leave the full-time workforce within three years of having children, and 19% leave the workforce altogether 'most often because their work cannot offer any flexibility or they cannot afford childcare'. However, the vast majority of mothers want to work[11].

The costs of this loss are financial (empty chair costs, recruitment costs and training costs), knowledge, expertise, lower innovation and productivity and lower representation and understanding of potential customer base. The loss of experienced female talent has both short-term and long-term consequences for their organisations:

- Small female talent pipeline from which to manage succession planning
- Lack of role models to attract new talent to the organisation
- Wide gender pay gap as a result of fewer women reaching senior roles

Research such as by McKinsey[12] continually reports that businesses with gender diverse Executive Committees are consistently and increasingly financially outperforming those with fewer women, (up to ten times more for organisations with a quarter of women on executive committees compared to organisations with no women at this level[13]). Gender diverse boards are also found to lead to better corporate culture[14]. Women Count summarised this at the end of their 2022 report: 'Each year, the UK is losing the equivalent of more than the defence budget, the entire schools budget, and triple the police budget, because of gender imbalance at the top of our companies'.

When we get the support right, this impacts not only the women retained by the organisation, but also the organisation itself. McKinsey identifies Gender Equality Leaders, which are organisations that foster inclusive cultures that support them and their mental well-being. Their Women in the Workplace[15] reports continue to show that women who work for Gender Equality Leaders show positive mental health, are more likely to recommend their employer, are happy with their working pattern, are less likely to experience microaggressions and plan to stay longer with their organisation.

Microaggressions

Microaggressions refer to comments or acts that can appear more subtle than obvious discrimination, but have a huge impact on well-being. Unfortunately, microaggressions during pregnancy and after returning to work from parental leave can have an impact on careers.

One survey respondent commented:

I did through multiple pregnancies have light-hearted comments and jokes made about my pregnant body or eating, my leave described as a 'break' or 'holiday', and my

> part-time work [being] commented on. I don't believe these were malicious but were relevant to the culture of not being taken seriously with family life balance.

Another shared:

> In my first week back I was told by a male colleague that I had taken the easy option by choosing a C-section (he had no children!) [I had] another colleague question the 'manlyness' of my husband if he was staying at home to look after our baby, and that it should be my job.

Against this backdrop of an increase in women and mothers' employment, society has become more 'child-centric' and, as a result, expectations of mothering have also changed. Women today are under an enormous amount of pressure to prove themselves to be 'good mothers' against a constantly moving goal.

Taking a holistic approach to supporting mothers in their career acknowledges the significant identity transition they have undergone, the competing pressures of work and home life and the want to work outside the home, and benefits not only mothers as individuals, but an organisation's bottom line.

The Importance of Supporting New Fathers

Working fathers are also under considerable pressure today. While fathers are increasingly taking on childcare[16], this societal shift is not being recognised and supported in the workplace[17]. Flexible working is open to all, but fathers are less likely than mothers to take advantage of flexible working arrangements[18] often due to microaggressions at work[19].

In addition, the common narrative of being a 'good man' is strongly correlated with being a 'good provider'. Ian Dinwiddy is the Founder of Inspiring Dads[20] and coaches new fathers. He sees this narrative come from the societal framework where the majority of lived experiences of fathers were in a family where their father was the 'provider' and mother the 'carer' (even if she worked) despite data that shows that the proportion of female breadwinners is steadily rising[21]. The pressure fathers feel to provide for their families may lead to fathers overworking which can impact physical and mental health and well-being.

For Dinwiddy, this narrative of being a 'good man' is no longer fit for purpose with men today being pulled in different directions, wanting to be more involved fathers as well as have a great career.

> It's easy to assume that a man in the workplace with young children is absolutely fine, but actually underneath [he's not] because he's not comfortable being vulnerable and sharing because of the fear [of] being seen as uncommitted to work . . . [and then losing] out on potential financial benefits, promotions and bonuses.

Research looking at the experience of fatherhood across four ethnic groups in the UK[22] found that there were more similarities than differences in the behaviours, attitudes, aspirations and challenges across fathers in the study. Fathers were expected to be involved in all aspects of raising their children, but the role of provider and protector was still found to be mainly the father's responsibility.

Taking a holistic approach to supporting new fathers in their careers acknowledges that they will feel pulled towards both their family and career as mothers are. Working fathers are now facing similar issues that working mothers have faced for a generation. However, having seen the impact talking about these issues has had on working mothers, fathers aren't comfortable being open because of the risk to their career if they are seen as uncommitted to their work.

Becoming a Parent

The (Sometimes Rocky) Journey to Parenthood

It's easy to overlook the emotional and physical rollercoaster of the journey to parenthood. People often romanticise the idea of becoming a parent, and mainstream and social media go a long way to feeding unrealistic images of the journey to parenthood, either glamourising it or showing it in such graphic detail that it feels like a storyline rather than reality.

While knowing the ins and outs of a colleague's journey may feel outside of the remit of the role of manager or coach, it's important to acknowledge that the journey to parenthood isn't always easy, and for some parents it can leave them with significant mental and physical scars that can be very much present when they return to work after parental leave.

Issues can often arise during pregnancy. Miscarriages are much more common than most people realise. Among people who know they're pregnant, it's estimated about 1 in 8 pregnancies will end in miscarriage[23].

Fear of childbirth can have a significant impact on women's well-being during pregnancy. One in ten women experience fear of childbirth[24] and this can be further compounded by the fear of prejudicial treatment[25], and norms concerning maternity, femininity and cisgender for lesbian, bisexual and transgender people[26].

Women who have experienced traumatic births might still be suffering from the physical or mental effects when returning to work, but worry about talking about them or even letting work know what is going on. Fathers may also experience trauma after watching the birth of their child and this could still be affecting them when they return to work.

A study by TENA of working mothers found that[27]:

- around 20% felt that their bosses and colleagues didn't understand what they had been through, either physically or mentally
- 14% worried that the effects of medical issues brought on by pregnancy and childbirth made them look unprofessional
- 53% kept their issues to themselves out of embarrassment
- 55% kept their issues to themselves as they didn't want others to think they weren't up to the job
- 25% of those who suffered long-term physical or mental effects of pregnancy and childbirth said it affected their career
- 32% felt like their colleagues or boss treated them differently as a result of their issues.

The 2024 MBRRACE-UK report[28] found that between 2020 and 2022, there was an 'almost three-fold difference in maternal mortality rates amongst women from Black ethnic backgrounds compared to White women . . . and there remains an almost two-fold difference amongst women from Asian ethnic backgrounds compared to White women'. Where women live also has an impact on the maternal mortality rate, with the mortality rate of women living in the most deprived areas more than double that of women living in the least deprived areas. Concern about this during pregnancy can cause stress and anxiety while preparing for parental leave.

Postnatal Mental Health

Starting a family increases an individual's stress levels, with over half of parents experiencing mental ill health, and 1 in 3 parents struggling to access support[29].

Statistics published by the NHS in May 2024 showed that a record number of women accessed perinatal mental health support over the previous year with up to 1 in 5 new and expectant mums experiencing some form of perinatal mental illness[30] (perinatal depression, perinatal anxiety, perinatal OCD, postnatal PTSD and birth trauma and postpartum psychosis). Perinatal depression may be more common among lesbian and bisexual women relative to heterosexual women[31]. Postnatal depression rates are 13% higher in Black mothers than in other groups[32] and Black and Asian women are less likely to seek help for postnatal depression and anxiety than white women[33].

Mental ill health doesn't only affect birth mothers. The huge life change can also take its toll on fathers and partners. The rate of depression in fathers in the first year after becoming a father is double the rate of the general population, with a quarter of fathers experiencing mild depressive symptoms and 10–12% receiving a diagnosis of depression. They are more likely to experience depression if their partner is depressed[34].

Adoptive parents can also experience mental ill health post-placement. Adoption UK's 2023 Barometer survey found that 58% of respondents said they had experienced stress, anxiety and/or symptoms of post-adoption depression[35].

How Does Becoming a Parent Affect Our Careers?

Becoming a parent can impact careers in a multitude of ways starting when parents-to-be first announce their news through to career management after they return.

Announcing the News and Planning Leave

People taking extended parental leave can feel the impact on their career immediately if they are sidelined after announcing their news. For this reason, individuals may delay announcing their news for as long as possible.

Sharing the news that they are going to become a father doesn't have the same statutory framework as becoming a mother in the UK, so managers might be informed relatively late on. There may be less time for fathers-to-be to understand and discuss the leave options open to them and prepare for their leave. Fathers-to-be are more likely to assume that statutory paternity leave is all that is available to them, as this is still the most common paternity leave in the UK.

Awareness of parental leave options, a culture of support for fathers taking paternity leave and support by line managers at this stage can be crucial in allowing fathers-to-be to make the right decision for them with regards to the type of leave they'd like to take.

It's important that managers are knowledgeable about their organisational policies so that they can support their colleagues as they prepare for leave. A lack of knowledge can add to the increasing stress parents-to-be can feel as they prepare for leave, and researching this themselves can add to their workload as they prepare to leave, which gives them less time to prepare. One of my survey respondents noted:

> I found various policies on our online system and navigated myself. Adoption leave was not well understood and as my manager was in America he was not clear on the UK allowances so expected I would be back sooner and working whilst I was out. He did learn and was supportive but it wasn't clear cut.

Another shared:

> I don't believe workplaces suitably support parents in a clear or consistent way. I have less confidence in the workplace due to negative experiences as a result of being a parent (despite feeling I gained a lot of incredible skills from being a parent). This started during IVF with unclear policies and managers that aren't trained to deal with these issues. The workplace expects more from managers who don't understand or have experiences on the complexities of these types of situations. There is very little direct contact with experienced HR professionals. Instead HR want these things to be discussed with managers. Managers say to go to HR. HR contacts only manage basic questions and send people back to their managers. And so on.

Another highlighted how important it is for employers to be actively involved in supporting their colleagues:

> I felt it was more up to me to ask rather than my company have a plan in place for things.

In the run-up to taking leave, people are typically focused on work, sometimes to the extent that they may not take advantage of support offered to them to help them prepare for their time away from work. One of my survey respondents noted:

> My employer was very encouraging but I personally was not so keen on talking about any plans / what happens when I return. My focus was on the leave.

At The Maternity Coach, the pre-parental leave coaching session, which is typically the most important for a smooth transition, is the one most often missed. When individuals focus on the operational side of work they don't make time to prepare to leave. Planning for the return to work during pregnancy has not only been found to be one of the most important predictors of returning to work as intended, and the ability to return to work full time, it also has a greater effect on return to work than income[36]. It is a key factor in enabling women to remain in work and their subsequent career progression.

Women can start to feel less relevant and visible at work as they approach their parental leave. They may be overlooked for opportunities or have responsibilities reduced or re-assigned. While managers may think this is helpful, this can impact their career as they start to lose 'career capital' before they've even become a parent. As one of my survey respondents noted:

> My manager tried to take the pressure off me in my last trimester. Although I really appreciated it I also felt slightly left out of the team.

Additionally, when a manager is focused on making sure operationally things run smoothly during the parental leave, they can forget to support their colleague who is leaving:

> Almost nothing was discussed except how the team would function in my absence. I had no preparation for leaving or returning.

A lack of support can cause people to start to question whether they will have a place in the organisation when they return to work:

> [Preparations were] very basic, what felt like absolutely essential information of which a fair amount of it I had to chase. Left me feeling guilty about going on maternity leave, unsure of my rights and nervous about returning.

My research found individuals had very mixed experiences in how they were supported in their preparation for parental leave. While the majority of respondents (74%) created a handover document, few were provided any other support to help prepare for parental leave.

In extreme cases, individuals had offers of new jobs or promotions withdrawn as a result of announcing their pregnancy, as seen in the case study below.

> Elizabeth was due for a promotion to a C-Suite role, but the offer was rescinded when she announced her pregnancy. After her baby was born by emergency C-section, her HR team called her multiple times a day to ask when she could go to the office for a KIT (keeping in touch) day. Her maternity cover was also heard to be undermining her position in the company as she was enjoying the role and wanted to stay on. Her experience of parental leave was so bad that she felt she had no choice but to leave her employer.

At The Maternity Coach we actively encourage clients to seek promotion if possible before going on leave as this not only provides an immediate boost to confidence but it also helps counteract the effect being away from work on parental leave can have on their career. One of my survey respondents noted:

> I was promoted before I left which made me feel relaxed and happy.

Even reassuring colleagues of their impact in the team and that they will be missed supports the preparation for leave and boosts confidence:

> [My Manager] reassured me [of] my worth, how they were going to miss me etc. so I felt confident in going.

The Impact of Fertility Treatment on Careers

Fertility treatments can affect the careers of those seeking treatment in multiple ways. They can cause a change in priorities as the treatment regimes are demanding and tough. They run based on the body's schedule so can't be neatly scheduled around work and other life demands and additional or last-minute appointments are common, impacting day-to-day work. The treatment regimes can become all consuming.

If people share that they are going through fertility treatment with their managers (which is recommended by organisations such as Fertility in the Workplace) it effectively gives managers a heads up that they are trying to start a family. Some managers might then start to sideline their colleague in a bid to manage their workload, even though there's no guarantee that the current, or even a future, cycle of fertility treatment will work.

Undergoing fertility treatment is hard on the body, which means that job performance might not be up to the level before treatment started. This can result in work being re-allocated to other team members and a loss of 'career capital' even before pregnancy.

Fertility in the Workplace says that for those undergoing treatment, it can be difficult to take time off for appointments, and there is the additional stress of not only managing workloads, but how much to disclose to your employer. On average, a woman needs eight days off per cycle for appointments. Of those going through fertility treatment, 83% felt sad, frustrated, worried often, or all the time[37].

Sania's story below illustrates these points and how difficult, but sometimes how important, it can be to try and maintain a career alongside fertility treatment.

> Sania was ambitious. After gaining her Masters she went to work in marketing. She wanted to reach at least Account Director level in her organisation. She was convinced she was going to conceive naturally so was still very much focused on her career while trying to get pregnant. After trying to start a family for two years her doctor put her on the waiting list for IVF.
>
> The shock of realising what she had to go through with IVF treatment made her immediately put her career on hold. She said if she could have given up her career then, she would have because the treatment was so consuming with regards to time, energy and headspace. Going through IVF was an emotional rollercoaster. She realises she was naive as she thought it would work first go, second at most. But after the two NHS rounds of treatment she had to seek private treatment.
>
> She didn't tell her boss because she didn't want him to assume she would be going on leave soon and start to sideline her at work. But she regrets this and said support at work is crucial when going through IVF. In the end, she gave up her job because she couldn't cope with undergoing the treatment alongside her role.
>
> She took a lower profile job, and her new boss was a woman. She was open with her manager straight away about the IVF. After three more rounds of treatment didn't work she started to think that maybe she wouldn't be able to have a child and sought promotion at work.
>
> Her new boss was a man, and he wasn't very supportive. He didn't understand the impact the treatment had on Sania and didn't offer her any flexibility at work. She had scans at 6am in the morning so she could be at her desk for 8.30am,

> often feeling upset. Some of the drugs made her feel unwell or dizzy, and her performance in meetings was criticised as a consequence. She said she cried a lot in the ladies toilets. But Sania still told him everything. She started to notice that he wasn't giving her as much work and she felt that he was making excuses about taking her off projects and re-assigning work to develop a more junior colleague. Her fifth round of IVF worked.
>
> After Sania returned from maternity leave, she was made redundant and the colleague who had been re-assigned Sania's work was given her role.

The Impact of Adopting Children on Careers

Adopting a child has the potential to disrupt parents' careers even more than becoming a parent biologically. The number of meetings required to become approved for adoption, which is much more time consuming than typical antenatal appointments, and often take place every two to three weeks over many months, can mean more time away from work. Adopted children are more vulnerable and can require more time and attention in caring for their often complex needs.

Statistics from Adoption UK show that in adopted children:

- 47% have social, emotional or mental health needs
- 65% of families experienced violent or aggressive behaviour in 2022

Most children who are adopted are between 18 months and three years old. They might be facing challenges sleeping, not accepting the care of their parents, emotional dysregulation, issues eating, low self-esteem and low confidence, lack of trust, trouble with attachment, and issues with transitions. These can all impact a parent's mental health, sense of well-being, and their ability to perform at work.

Luke shared his story of adopting his son and how it impacted him and his husband.

It took 20 months from when Luke first started the adoption process to Mitch coming to live with them. During the approval process they met a social worker every two weeks, for 2–3 hours each time, which required flexibility from both employers. His employer had a family comes first policy so he felt very supported with regards to the number and length of the meetings.

Becoming a father coincided with a change in job, so he didn't have to take parental leave, while his husband took a six-month sabbatical to help their son settle. It's advised to limit contact in the first few months to just the immediate family, so it was a lonely and overwhelming time. Mitch was three and a half years old when they became a family and had multiple additional needs. He had already been in multiple foster families in the care system and while he bonded with Luke quite quickly, it took longer for him to bond with Luke's husband.

The first 12–18 months were really hard emotionally for Luke and his husband as they felt like they had a stranger living in their house who didn't want to be there. They also felt like they were grieving for the child they didn't have. There was still a lot of involvement with social services, plus additional assessments and support Mitch needed, from occupational therapy to speech therapy to doctor's appointments. Mitch had behavioural issues and regularly spat at and kicked Luke and his husband, and bedtimes would go on for hours. He said that if he had needed to pretend things were OK for the sake of work it would have been really hard.

Becoming a parent through adoption had a big impact on Luke's productivity at work, both immediately and then through Mitch's life transitions such as starting school. He is prepared for the teens to be even harder as the rate of anxiety and mental health conditions, exclusions, and drug and alcohol problems is higher for any child that's been through the care system.

Managing Careers Through Parental Leave and Returning

When new parents are on parental leave they can feel like they are living in a bubble. Life has changed immensely. It can be hard to remember what their life was like before becoming a parent. Their day-to-day tasks have changed so much it can feel like they are learning a new language, which in fact they are. The language of their new child. Birth parents are getting to know a new person who can't speak and whose only way to communicate at first is to cry.

Neuroscience[38] has shown that the hormones circulating a woman's body while pregnant not only support the development of her baby, but also optimise her brain to take care of her baby after birth and help develop the bond between mother and baby. Mothers aren't alone in experiencing brain changes when becoming a parent. Fathers' brains also undergo remodelling to support the adaptation to fatherhood[39].

So it probably isn't a surprise that most parents want to spend their parental leave focusing on their baby. It's important they do as this is a key bonding time, as well as an important step in their identity transition to 'parent'.

This time out of the office, focusing on their new baby or child, can have a huge influence on parents' subsequent careers. There are a number of factors that can impact a parent's career at this time.

A Lack of Preparation Before Leaving for Leave

Parents who don't have a return to work plan before they go on leave can feel like the idea of returning is too much to think about. This can lead to procrastination, last minute panics, a return that doesn't work for either employer or parent and ultimately an increased chance in either not returning or leaving soon after their return.

A Lack of Communication Plan Between Employer and Parent

Communication between employer / line manager and parent is key in supporting a successful return and the nature and frequency of the communication during leave should be agreed before they go on leave. Full details on the communication required by law in the UK can be found on Legislation.gov.uk.

The impact of not having this agreement in place causes problems for both the manager and parent on leave. The manager can feel uncertain about whether to contact their colleague or not – pulled between wanting their colleague to know they're not forgotten but not wanting to intrude into their parental leave. It may also slip their mind that they do need to stay in touch as day-to-day work and managing the team distract them from their colleague on leave.

A lack of contact from a manager can feel like a break in the psychological employment contract. It can cause parents emotional distress, to feel neglected, no longer valued or part of the team. It can also cause logistical problems as they are unprepared for their return. A worst case scenario is that it contributes to parents not returning to work at all. These points are illustrated by my respondents' comments below:

> 'There was little to no support on returning, what to expect or contact in the run up to me walking back into the office which made it feel quite overwhelming'.
> 'I had one call with my mentor and one call from HR. I felt that they didn't want me back'.
> '[My employer was] completely silent on the issue. On my return I was blocked from all systems and no HR / manager catch up was held'.
> 'There was no preparation and no discussions with me. The only phone call to confirm my return date and what I needed to do on the first day was initiated by me'.
> 'My employer didn't contact me at all when on leave. I ended up not going back and going self-employed'.
> 'I heard nothing about returning to work, until I went in to hand my notice in'.
> 'My cover had been hired full-time and while there was a meeting to delineate the workload on my return, in practice, this was not the case. It left me feeling worthless and not only replaceable, but

confirmed that I had actually been replaced'. (Respondent was made redundant eight months after return.)

'Catching up on processes that had changed outside my team was hard and I think in some ways that would have been helpful to be treated like a new starter by HR'.

The Pause in Career and Loss of Business Network

Typically during parental leave, parents don't spend much time thinking about work or staying up to date with developments in their field. Parenting a new child is a full-time job which doesn't normally leave much time for anything else. Parents also want to fully immerse themselves in their new role, which is key to integrating being a parent into their new identity. This can mean that they feel out of touch with their role, industry and career.

Parental leave can deplete someone's 'resources' such as status, money, support, personal/professional development, skills and knowledge. They feel like they have lost 'career capital'. A loss of resources can cause stress, which can lead to anxiety and attempts to minimise the loss. Ways of doing this include refocusing on what has been gained, devaluing what has been lost or investing in new (valued) resources[40]. This can lead parents to think about leaving their job.

KIT days can be critical in helping parents stay in the loop at work, and boost 'career capital' (e.g. reconnecting with their network, boosting skills through training or refreshing knowledge of work projects), as highlighted by some of my respondents:

'Keeping in touch was critical [in supporting my return to work]'.

'I arranged a KIT day meeting with my maternity cover in advance of returning so that I could get up to speed, which was helpful (although led by me rather than the organisation)'.

'[I wish my organisation had] helped me plan KIT days better. They seemed quite surprised I wanted some kind of plan and it was quite an effort to find any days that would work. I also had to hand back my laptop while on maternity leave which made taking part in KIT days remotely very difficult'.

Another way to boost 'career capital' while on leave is for parents to be offered a promotion to return to.

A Change in Line Manager

The discontinuation of line management can have a significant impact on whether the return to work is successful, as illustrated by the comments made by my respondents below:

> 'There was a restructure whilst I was on mat leave. My manager went on mat leave and my new manager did not contact me. I was sidelined significantly when I returned from mat leave with my job share partner (maternity cover) preferred. My return to work was terrible and caused me to leave the organisation as I was miserable'.
>
> 'I had a new line manager. I wasn't supported. I almost put in a grievance to be allowed to work KIT days. I felt isolated'. (Respondent resigned three months after return due to the team/company culture.)
>
> 'I had a new manager during my leave and she organised a couple of meetings to get to know me – [this] made me feel very much included'.

A Loss of Confidence

A loss of confidence is one of the issues most frequently cited by The Maternity Coach clients. Individuals report a lack of self confidence in their ability to return to work and manage motherhood and a lack of confidence in their ability to do their job again. Even clients who have received excellent performance reviews and appraisals before work can experience this.

While on parental leave, parents can feel that the skills they rely on at work have become rusty, and they often forget their previous successes at work. The change in identity can change the way parents feel about their ability to perform in their role again and their support network has often shrunk. As noted earlier, a loss of confidence impacts women significantly more than men and can have an impact on the success of the transition back to work as well as whether someone returns at all.

A Change in Priorities and Values

Becoming a parent can act as a 'career shock' to a parent's career. A career shock is 'a disruptive and extraordinary event that is at least to some degree caused by factors outside the focal individual's control and that triggers a deliberate thought process concerning one's career'[41].

Career shocks can impact careers in different ways. For some people it makes them commit further to what they know and to stay in their comfort zone. For others, it can highlight latent disquiet which can prompt a career change.

The transition to parent and accompanying identity change can cause a re-evaluation of priorities and values, and the reality of what this means can only be fully understood once the baby or child is finally here. The disruption this can cause to priorities and values can lead to dilemmas over whether returning to work, to the former career, is aligned with the new priorities and values.

The Experience of Parental Leave

Parents' experience and how they use parental leave can have a big impact on the return to work experience. When parents who are bringing their children up bilingual, or with a dual culture, spend time immersed in their family culture and mother tongue while on parental leave, they can experience a culture clash when they return to work, as can be seen by Ishani's experience below.

> Ishani is from a British Punjabi family. She wanted to switch off from work completely while on maternity leave and took her full year entitlement. She is raising her son to be bilingual and speaks to him exclusively in Punjabi. She also loves Bollywood and watching Indian content on streaming services. She spent

> her whole maternity leave immersed in her Indian and Punjabi culture.
>
> While she loved her time in her maternity leave bubble, it had a significant impact on her return to work despite using her KIT days, as it felt strange returning to her office where everyone was white and spoke English. She feels like she has always masked her true self at work, and that she hides the side that speaks Punjabi, has a big Punjabi family and loves Bollywood, and her maternity leave enhanced these feelings. She considers Punjabi her mother tongue and found it hard to express herself in English when she returned to work.
>
> Ishani shared how she felt at her most vulnerable when she returned to work. Her maternity cover was well established in her role and had built excellent relationships with her team. This knocked her confidence and impacted her self-esteem. She found it hard to catch up with both the work she had missed while she was away, and also the trends and culture she had missed through caring for her baby and immersing herself in her culture.

Emotions and Mental Health

The transition to parenthood can cause a strong emotional change, and this can cause anxiety around whether a parent will fit in their organisation anymore. Parents can feel emotionally torn between the love of their work and career and their love for the child they will need to leave behind to return to it. This can be so extreme that a parent might feel they can't leave their baby. However, some women who express a 'deep sense of sadness about leaving their babies also identified that they would not be happy being a full-time mother'[42].

Parents can experience feelings of insecurity and uncertainty about their role while they are on leave, and whether they are still needed by their organisation. The return to work after parental leave can be an emotional journey. Line managers need to be aware that returning to work is a time of vulnerability – and potentially grief (for the loss of time with their child) and have support systems in place to ease this transition.

Respondents shared:

'[I felt] apprehensive and unsure that I really wanted to return and put my daughter in childcare'.
'I was loving my cocoon and I was looking forward to returning but I was very insecure and worried about where I would fit in when I came back'.
'[I felt] sick with worry'.

Societal or Family Pressures Around What a 'Good' Mother/Father Should Do

Societal norms and an individual's beliefs around what a good parent does can impact the return to work and be felt strongly enough to cause a parent to decide not to return to work at all. Parents who return can feel overwhelmed by a sense of guilt at leaving their baby or child in the care of someone else. These feelings of guilt often come from the sense that they are not living up to society or family ideals of a 'good mother' or 'good father', and they feel judged for this.

Sleep Deprivation

The effects of sleep deprivation in new parents should not be underestimated, and this can affect both new mothers and fathers. Sleep deprivation causes slower reaction times, increases the chances of 'microsleeps' (a momentary lapse in concentration when eyes may partially or fully close) and people consistently underestimate how sleep deprived they are[43].

After ten days of six hours of sleep at night, people's performance is as impaired as if they have been up for 24 hours, and 11 days of four hours of sleep at night matches someone's performance who's been up for 48 hours. Lack of sleep also makes it harder to manage emotions and people can react more emotionally. It affects the ability to learn as well as impacts mental health and well-being[44].

As many as 62.5% of parents have reported suffering from sleep deprivation when returning to work and nearly half of parents weren't able to share how bad their sleep deprivation was with their managers; 17.4% have reported being unable to perform efficiently or safely in their roles in the workplace due to lack of sleep[45]. Sleep deprivation can significantly impact both parents' day-to-day work and subsequently their careers.

The Second Shift and Mental Load

With parental leave often comes an expectation that being at home with the baby also means picking up all the chores. Women are still taking the majority of parental leave[46] and assuming the majority of the second shift of chores. Managing the second shift of work at home, together with remembering what needs to be done at home and for the children, creates a heavy mental load, mostly carried by women in a heterosexual relationship[47].

One of the biggest challenges for women's successful return to work and continuation of their career, and the number one issue for The Maternity Coach clients, is how to manage things at home after they return to work. The impact of this inequality at home can affect women's well-being as well as their ability to manage their workload. This can lead them to reduce their hours at work which typically affects their career development opportunities.

The Availability and Cost of Childcare

The cost and lack of childcare is causing problems for parents in the UK[48]. Only a third of English counties offered enough childcare places to enable parents to work full time and costs increased 7% over the last year. The UK is (unfortunately) seen to rank highly in OECD countries with regards to the cost of childcare as a percentage of salary. The cost of childcare in the UK is currently limiting mothers in their participation in the workplace (40% of mothers would prefer to increase their hours of work if childcare was affordable and accessible[49]).

A lack of childcare or unaffordable childcare therefore has a huge impact on not just how a parent returns to work after parental leave, but whether they can return at all.

Lack of Support for Ongoing Breastfeeding

The WHO and UNICEF recommend exclusive breastfeeding for the first six months of a baby's life as it provides benefits both to baby and mother[50]. Many women would like to follow this recommendation and some want to breastfeed for even longer. Returning to work within this time period can make breastfeeding very difficult to maintain unless an employer supports a mother in expressing milk while at work, and inadequate provision of space to do this can cause mothers considerable stress when they return to work, as noted by my respondents:

> 'I also found it incredibly difficult to return to work and continue to breastfeed. It felt as though I was being frowned upon for having to leave early to get back home and feed my child. And, I had to miss many work travel trips due to breastfeeding. It went down "ok" with my colleagues, but not embraced or supported'.
> 'I was the first person I know of to express milk in the office so that felt like a lonely journey at times but important to me. Unexpectedly as I work in a majority female office'.
> 'The breastfeeding discussion was difficult as expressing several times a day isn't practical with what I do'.

Where breastfeeding isn't supported, mothers have the unenviable decision of either having to stop breastfeeding before they want to or leave their roles.

Lack of Acknowledgement of the Significance of the Life Transition

By taking a holistic approach to supporting parents in their careers, it is important that a parent's changed circumstances and needs are acknowledged when they return to work after parental leave. They aren't the same person they were before and bring a wealth of new skills and experience back to work. They are likely to need compassion as they adapt to their new identity of 'working parent' and unlikely to be able to 'hit the ground running' as many organisations expect them to. One of my respondents noted:

> The day I returned, my squad hit me with wanting to know which projects I could take immediately and took no notice, nor showed much compassion [that I had just returned from parental leave].

The Ability to Successfully Combine Work Life with Home Life

With the average commute time in England in 2022 being 28 minutes[51], and a mismatch between the opening hours of school (typically 9am–3pm) and work (typically 9am–5pm) it doesn't take much common sense to see that parents require some flexibility in the hours they work. Next take into account that the average UK worker gets 5.6 weeks holiday a year[52] (including bank holidays) and school holidays are 13 weeks long, the need for flexible working for parents increases. Managing school holidays can be particularly tricky for solo or separated parents. Careers After Babies found that 19% of mothers who returned to work leave the workforce altogether often because their work cannot offer any flexibility or they cannot afford childcare. They found that the majority of mothers want to work three or four days a week in a hybrid way (some home working, some in the office) but importantly, want to be treated with the same respect as full-time office-based employees.

My respondents shared their experiences of flexible working in their return to work.

> 'I requested part time working with non-standard hours, which was rejected with no valid reason. Verbal feedback was that if I did compressed hours, I wouldn't be able to do the "extra hours

I needed to do at my level" (unpaid, and unappreciated hours, that are not part of contract, and that many staff put in because there is not enough resource)'.

'[My] flexible working request was a tricky process. [I was] massively helped by my external maternity coach that my employer gave me access to. [My] employer didn't respond with the decision within [the] time period laid out in their policy – I had to follow up. The process (as laid out by the policy) should have involved a meeting to discuss how this would work / workload managed / role changed due to coming back part time. This never happened which meant this crucial conversation was skipped. Transitioning to part time was very challenging because of this and remains a continued challenge'.

'I was given the understanding that if I needed flexible hours due to childcare, then that was OK. [However] I was made redundant after returning from maternity leave. My maternity cover ended up getting my permanent role'.

'I did not return as I decided to work part-time hours and could not take the pay drop, so became self-employed'.

Ian Dinwiddy notes that this is an important concern for fathers. Their concerns are more about logistics, such as 'How do I get the four day working pattern?' and 'How do I persuade the business that that's OK without it screwing my career?'

Impact of Managers and Colleagues

Co-workers' and managers' support during pregnancy is hugely beneficial to mothers-to-be and new mothers. It is associated with lower levels of prenatal stress which is associated with lower levels of postpartum depression after returning to work and quicker recovery times from injury during birth.

Postpartum allyship (behaviours that support and advocate for working mothers when they return to work) has also been found to reduce turnover intentions and postnatal depressive symptoms[53].

My respondents' experience of supportive (and unsupportive) managers and colleagues supports this.

> 'I had a difficult and high risk pregnancy and my manager enabled me to work from home from month 4 (before working from home was a widely available thing). He also found a way so I could join team meetings remotely. We had phone one-to-ones on a weekly basis. He was very supportive'.
>
> 'I didn't have any specific conversations with my manager about preparing before maternity leave – as it was the second time it was just assumed I knew'.
>
> 'My line manager had recently come back from maternity leave herself and this made a big difference'.
>
> 'I remember feeling like it was always me bringing up the topic with my manager, or asking HR questions, and I would have liked them to be a bit more proactive'.
>
> 'My manager kept me abreast of any major changes in the team whilst I was on parental leave. She was conscious to not contact me too much. She was also very supportive about my return, allowing me to come in late etc. for the first few weeks as I established a new routine with childcare / school etc.'.

For new fathers, Dinwiddy sees managers' key role in 'creating that space to support them with this transition that has emotions attached. They're not the same person when they come back to work' in the same way as mothers aren't. Fathers need to be able to have time to take a step back and know it's not going to affect their career. He also notes that line managers have a big impact on men's experience of taking parental leave and whether it goes smoothly or not.

Managing Careers After Parental Leave

While the transition back to work is often the focus of supporting parents after parental leave, the first year or two back can be particularly hard for someone who has taken long parental leave. The 9–12 month period after return can be a very critical period when women feel they have reached a crunch point and need further support[54].

Beyond this period, it is easy to assume that working parents are settled into a routine and it's now business as usual. However, children's transition from childcare to school is another crunch point where parents are typically faced with big decisions around how to manage working hours around the shorter school day. While their children are at school, particularly junior school, there will also be memory-making events parents will want to attend such as school plays, sports days and parent teacher events. Ultimately, until children reach adulthood, they will be their parents' priority.

Ian Dinwiddy sees the key to helping fathers manage their careers after parental leave is to help fathers acknowledge and manage any emotions and difficulties they have to ensure good mental health. It's important to allow fathers to be parents in the workplace, which also provides positive role models for younger colleagues who aren't yet fathers. While it's becoming increasingly common for men to take parental leave, their careers after parental leave don't seem to be affected by taking leave. Research in Norway[55], where fathers take more parental leave than in the UK, found that even though fathers became more involved in childcare due to their leave, it didn't seem to affect their working hours after their leave was over, with men infrequently working part time.

Company Culture

The culture of a company, and whether it is family-friendly, can overwhelmingly have the biggest impact on parents' careers. Long hours of work don't recognise that parents need to take their children to childcare or school and collect them at the end of the childcare/school day. An 'always-on' culture expects employees to respond to communications or work outside of their contracted working hours when they want to spend time with their child(ren). An early morning or late afternoon meeting culture clashes with childcare needs such as drop-off and pick-up times, as do networking socials before or after work. A 'last minute' culture where employees regularly receive requests to work late the same day also clashes with childcare commitments. The lack of flexibility either with regards to hours or location, as well as a lack of last-minute flexibility to deal with child illnesses, makes it hard to juggle work and childcare. Valuing 'facetime' over output as a measure of employees' success and achievement discriminates against parents who are most often working flexibly or remotely to help them manage their work and life responsibilities.

Line Manager

Line managers not only are directly responsible for the support and progression of their reports, they are also key in setting the culture of the team. As a result, poor line management can impact parents' careers by creating or allowing a culture that doesn't allow the discussion of or support parents' needs, having a lack of knowledge of parents' needs, not acknowledging that parents have specific needs, creating an environment that lacks the psychological safety needed for parents to thrive and not supporting healthy work–life boundaries.

Research has found that while 69% of parents feel supported by their managers, 27% are uncomfortable discussing their needs[56].

The impact of an unsupportive manager can have long lasting effects on a parent's career. Returning to Elizabeth, when we asked about how ambitious she feels now, she said:

> I would say less ambitious now, because the realisation is that as a woman in particular you are just a number for businesses and they will replace you in a heartbeat.

Career Development Paths on Offer

The preferred model of working that supports career development in most organisations is one of working full time in continuous employment. Breaks in careers, working part time or home working can all have a detrimental impact on employees' careers through a loss in salary, missing out on promotion, assumptions around ambition, valuation of input or a loss of responsibilities from their roles.

Two-thirds of mothers feel that motherhood has negatively impacted their career development[57]. Often this is through a reduction in job responsibilities (mothers' responsibilities are twice as likely to be reduced compared to fathers').

My own research found that fewer than half of parents felt their manager values their opinions and contributions as much as before they went on parental leave and only 14% felt like they are given the same opportunities (or better) than before they went on leave.

Careers can also be affected by a lack of career development conversations, and only one in five of parents I surveyed had discussed how to develop their career in their organisations with their managers despite over three-quarters feeling as ambitious or more ambitious than before they became a parent.

Over half of parents surveyed felt that being a parent has or will hold them back in their career progression. In particular, respondents shared:

> 'My manager was clear that working a 60% pattern would hold back my career as certain opportunities weren't possible. I was not given performance appraisals or goals and no opportunity for discussion of pay reviews in this new role. I pushed hard for this to be rectified the longer time went on and felt very demoralised and poorly treated directly related to having children and working a part time pattern'.
>
> 'They supported me returning in the pattern and short-term capacity I wanted, but because it was a less valuable role to them I was then sidelined longer term. This worsened upon announcing a subsequent pregnancy. I'm very grateful I wasn't pushed out of the company like other friends had been (in different companies)'.

Another simply said,

> '[I] feel like I've been shafted a bit as [I've] been moved to a different less interesting work stream'.

There were some positive stories:

> 'I was promoted when I came back from leave as my job had been split with others'.
> 'I was offered opportunities and different areas to work and grow'.
> 'I've been promoted to a line manager since returning and I'm leading on a new programme development now too'.

Ultimately, the picture emerging from my research supports that of wider research – that organisations are wasting the skills and potential of parents, particularly mothers returning to work after parental leave. This has an impact on their career, the UK workforce and the economy.

Work–Life Balance

Balancing the demands of work and home life is typically a struggle for parents throughout their child(ren)'s childhood, particularly for solo and separated parents who are typically managing things without the support of a partner. Flexible working is one way to support parents to achieve the balance that works for them.

There is an assumption that it is predominantly women who seek work–life balance, but men are becoming increasingly involved in caregiving; they seek improved work–life balance as much as women[58]. It is likely that all parents at some point will need to stop and evaluate the reality of how they will or are coping with juggling being a good parent and a good employee. And when work and family life collides – children are women's number one priority[59].

If women are given the flexibility they need at work, it leads to increased commitment to the organisation and productivity[60], as illustrated by one of my respondents:

> The support and flexibility (beyond the standard policy) once I returned to work had enabled me to continue working and made me feel valued. Their flexibility and help has meant I feel more motivated to give them my best.

However, negotiating and finding roles with the right flexibility is still proving difficult with 85% of mothers and 81% of fathers struggling to find jobs that accommodate their childcare needs[61].

Without flexibility, people (generally women) are forced to choose part-time roles. While on the surface, these roles fit their needs, part-time roles can be career limiting. They generally leave little or no time for personal and professional development, focusing purely on the operational side of the role. There is an assumption that people working part time are less interested in career development and two-thirds of women who worked part time had restricted their careers[62]. Part-time roles are often less attractive positions for these reasons.

Becoming a parent means that there is often a need to pass on career development opportunities if the parent feels it will have a negative impact on their delicate balance between work and family life. Trying to find harmony in how work life and home life fit together is an ongoing struggle for most parents, and my research supported this. Only 45% of respondents felt that it is possible to be a good enough parent and a good enough employee.

Boundary Management

Managing the boundary between work and home life is a key part of healthy work–life balance. When boundaries can be managed effectively, parents can enjoy and thrive in both their home life and work life. When these boundaries become blurred, this can lead to overwork, burnout and eventually dropping out of the workplace.

One of the main factors keeping women in work after parental leave is their need for intellectual stimulation and creativity. Wanting to be successful at home and at work can give them meaning in their lives[63]. However, women who have taken longer parental leave often feel the need to prove themselves in the workplace after they return. They try to work at the same level as they did before leave and make up for taking time off. These two factors can combine and lead to overwork and even burnout.

My respondents noted:

'I was thrown in[to] the busy end very quickly on [my] return to work. I embraced this, and wanted to feel as though I was contributing and "making up for the time I was off"'.

'I was overworked and working a lot [of] over time. Unable to leave the computer even when my son returned home. My employer could not care less. I ended up on medical leave for mental health and never returned'.

'I was reassured that I could keep my workload manageable, though in practice I find it difficult to resist agreeing to additional tasks due to anxiety around how competitive the industry is'.

Parents can sometimes feel like they aren't working hard enough. This can contribute to a loss of confidence and can cause working mothers to feel unsure about their skills and abilities and impact their career development prospects.

Parents of Children with Additional Needs

No matter the route to parenthood, parents rarely know in advance if their child will have additional needs. Biological parents might gain an inkling from scans during pregnancy, and parents adopting might be told some of the needs of the child being placed with them. It's very common, though, to become aware of children's additional needs as they grow.

Whatever a child's additional needs, they are likely to need extra support and attention from their parents. Children may need more medical appointments or other types of support and these will generally happen during office hours. Parents may need to work flexibly around these appointments, or even reduce their hours, both of which can have an impact on their career.

One of my respondents adopted a young girl with additional needs.

She has Down syndrome, developmental delay, severe sight impairment and a brain tumour. [This required] multiple hospital appointments and sudden admissions [into hospital] make [holding a] career difficult, particularly as a single mum. My work are very supportive and I am able to work from home and around appointments but it is exhausting and makes it difficult to even want to progress and develop whilst also trying to keep [my] head above water.

Neurodiverse Parents

While some parents may be aware of their neurodiversity going into parenthood, it's very common for adults to have found a way to manage and mask their undiagnosed neurodiversity, particularly if it hasn't caused too big an impact on their day-to-day life before becoming a parent. Undiagnosed neurodiverse adults often become aware of their potential (or actual) diagnosis when their child receives a diagnosis.

The effects of becoming a parent on sleep, sensory demands, time to oneself, time for leisure activities and hobbies, time to exercise and ultimately the ability to stop and take downtime when needed can create overwhelm in all parents. For undiagnosed neurodiverse parents it can lead to chronic fatigue, burnout and affect their wellbeing. Among autistic individuals, 96% experience sensory processing difficulty[64], so the increased sensory demands of becoming a parent can be especially challenging.

Ultimately, becoming a parent whether they have diagnosed or undiagnosed neurodiversity can affect their ability to manage their workload and juggle their competing work and home priorities.

Typical Assumptions and Biases

Biases towards parents can affect the way they are treated at work. Gender stereotypes are a key bias to be aware of, particularly as they can lead people to make assumptions that disadvantage the parents they work with.

One of the most impactful assumptions sparked by parenthood is that taking parental leave is like taking a long holiday, and that people can return and 'hit the ground running' with little to no time needed to re-integrate back into their role. The reality is that parental leave is a complicated multilevel transition of identity that runs alongside a significant break from work and a (sometimes subconscious) re-evaluation of career and life plans. As a result of this assumption, preparations in most organisations focus on the HR admin, the logistics of who is covering the work and how long this will be for, leaving new parents unsupported and left to figure out the transition for themselves.

Another big assumption triggered by parenthood is the 'Maternal Wall'. This is the assumption that mothers are less competent and less committed at work. It is one of the biggest biases that women can face, even if they aren't mothers. Women with children are less likely to be hired, promoted and are paid less (known as the 'Motherhood Penalty'), and may even be held to higher standards than women without children. 'A third [of employers] believe that women who become pregnant and new mothers in work are "generally less interested in career progression" when compared to other employees in their company'[65], known as the Gender Ambition Gap.

The contrasting assumption about fathers, the 'Fatherhood Bonus', sees working fathers benefit both with regards to their salary and perceived competence when compared to either working mothers or non-fathers. The assumption or belief being that fathers are more committed to work, are looking for more stability and are even more deserving of a higher salary.

A commonly held gendered assumption is that mothers don't value training and progression, and that fathers don't have family responsibilities[66]. This can directly impact the experience of mothers and fathers in the workplace.

Research has found that female managers will be more supportive than male managers of a larger number of flexible working arrangements, and that managers of both sexes will be more supportive of flexible working for women employees than for men[67].

In addition to the assumptions around career and ambition, another commonly held assumption about pregnant women and mothers who have given birth is 'baby brain'; that pregnant women and mothers have lower cognitive abilities or lose their cognitive abilities as a result of being pregnant or having a baby. The good news for all is that developments in the field of neurobiology and neuroscience have been able to disprove this. No evidence has been found that mothers lose any cognitive abilities and the phenomenon of 'baby-brain' is a subjective experience with 'poorer sleep, higher anxiety and higher depression related to reports of poorer subjective memory in mothers'[68].

There is a commonly held assumption that mothers don't really want to be at work, and that if they had the choice they would rather be at home with their baby, while fathers want to be at work and don't want to be home with their baby. The reality is that 98% of mothers do want to work, and 52% want to work four days or more[69].

Mothers may themselves hold their own assumptions and biases about returning to work after parental leave. They may hold self-limiting beliefs about their ability to navigate their return to work and whether they are able to combine working and family life effectively.

This bias against women can have a massive impact on their return to work and subsequent career progression. It can be less likely that they will be offered stretch work or promotions due to the misguided assumption that they are less interested in progressing their career now they are a mother, or that they simply won't have the time.

For new fathers, there are two commonly held assumptions: that fathers don't want to take parental leave to be home with their children, and that fathers want to be the main 'bread winner' and fill the stereotypical role of 'provider'. Research has shown that men do want to take paternity leave, but 50% of fathers felt they couldn't take enough leave to support their families and 53% of families said they struggled financially when the father took paternity leave[70].

Ian Dinwiddy of Inspiring Dads says that the clients he works with who take parental leave are often struck by how much their priorities have changed as a result, and it makes them realise that 'work isn't everything' when they used to be 'all in'. By being an active parent, it's opened their eyes and they realise that while their career is great, it's not the 'be all and end all'. They want to balance work and home life. He also notes that some clients who have taken on caregiving at some stage have said to him that they no longer feel as ambitious as they used to be and have been disconcerted about that. They have enjoyed the connection they have formed with their children and they don't want to give it up. They want to have it all.

How Do Personal Experiences Affect Our Assumptions and Biases?

Our personal experiences, attitudes and values can affect the way we regard our teams and colleagues, and how we respond to them when issues arise between home and work responsibilities.

A manager who is a parent might be particularly sensitive to the needs of a sick child or the priority most parents will want to give to illnesses or accidents that affect their children. A manager whose partner took care of all domestic situations might expect a similar situation to be the case with members of their team experiencing issues that need their attention at home.

A manager who took very little parental leave might expect team members they see as being in their 'group' to behave in the same way, while a manager who returned to work full time or part time after their parental leave might assume other parents are able to and want to manage their return the same way.

A manager who had very little help in returning to work after parental leave might expect others to feel or need the same and a manager who has chosen not to have children might feel that those who have chosen to have children have prioritised children over their career and so chosen the difficulties juggling the career and children brings.

How Can We Avoid Making Assumptions and Reduce Unconscious Bias?

It can be hard to change biases that impact decision making as this means changing behaviour and beliefs that are deeply rooted and often unconscious. But it is feasible to try and reduce the impact our biases and assumptions play in decision making and managers are perfectly placed to become advocates for people returning to work after parental leave.

Top Tips to Avoid Making Assumptions and Reducing Unconscious Bias

Raise Awareness of Our Own Assumptions and Biases

The first step to limiting the impact of biases and assumptions is to accept that they exist and understand your most significant stereotypes. For example, do you believe women are more emotionally intelligent? Do you believe that men are more confident in the workplace? Acknowledging biases are there and might impact the efforts of a supportive line manager makes it possible to put them aside prior to conversations with a team member.

Try Not to Treat Someone as a 'Friend or Foe'

When looking at candidates for a promotion, remember you might look upon someone more favourably if, for example, they went to your university, or have similar hobbies.

Be Objective

When making a comparison between candidates, separate out the key information you need to make the decision so you can be fair and unbiased. In the case of promotion, this might be the performance and skills record.

Don't Make Decisions When You Are Tired or Stressed

When you have low energy, your brain is more reliant on biases and assumptions. Leave decisions until after you've had a good night's sleep.

Use Your Imagination

Interestingly, the brain responds the same to something whether it is real or imagined. So if you imagine the 'perfect person' making the decision you are trying to make, you are less likely to default to or rely on your biases.

Build a Support Group

Create a support group with other managers to help support you with making fair decisions and challenge you if they feel unfair assumptions or biases are coming into play.

Put Processes in Place to Support Behavioural Change

Spending time thinking about what you can put in place to ensure your biases aren't affecting the decisions you make can help reduce their impact. Treat employees as individuals and all problems as if you are hearing them for the first time. Ask individuals how they are feeling before you rely on how you'd feel in their situation or how you dealt with a similar situation previously. Avoid making comparisons between individuals in similar situations. Check in with your own support group regularly to ensure you're not making decisions based on your biases. Challenge others if you hear negative comments or see negative behaviour and regularly check on your own mindset.

The Hidden Strengths of Parents

Caring for a child has impacts on the brain that not only make us better able to care for our children, but benefit us in our wider lives.

For example, women with a higher number of children show less apparent brain ageing[71] and there is also evidence of a positive relationship between number of children and brain ageing in fathers[72].

Time away from work caring for children enhances skills that can bring real value to the workplace.

For mothers, there's evidence of 'professional benefits from the psychological rewards, social support and skills acquired through personal roles'. Women gained 'satisfaction, confidence, self-esteem and a well-rounded perspective that helped them cope with work related issues' and the more women invested in multiple roles, the more they were rated as having managerial skills[73].

Being a mother has also been associated with improved empathy skills, feeling more efficient and productive, more understanding, more tolerant and more compassionate. A changed perspective on life can make mothers feel more positive, motivated and better communicators[74].

The effects of parenthood on fathers are just as interesting. Research in Norway with fathers taking parental leave found that they felt they gained experience in 'tolerating trivialities and chaos'. They reported growing 'calmer, more harmonious, more patient, more humble and less selfish'. The experience of being responsible for taking care of their child made them 'a little bit more tolerant and flexible, more willing to compromise', that their 'emotional register had expanded'. They felt that 'being more open to others and having more empathy . . . made . . . them feel that they were developing as people'. One father noted that his fathering experience was useful in his work situation. His experience of caring for his son 'helped him develop a greater understanding of other ways of seeing and doing things in a work related context' and becoming a father had influenced his managerial style to be more inclusive and softer[75].

Being a parent often requires regular switching between parenting styles depending on the time of day and situation, even more so when parenting multiple children with different personalities. This can benefit leadership skills on returning to work as parents can adapt the flexibility they develop in parenting styles to flexibility in leadership styles. Research in Canada and Belgium found that childcare helped fathers develop their managerial skills through learning to 'master a greater diversity of tasks and solve conflicts'[76]. Other research has shown that when fathers learned 'needs-orientated communication and care rationality' it appeared to make their interactions with people other than their children easier too[77].

Research into the wider benefits caregiving in general brings to the workplace identified three main areas of benefit as reported by caregivers[78].

- **Humanity**: Caregiving was found to benefit empathy, teamwork, emotional intelligence, collaboration, encouraging others and commitment to employer; it also made people feel like a kinder manager, a better co-worker and a more understanding leader.
- **Productivity**: Caregiving was found to improve efficiency, persistence, patience and resilience.
- **Cognitivity** (the mental and emotional work needed to maintain culture, connect people and allow for smooth operations in organisations): Caregiving was found to benefit prioritising, anticipating needs, flexibility, multitasking, project management and focus.

The skills highlighted above, developed through parenting and caregiving, not only benefit the individual parent, but also their employer. When parents return to the workplace after parental leave they are doing so after a skills boost. While they may feel that their job-specific skills have become a little rusty due to their time away from work, the enhanced skills they bring with them more than compensate for this loss which can soon be fixed through training and their experience back in the office.

Unfortunately, more than half of respondents (57%) to my survey reported that they don't feel that the skills and strengths they bring to their organisation are recognised, and this is one factor that can cause parents to look for alternative employment where they feel they have impact and are valued.

How to Get the Best Out of Parents

The transition to working parent can be a time of stress and vulnerability which can significantly impact a parent's career immediately and in the long term. There are things that employers can do both at an organisational and individual level.

The main issue for an employer when supporting women becoming parents is increasing retention after parental leave and providing the support and environment they need to thrive as working mothers. For men, it's giving them time to adapt to their new identity and supporting them to be the father they want to be alongside continuing in their career.

There are clear issues that affect the retention of women: career development paths that recognise the impact maternity has on them, working conditions that enables them to meet their childcare needs and engage in work they find intellectually stimulating that adds to their career capital, and a corporate culture that supports their needs and acknowledges their need for balance in their lives. But ultimately, women opt out of work for similar reasons to men: the lack of opportunity, dissatisfaction with their role and lack of organisational commitment[79].

The biggest barrier that organisations present to meeting men's needs is inadequate paternity leave. This means they miss out on the time they want to bond with their baby or child and support their partner, to develop their parenting skills and support the development of equity with their partner in managing childcare and the domestic load. Just 32.3% of fathers who took two weeks or less paternity leave said they were ready to return to work physically after their paternity leave, 14% said they were ready to return mentally and 12.8% said they were ready to return emotionally[80]. Providing equality in parental leave is key to supporting mothers' career development.

What Can Employers Do?

Organisational culture is one of the key factors in supporting parents in their careers through parental leave and in the years following their return. Without a culture that is positive, inclusive and parent-friendly, policies and other interventions can only act like a bandage and will ultimately fail, as half of departure issues for women relate to organisational culture[81]. The following practical changes can impact retention of parents and support them in their careers.

1. Provide equal parental leave for all parents. As we have seen, fathers want to actively parent and mothers want to work. Inequality in parental leave maintains the stereotype that caring is a mother's issue to juggle around their career.
2. Ensure senior management role-model and express inclusive, parent-friendly values and are accountable for the advancement of parents in their careers.
3. Involve parents in designing support programmes to ensure their needs are met as far as possible.
4. Embrace flexible working, providing as much autonomy as possible on working hours and location. In 2019 Zurich UK started offering all roles on a part-time or flexible basis. Since then they have seen the number of female part-time hires increase by four and male part-time hires double. In 2023 they hired twice as many women into senior roles compared to the same period in 2019. This has also benefited career progression, with part-time internal promotions increasing by 167%[82].
5. Ensure that part-time roles are more than just operational/functional roles and provide meaningful work and opportunities for people to increase their career capital.
6. Introduce inclusive measures of performance that support non-linear career progression.
7. Create a hiring and promotion policy based both on merit and potential, not the amount of time spent in the office.
8. Improve psychological safety at work by supporting zero tolerance of microaggressions towards parents.
9. Notice and challenge assumptions and biases and develop a policy to support this.
10. Respect employees' time outside of working hours and move away from the 'always on' culture that has become so widespread.
11. Remove early and late meetings as much as possible to allow parents to manage childcare arrangements.

12 Provide qualified, experienced, external coaching support to help parents navigate their transition to and from parental leave and continue to support their needs for at least the first 12 months after they return. While Maternity Coaching doesn't significantly increase the numbers of mothers returning to work after parental leave it does increase retention for the two years after return. Encourage men to seek support, as women are more willing to admit they need help and seek it out[83].
13 Provide internal mentors for all parents to support them and advocate for them in the organisation.
14 Develop and invest in physical and mental spaces (such as Employee Resource Groups) for parents at work. Ian Dinwiddy notes the importance of intentionally creating environments for fathers to be able to talk to other fathers, whether through one-to-one internal mentoring or coaching as well as support groups, even if there are very small numbers interested to start with.
15 Create informal social and networking events during normal working hours as these can be a key support for career development. Mothers in particular can find themselves excluded from such events when they clash with childcare commitments, particularly solo mothers.
16 Invest in childcare solutions as much as possible, whether physically through providing on-site facilities, to providing backup / emergency childcare solutions. On-site childcare has been found to increase the retention of parents and create more loyalty to the organisation[84].
17 Train line managers to:

- understand organisational policies and support available
- understand the general needs of working parents
- help parents in their team develop their support network
- understand and help their team implement healthy and effective boundary management
- recognise the signs people might be moving towards overwhelm and burnout
- foster a culture of open communication.

I talked to Adam (see case study below), who was only able to take two weeks of paternity leave and feels that although he and his wife were happy with the arrangements they made around parental leave, if their needs aren't met in the future they won't hesitate to move to organisations that will meet their needs.

> Before he became a dad, Adam didn't think much about how to juggle being a dad around his career. He knew he would only have two weeks of leave, and his time was spent making sure his wife was set up to look after their baby for her maternity leave. He remembers the shock of having his son but as he returned to work so quickly it had no impact on his role or career. It was only when his wife also returned to work that he experienced how tricky the juggle was going to be.
>
> When his daughter was born he took another two weeks of paternity leave, and when his wife returned to work this time the logistics and organisation needed to juggle work and family really hit home. Each weekend they planned the drop-offs and pick-ups for the coming week. Sometimes he would be at the nursery before it opened so he could be the first to drop off then dash to get the train to London. Delays resulted in being late for work, but the greater acceptance of flexible working since the Covid pandemic have made things easier for him.
>
> He doesn't think his parental leave or becoming a parent has had any real impact on his career. He was keen to carry on with his career plans and try to find balance between career and being a parent. He doesn't think his organisation supports him being a father and that generally organisations want people to do their job well and don't take personal circumstances into account. He says that managers are understanding if a parent has to leave work to collect their child if they're unwell, but at the end of the day if parental duties encroach on the ability to do the job, this diminishes career prospects. However, he feels

> that if an organisation isn't open to approving flexible working options, or benefits such as buying more annual leave, they will struggle to hold on to people.
>
> If in the future he feels that his needs aren't being accommodated, he will choose to work for a company that does meet his needs. Ultimately he feels that it is important for organisations to support parents as individuals and work out what will work for both the parent and organisation. That way dads can work effectively knowing their way of working is accepted in their organisation.

What Can Managers Do?

The following interventions can be implemented by managers at each stage of the transition to and from parental leave:

Pre leave:

The focus is on planning for leave and the return.

1. Involve the parent-to-be in the decision as to how their work will be covered while they are away, including helping to find their cover and their cover starting before parental leave starts to allow for an 'in-person' handover.
2. Support the production of a handover document that includes a return to work plan of how the parent will phase back into their work and responsibilities.
3. Discuss and agree priorities for the run-up to leave starting.
4. Help in the creation of a work support network, including colleagues who will advocate for the parent-to-be in their absence, a mentor and someone who will keep them up-to-date with key information while they are away/ready for their return.
5. Schedule in regular meetings to discuss preparations for leave.
6. Create a joint communication plan to agree how to stay in touch during parental leave.

7. Discuss and agree how KIT/SPLIT days can support the return to work, and create a plan for how these can be used to support the return to work including any training that might be useful.
8. Provide an appraisal/review before leave starts which includes a career development discussion and plan for after leave.
9. Discuss any opportunities for promotion before or after leave.
10. Create a contingency plan in case leave needs to start earlier than anticipated or the return to work can't go as planned.

During leave:

The focus is on facilitating parents' smooth return to work.

1. Follow the communication plan as agreed before leave.
2. Encourage and support parents in their KIT/SPLIT days to reconnect with their role and industry.
3. Revisit the return to work plan and discuss new parents' needs for their return, including changes to working pattern (phased return, days and hours of work, re-induction).
4. Check in with regards to and provide training as needed.
5. Support parents to reconnect with colleagues while on leave to enable a smooth return to work.
6. Support parents to reboot their reputation through internal and external communication channels as appropriate.
7. Discuss and agree boundaries for maintaining a healthy work–life balance and how to use technology to support these.
8. Create clear priorities for the return period and a plan for building up workload alongside a phased return.

Post-leave:

The focus is on helping parents re-integrate with working life and their career at the speed that works for them. It's also important to recognise and acknowledge the transition as significant and impactful – life has changed dramatically and parents are returning as different people to who they were before they left.

1. Be present on the first day back both to welcome parents back, acknowledge the significance of the transition back to work, and ensure that they feel supported and that things run smoothly.

2 Check in daily for the first week or so to see how things are going at work and at home, set confidence boosting goals and be there to help with any issues quickly, before moving to weekly one-to-ones for at least the first three months.
3 Book in a career development conversation within the first month of the return to discuss goals, projects, stretch work, training requirements, promotion opportunities, gaps in experience or skills, new skills that they developed that can be useful back at work, mentors for career development, and internal groups that can support career development. Look at alternative career paths and encourage broader definitions of career success.
4 Be aware that while the return could go smoothly, that the danger period is often a few months after the return when parents can start to question their decisions and the needs of their child(ren) shift and change, for example following the birth or adoption of additional children, starting school, and any medical or neurodiversity diagnoses. Look out for signs of overwhelm or burnout if boundaries aren't being managed or if they are trying to take on more than they can cope with.
5 Encourage parents to recognise successes in both their home and work spheres, and acknowledge the skills they have developed through parenting that are beneficial to their role.

Evie knew she was going to be a solo parent early on in her pregnancy. Her experience of parental leave (see case study below) highlights how important the line manager relationship is, and how difficult it can be for solo parents after they return to work:

> Evie's relationship broke down when she was ten weeks pregnant, so she knew she would be solo parenting from early on in her pregnancy. She had been with her organisation for a few years and had a great relationship with her manager, and a really supportive team. When she shared her news with her manager he was 'overwhelmingly' supportive and just asked what she needed.

Before going on maternity leave she was conscious of how important childcare was going to be for her parenting on her own. As a result, she needed to create a return-to-work plan before going on leave so she could book her childcare place but at the time her organisation didn't allow the agreement of working plans at this early stage. She had to make a plan regardless and hope that her flexible working request was agreed when she returned, which fortunately it was.

The return to work was very hard emotionally and mentally as Evie had been the sole carer for her baby, who suffered from quite severe separation anxiety when left with her childminder. When she collected her in the evening, this made for a disruptive evening and very disrupted sleep.

Three months in this caused Evie's confidence to take a nose dive when the reality of working life sank in as she tried to balance everything. It was at this time, when she was trying to be the best at everything, that she burned out and started to experience what she now knows were autistic meltdowns from the overwhelm and exhaustion. As is common with undiagnosed autistic women, becoming a mother was particularly overwhelming for Evie and resulted in a particularly difficult return to work. She sought coaching from internal coaches at her organisation and became involved in setting up an Employee Resource Group to support parents.

School holidays are particularly tricky to juggle being a solo parent, and the only solution is holiday clubs, the cost of which is hard to cover with one salary. It's also hard for her to travel for business as she has sole responsibility for her daughter. She feels her career has definitely been impacted by becoming a mother, although flexible working has made it easier to manage being a mother and have a career.

Supporting the Adoptive Community as Employers

Adoption UK provide these additional tips to support the adoptive community in the workplace and their careers:

1. If you are unsure about the process and how you can be supportive, ask.
2. Ensure your adoption policies and flexible working policies support the needs of adoptive parents.
3. Provide managers and colleagues with an understanding of adoption to help create an inclusive culture.
4. Consider tailoring your employee assistance programmes to provide particular support to those parenting care-experienced children or who are themselves care-experienced.
5. Consider how you can create a community for adopters in the workplace and whether your processes and systems are sensitive to their needs.

Supporting the Fertility Journey as Employers

Fertility in the Workplace provide these additional tips to support parents on their journey through fertility treatment:

1. Create a company Fertility policy which will help improve productivity and reduce lost hours.
2. Offer support, guidance and reasonable adjustments, including time to attend appointments or recover from treatments.
3. Include all employees in the wider conversation.
4. Provide training and awareness of the fertility journey.

Final Thoughts

There's a common narrative in the media today that women are damaging their careers when becoming a parent. This is extremely harmful to women and detrimental to their ability to be a successful working parent as it individualises structural and organisational issues and puts the emphasis on parents having to find a solution to balance work and family needs.

Organisations rely on people becoming parents to provide the next generation of workers. The narrative needs to be changed to one where organisations that don't support parents at work are damaging themselves, and a society that doesn't support working parents is one that is going to fall behind globally both with regards to GDP and HDI (Gross Domestic Product which measures value created by goods and services and Human Development Index which measures a country's social and economic development).

Questions for Reflection

Biases and Assumptions

What biases or assumptions do you hold about working mothers and fathers?

What can you do now to ensure that these don't impact the careers of those you manage?

Culture

How does your company and team culture currently impact the parents in your team?

What opportunities do parents miss out on as they happen before or after regular working hours?

What could you change about your culture to help maximise parents' career development opportunities?

Skills and Strengths

What new skills and strengths have you noticed and valued in parents who have returned after parental leave?

What changes in management and leadership skills have you noticed in new parents?

How can you make better use of the skills new parents bring back to your team?

Managing the Transition to and from Leave

What are the issues you've noticed your colleagues struggling with in their transition to and from parental leave?

What changes can you make to better support them?

Career Development

How do your colleagues' careers typically develop after they return from parental leave?

What differences do you notice in the career paths of mothers and fathers?

What could you do to better support mothers and fathers in their careers after parental leave?

Work–Life Balance

What work–life balance issues do you notice colleagues struggling with after they return from parental leave?

What causes these issues?

What can you do to help solve these issues?

Notes

1 Martínez García M, Cardenas S, Pawluski J, Carmona S, Saxbe D. Recent neuroscience advances in human parenting. *Advances in Neurobiology*. 2022;27:239–67. doi:10.1007/978-3-030-97762-7_8.
2 www.statista.com/statistics/280120/employment-rate-in-the-uk-by-gender/
3 www.careersafterbabies.org/careers-after-babies-report
4 www.ons.gov.uk/employmentandlabourmarket/peopleinwork/employmentandemployeetypes/datasets/familiesandthelabourmarketuk maindatasetusingthelabourforcesurveyandannualpopulationsurvey
5 https://newscentre.vodafone.co.uk/app/uploads/2021/05/Lost-Connections-2021-180521-Pages-Web-1-1.pdf
6 Schlossberg, N. A model for analyzing human adaptation to transition. *The Counseling Psychologist*. 1981;9:2–18. doi:10.1177/001100008100 900202.
7 Brandth B, Kvande E. Changing fathers and work–life boundary setting. In: *Designing Parental Leave Policy: The Norway Model and the Changing Face of Fatherhood*. Bristol University Press; 2021. pp137–52. doi:10. 46692/9781529201598.009.
8 Lee J, Lee S. Caring is masculine: Stay-at-home fathers and masculine identity. *Psychology of Men & Masculinity*. 2016;19. doi:10.1037/men 0000079.
9 https://ftsewomenleaders.com/latest-reports/
10 www.fawcettsociety.org.uk/paths-to-parenthood-uplifting-new-mothers-at-work
11 www.careersafterbabies.org/careers-after-babies-report

12 www.mckinsey.com/featured-insights/diversity-and-inclusion/women-in-the-workplace
13 https://data.unwomen.org/women-count
14 www.frc.org.uk/news-and-events/news/2021/07/diverse-boards-lead-to-better-corporate-culture-and-performance/
15 www.mckinsey.com/featured-insights/diversity-and-inclusion/women-in-the-workplace
16 www.fatherhoodinstitute.org/post/closing-the-gap-uk-fathers-doing-18-more-childcare-since-pre-pandemic
17 www.peoplemanagement.co.uk/article/1870794/working-fathers-let-down-equality-act-workplace-banter-panel-argues
18 www.ons.gov.uk/employmentandlabourmarket/peopleinwork/employmentandemployeetypes/articles/familiesandthelabourmarketengland/2021/
19 www.peoplemanagement.co.uk/article/1870794/working-fathers-let-down-equality-act-workplace-banter-panel-argues
20 www.inspiringdads.co.uk/
21 www.royallondon.com/about-us/media/media-centre/press-releases/archive/female-breadwinner-rise/
22 www.jrf.org.uk/care/understanding-fathering-masculinity-diversity-and-change
23 www.nhs.uk/conditions/miscarriage/
24 www.nct.org.uk/pregnancy/how-you-might-be-feeling/fear-childbirth-and-tokophobia
25 Malmquist A, Jonsson L, Wikström J, Nieminen K. Minority stress adds an additional layer to fear of childbirth in lesbian and bisexual women, and transgender people. *Midwifery*. 2019;79:102551. doi:10.1016/j.midw.2019.102551.
26 Malmquist A, Wikström J, Jonsson L, Nieminen K. How norms concerning maternity, femininity and cisgender increase stress among lesbians, bisexual women and transgender people with a fear of childbirth. *Midwifery*. 2021;93:102888. doi:10.1016/j.midw.2020.102888.
27 www.tena.co.uk/women/living-with-bladder-weakness/everyday-life/back-to-work-how-mums-really-feel
28 www.npeu.ox.ac.uk/mbrrace-uk/data-brief/maternal-mortality-2020-2022
29 www.unicef.org.uk/new-survey-reveals-over-half-of-all-parents-with-young-children-in-britain-over-2-million-families-are-struggling-financially-or-with-their-mental-health-as-1-in-3-struggle-to-get-profess/
30 www.england.nhs.uk/2024/05/record-numbers-of-women-accessing-perinatal-mental-health-support/

31 Ross L, Steele L, Goldfinger C, Strike C. Perinatal depressive symptomatology among lesbian and bisexual women. *Archives of Women's Mental Health*. 2007;10:53–9. doi:10.1007/s00737-007-0168-x.
32 www.mentalhealth.org.uk/explore-mental-health/stories/black-maternal-mental-health
33 Watson H, Harrop D, Walton E, Young A, Soltani H. A systematic review of ethnic minority women's experiences of perinatal mental health conditions and services in Europe. *PLOS One*. 2019;14(1):e0210587. https://doi.org/10.1371/journal.pone.0210587
34 www.nct.org.uk/life-parent/emotions/postnatal-depression-dads-and-co-parents-10-things-you-should-know
35 www.adoptionuk.org/the-adoption-barometer
36 Houston D, Marks G. The role of planning and workplace support in returning to work after maternity leave. *British Journal of Industrial Relations*. 2003;41:197–214. doi:10.1111/1467-8543.00269.
37 https://fertilitynetworkuk.org/fertility-in-the-workplace/
38 www.pregnancyandthebrain.com/research/
39 Saxbe D, Martínez García M, Cardenas S, Waizman Y, Carmona S. Changes in left hippocampal volume in first-time fathers: Associations with oxytocin, testosterone, and adaptation to parenthood. *Journal of Neuroendocrinology*. 2023;35. doi:10.1111/jne.13270.
40 Bon A, Mohamud A. Review of conservation of resources theory in job demands and resources model. *International Journal of Global Optimization and Its Application*. 2022;1:236–48. doi:10.56225/ijgoia.v1i4.102.
41 Akkermans J, Seibert S, Mol S. Tales of the unexpected: Integrating career shocks in the contemporary careers literature. *SA Journal of Industrial Psychology*. 2018;44. doi:10.4102/sajip.v44i0.1503.
42 Moffett J. 'Adjusting to that new norm': How and why maternity coaching can help with the transition back to work after maternity leave. *International Coaching Psychology Review*. 2018;13:62–76. doi:10.53841/bpsicpr.2018.13.2.62.
43 Walker, M. (2018). *Why We Sleep*. Penguin Books.
44 Walker, M. (2018). *Why We Sleep*. Penguin Books.
45 https://baby2sleep.co.uk/wp-content/uploads/Breaking-The-Silence-Revealing-The-Truth-about-Parenting-and-the-Workplace.pdf
46 www.ons.gov.uk/employmentandlabourmarket/peopleinwork/employmentandemployeetypes/articles/familiesandthelabourmarketengland/2021
47 Ciciolla L, Luthar SS. Invisible household labor and ramifications for adjustment: Mothers as captains of households. *Sex Roles*. 2019;81(7–8): 467–86. doi:10.1007/s11199-018-1001-x.

48 www.coram.org.uk/news/families-facing-growing-childcare-shortages-while-costs-rise-by-7/
49 www.fawcettsociety.org.uk/Handlers/Download.ashx?IDMF=d73d0c92-19af-479c-a206-0807ec008bf1
50 www.who.int/news-room/fact-sheets/detail/infant-and-young-child-feeding
51 www.gov.uk/government/statistics/transport-statistics-great-britain-2023/transport-statistics-great-britain-2022-domestic-travel
52 www.gov.uk/holiday-entitlement-rights/holiday-pay-the-basics
53 Chawla N, Gabriel A, Prengler M, Rogers K, Rogers B, Tedder-King A, Rosen C. Allyship in the fifth trimester: A multi-method investigation of women's postpartum return to work. *Organizational Behavior and Human Decision Processes*. 2024;182:104330. doi:10.1016/j.obhdp.2024.104330.
54 Bussell J. Great expectations: Can maternity coaching affect the retention of professional women? *International Journal of Evidence Based Coaching and Mentoring*. 2008;S2:14–26.
55 Brandth B, Kvande E. Changing fathers and work–life boundary setting. In: *Designing Parental Leave Policy: The Norway Model and the Changing Face of Fatherhood*. Bristol University Press; 2021. pp137–52. doi:10.46692/9781529201598.009.
56 www.fawcettsociety.org.uk/Handlers/Download.ashx?IDMF=d73d0c92-19af-479c-a206-0807ec008bf1
57 www.fawcettsociety.org.uk/Handlers/Download.ashx?IDMF=d73d0c92-19af-479c-a206-0807ec008bf1
58 Kossek E. Managing work–life boundaries in the digital age. *Organizational Dynamics*. 2016;45:258–70. doi:10.1016/j.orgdyn.2016.07.010.
59 Grady G, Mccarthy A. Work–life integration: Experiences of mid-career professional working mothers. *Journal of Managerial Psychology*. 2008;23:599–622. doi:10.1108/02683940810884559.
60 Grady G, Mccarthy A. Work–life integration: Experiences of mid-career professional working mothers. *Journal of Managerial Psychology*. 2008;23:599–622. doi:10.1108/02683940810884559.
61 www.fawcettsociety.org.uk/Handlers/Download.ashx?IDMF=d73d0c92-19af-479c-a206-0807ec008bf1
62 Gash (2008), cited in McQuaid R, Munro A, Dabir-Alai P. Motherhood and its impact on career progression. *Gender in Management: An International Journal*. 2012;27:346–64. doi:10.1108/17542411211252651.
63 Grady G, Mccarthy A. Work–life integration: Experiences of mid-career professional working mothers. *Journal of Managerial Psychology*. 2008;23:599–622. doi:10.1108/02683940810884559.

64 Talcer MC, Duffy O, Pedlow K. A qualitative exploration into the sensory experiences of autistic mothers. *J Autism Dev Disord*. 2023;53:834–49. https://doi.org/10.1007/s10803-021-05188-1
65 www.equalityhumanrights.com/guidance/business/pregnancy-and-maternity-discrimination-research-findings
66 https://workingfamilies.org.uk/publications/working-parents-flexibility-and-job-quality-what-are-the-trade-offs/
67 Yeandle S, Phillips J, Scheibl F, Wigfield A, Wise S. *Line Managers and Family-Friendly Employment: Roles and Perspectives*. Family and Work Series. Policy Press; 2003.
68 Orchard E, Ward P, Egan G, Jamadar S. Baby-brain phenomena is a subjective experience: Absence of evidence for cognitive deficit in new mothers at one-year postpartum. 2021;preprint. doi:10.1101/2021.06.07.447303.
69 www.careersafterbabies.org/careers-after-babies-report
70 www.workingdads.co.uk/50-fathers-take-less-paternity-leave-than-they-want/
71 De Lang et al. (2019), cited in Martínez García M, Cardenas S, Pawluski J, Carmona S, Saxbe D. Recent neuroscience advances in human parenting. Advances in Neurobiology. 2022;27:239–67. doi:10.1007/978-3-030-97762-7_8.
72 Orchard et al. (2021), cited in Martínez García M, Cardenas S, Pawluski J, Carmona S, Saxbe D. Recent neuroscience advances in human parenting. Advances in Neurobiology. 2022;27:239–67. doi:10.1007/978-3-030-97762-7_8.
73 Ruderman M, Ohlott P, Panzer K, King S. Benefits of multiple roles for managerial women. *Academy of Management Journal*. 2002;45:369–86. doi:10.2307/3069352.
74 Kurt B, Ucel E, Dalkılıç O. So many challenges, so many regrets: Motherhood decisions of career-oriented women. *Gender Issues*. 2024;41. doi:10.1007/s12147-024-09326-8.
75 Brandth B, Kvande E. Changing fathers and work–life boundary setting. In: *Designing Parental Leave Policy: The Norway Model and the Changing Face of Fatherhood*. Bristol University Press; 2021. pp137–52. doi:10.46692/9781529201598.009.
76 Doucet and Merla (2007), cited in Brandth B, Kvande E. Changing fathers and work–life boundary setting. In: *Designing Parental Leave Policy: The Norway Model and the Changing Face of Fatherhood*. Bristol University Press; 2021. pp137–52. doi:10.46692/9781529201598.009.
77 Waerness (1984), cited in Brandth B, Kvande E. Changing fathers and work–life boundary setting. In: *Designing Parental Leave Policy: The*

Norway Model and the Changing Face of Fatherhood. Bristol University Press; 2021. pp137–52. doi:10.46692/9781529201598.009.

78 https://hbr.org/2023/08/research-caregiver-employees-bring-unique-value-to-companies

79 Bussell J. Great expectations: Can maternity coaching affect the retention of professional women? *International Journal of Evidence Based Coaching and Mentoring*. 2008;S2:14–26.

80 https://pregnantthenscrewed.com/70-of-dads-who-didnt-take-their-full-paternity-leave-entitlement-had-to-cut-it-short-due-to-cost/

81 Bussell J. Great expectations: Can maternity coaching affect the retention of professional women? *International Journal of Evidence Based Coaching and Mentoring*. 2008;S2:14–26.

82 www.zurich.co.uk/media-centre/zurich-quadruples-part-time-hires

83 Ludeman K. Coaching with women. In: Passmore J, editor. *Diversity in Coaching*. Kogan Page; 2013. pp. 199–215.

84 https://bestplace4workingparents.com/wp-content/uploads/2024/06/national-trends-report-2023-6_7_24_sm-compressed.pdf

Chapter 8

Talking About the Menopause at Work

Kate Mansfield

Introduction

Definitions of menopause, perimenopause and menopausal transition can be found at the end of this chapter. The term menopause is used as an all-encompassing term to describe all three. A reference to how I am using the terms woman and women inclusively can also be found there.

'Menopausal women are the fastest growing demographic in the workforce', according to Professor Jo Brewis[1]. Our workforce is ageing with eight out of ten women now experiencing menopause whilst working[2]. The menopausal transition usually occurs between the age of 45 and 55, although for some women it occurs much earlier, with symptoms lasting on average seven years[3]. Mid-life can be a vulnerable time for both men and women as explored in Chapter 3. Yet for women also experiencing the biological transition of menopause, alongside other mid-life challenges such as parenting teenagers, eldercare, wider health issues, divorce and bereavement, it can be a particularly bewildering and destabilising period in their careers and lives.

This coincides with the time in their professional lives that organisations can really benefit from their valuable skills and strengths as leaders and subject matter experts. If 10% of women are leaving the workplace due to menopause, this is over 300,000 women lost in the UK alone[4], undermining organisations' efforts elsewhere to retain talented women. It is not only the issue of female retention to consider but also how the experience of menopause may be

DOI: 10.4324/9781003510475-9

impacting the careers of the women who stay. In my experience, it can connect with a wide range of career related areas such as women's levels of engagement and motivation; commitment to their employer, confidence, perceptions of performance and whether they apply or put their hands up for development opportunities.

Take Charlotte, 50, for example, who had always been keen to develop and learn and who could not make sense of why work she previously would have relished now felt beyond her capability.

> My manager asked if I would like to take on a new research project and instead of feeling excited, I felt desperate. I was waking up each morning feeling as if I hadn't slept at all. I was getting anxious about the smallest of things and doubting my ability to stay on top of day-to-day tasks like emails. I was so over-tired; I would feel like crying constantly but I felt I had no choice but to put my mask on, smile and bear it as best as I could to get through the day.

Charlotte is a good example of someone who struggled with her identity and its impact on her work during her menopausal transition. She did not feel herself and came to career coaching to try to make sense of what she was feeling about her career. Charlotte said she felt invisible, which is something I often notice about the menopausal women I coach. As a result, she was unable to see the strengths, skills, wisdom and role modelling that she was able to offer her employer.

Not all women experience menopause negatively however, and some claim to experience no symptoms at all, but of those with symptoms, over half self-report a negative impact at work, and 30% claim it negatively impacts their career progression[5]. This suggests that something significant is happening at this stage of life.

It is an exciting time to write on a previously taboo topic that is now receiving more attention than ever before. Covid-19 accelerated menopause conversations helped by documentaries fronted by celebrities such as Davina McCall. The UK is leading the conversation; we have a Government Menopause Champion working with employers[6], including SMEs and unions, and a government created employer resource hub[7]. Increasingly employers are paying attention: 25% now have a menopause policy from a zero start in 2017[8]. Henpicked launched the 'Menopause Friendly Accreditation' in 2021 with over 500 UK employers working towards becoming menopause friendly[9].

So, whilst there is much progress, menopause policies and good intentions will not be enough. This chapter makes the case that it is not menopause itself, but how women experience the menopausal transition at work that influences their career and development decisions. Research by Encompass Equality strongly suggests that negative experiences of menopause can be rebalanced positively by culture and line managers[10]. How organisations respond to the career needs of menopausal women is indicative of how their culture enables those within the workplace to be at their best whatever their life stage and issues. It is of equal importance to other topics covered in this book, reflecting the overlap between life and work.

For this chapter, I have considered academic studies; research by menopause workplace experts such as Over the Bloody Moon[11] and Henpicked[12]; my own coaching experience; as well as asking 15 employers about how they were approaching menopause conversations at work. I want to first pose a few challenges for consideration on menopause in the workplace before sharing some practical ideas in the last section, on what employers and managers can do to more holistically address the topic.

Before I share the challenges, let's return to Charlotte who was feeling desperate about her manager wanting to her to take on a new development project and was so tired she wanted to cry. Charlotte's story is complicated by some other factors, however. In addition to being exhausted from lack of sleep caused by perimenopausal symptoms, Charlotte has three teenagers and an elderly father living alone one hour from home.

> There was so much support when the children were small. I had maternity leave for all three children. I worked part time on my return whilst they were very young. Now I am more senior, I agreed to full time and there is no support or flexibility to take time off because I haven't slept all night or because I need to go and sort out my father because he has had a fall again.

Charlotte's story illustrates that for many women it is difficult to separate their experience of menopause from other mid-life challenges faced by men too. Plus, as the sandwich generation, they may be bearing the brunt of caring responsibilities, for children and elderly family. Based on her research into the careers of mid-life women and her resulting book, *Revolting Women*, Lucy Ryan coined the term 'mid-life collision' to highlight the dynamic interaction of factors that may be at play during this stage of women's life and careers[13].

> As Charlotte also said: 'How can I possibly know how the menopause is really affecting me? I have no time to stop and work it out. I have such a busy job, three children and my elderly Dad to look after. No wonder I am exhausted permanently. Any woman I know my age is the same.

Brewis et al. in their aggregate report of all the menopause research in 2016 noted that most studies also concluded menopause is experienced contextually and impacted by many diverse factors[14]. These factors can include employment conditions, socioeconomic/life course factors as well as overlapping social identities such as race, ethnicity, class, sexual orientation, disability and age[15]. Intersectionality is therefore an important lens from which to consider menopause, recognising how the existence of multiple identities can shape women's experiences. For a further exploration of intersectionality, please see Chapter 5.

What is encouraging is that if menopause is experienced contextually, however, this suggests that by positively influencing context employers can make a difference.

Here are some of the challenges that employers and managers having career conversations with menopausal women might want to bear in mind:

1 All women experience menopause differently. There is no one-size-fits-all menopause!
2 How women experience menopause is influenced by many contextual factors including other mid-life challenges.
3 Women are often woefully unprepared for the impact of menopause and how it might affect their feelings and perceptions of work.
4 For those who do recognise the impact, the thought of sharing this with managers and colleagues is excruciating – perceived career suicide!
5 Others in the workplace may find discussing the topic extremely embarrassing especially male or younger female managers.
6 Unconscious biases relating to how menopausal and older women are perceived at work may undermine your efforts to create a positive culture that discusses menopause (and they link to women's own limiting beliefs).

Why Should Organisations Talk About Menopause?

According to Lesley Salem, 'the more people talk about menopause the better their experience'. Menopause is a workplace and female health issue that intersects with an employer's approach to careers, inclusivity, productivity, lived values and competitive advantage. Although there are currently no menopause-specific laws, increasingly there have been successful employment tribunals brought under sex discrimination and disability laws in relation to the treatment of women managing menopause at work[16,17]. The Equality and Human Rights Commission has published guidelines about the risks that a lack of awareness could pose to employers[18]. However, a change in perceptions and attitudes is more likely to occur when the approach is less stick and more carrot.

Ultimately evidence suggests that it is optimum for women to have alternative touchpoints within an organisation to talk about menopause[19]. Plenty of studies point to the fact that negative experiences of menopause are offset by support groups where safe conversations can take place[20]. Indeed, this has led to the Menopause Café concept[21], which many organisations are adopting, which brings communities of people together safely to share their experiences of menopause.

However, studies also repeatedly suggest that the response of individual managers plays a critical role in positively or negatively validating how a woman feels through the menopause[22]. In addition to organisation-wide education and initiatives, the conversation between women and their managers can really make a difference. Managers have much on their plates already though and may feel this is yet another burden for which they are unqualified. Yet they do not need to be menopause experts. Small steps and actions which support menopausal policies may have a big impact. Greater awareness, empathy and understanding is what women want.

Yet to commit to small steps, managers need to understand how talking about menopause benefits them, the business and their teams. This is a better starting point from which to tackle barriers of discomfort. They may also have concerns about whether menopausal symptoms are impacting women's productivity, performance and team relationships and need further reassurance.

Menopause is a temporary phase. A transition. Women come out the other side, and there is a good deal of evidence (explored in the strengths section) to suggest that women bring multiple strengths both during menopause *and* post-menopause. It is a time in fact of significant personal growth. There is little evidence to suggest that menopause impacts performance and productivity negatively[23], instead it is women's perceptions that it does which causes them increased stress and anxiety, and impacts confidence and their perceptions of their career opportunities. Research suggests that women experiencing menopausal symptoms self-scored more negatively on many work-related metrics including line manager support, team culture, work itself, amount of work and flexibility[24].

Performance management processes which place a lot of emphasis on being physically present have caused difficulties for menopausal women, for example the National Union of Teachers found that performance measures giving a lot of weight to absences left no room to acknowledge the strengths of menopausal women[25].

Surveys have suggested that many women claim to have taken some sick leave due to menopausal symptoms (62% according to Over the Bloody Moon and Kantar)[26]. The US and Canada have attempted to quantify this sickness absence into lost annual revenue ($1.8 billion and $3.5 billion respectively)[27,28]. I am a huge advocate that working structures need to better allow for flexibility to avoid sick days but sceptical about how quantifiable this is in relation to performance. Other studies and my own experience confirm that many women spend a lot of time masking symptoms[29], or over-compensating through additional work to try to minimise the impact of menopause which might lead to enhanced productivity. Additionally, it is worth noting that beyond the menopause many women describe a period of menopause zest, coined by anthropologist Margaret Mead, to describe a time of life when women feel most energised and feel at their most productive, committed and motivated[30]. It is here that they often reflect on their careers, feel at their most assertive and able to say no, and the age of life where many women start their own businesses[31]. It is also a time for many who have taken career breaks, as outlined in Chapter 6, to want to resume their careers. It is often a time of reinvention.

Any business case must be relevant to your own context rather than to be assumed as universally appropriate. I suggest a few ways below in which creating cultures that talk openly about menopause might benefit organisations.

The Business Case for Supporting Mid-Life Women with Menopause

1 Contributes to female retention balancing gender diversity which boosts innovation.

> 2 Reduces attrition and recruitment costs.
> 3 Underpins talent strategies – positively impacts female retention and development at all levels.
> 4 Supports the diversity and inclusion goals of the organisation.
> 5 Reduces potential risk of employment tribunal costs.
> 6 Reduces risks to productivity and performance.
> 7 Contributes to organisation's skills and capabilities for the future (experienced women).
> 8 Contributes to the employer value proposition – how an organisation is viewed by existing and prospective employees.
> 9 Contributes to well-being at work which can impact productivity and engagement.

Employers who wish to explore the case within their own environments might start by investigating the experiences of their own women's views on menopause and career. Many organisations I approached were leading the conversation from their equity, diversity and inclusion (EDI) agendas and particularly interested in the case that cuts across both gender and age with menopausal women.

Other chapters in this book have highlighted the business cases for both gender and age diversity made by McKinsey Women in the Workplace plus others (Chapters 6 and 7) relating to the efforts of organisations at retaining equal numbers of men and women in early career programmes being undermined when organisations start losing women at mid-career[32,33].

Many organisations struggle to encourage more women into leadership roles. McKinsey Women in the Workplace confirms that for every female director who gets promoted in the US, two other female directors leave the organisation[34]. However, it is not just about formal leadership. Women of menopausal age have much to offer through their skills, strengths, knowledge, wisdom and powerful role modelling. I encourage employers to make use of the following prompts to aid reflection on their business case.

Reflection Questions to Build the Case

1. What is the current gender balance of employees at mid-life (age 40–60)?
2. What percentage of women are leaving the organisation ages 40–60?
3. Is there a menopause policy in place?
4. What do female employees ages 40–60 say about their experiences of menopause at work?
5. Do exit interviews provide information on those leaving in this age bracket?
6. Can exit interviews include questions relating to experiences of menopause at work?
7. What are peer organisations doing in relation to menopause at work?
8. Are the menopause resources created by the government Hub useful?
9. Does the organisation offer private healthcare to employees and is there a menopause provision?
10. Can the organisation run a focus group to better understand the experience of menopause?
11. Do performance management criteria and process allow for any temporary impact that may be due to menopausal symptoms?

Much of the challenge for employers is to educate managers in the workplace about menopause *and* to also convince women that it will not harm their careers by talking about menopause. They will need convincing that policies are embedded into the fabric of the organisation culture and demonstrated in the attitudes and behaviours of colleagues and managers. Thus, learning and understanding more about the lived experiences of menopausal women is important.

Lived Experiences: How Does Menopause Impact Women at Work?

Vodafone published independent research conducted by Opinium, surveying 5,012 people in five countries aged 18+ who had experienced menopause while at work[35]: 62% said that their symptoms had negatively impacted them at work with the most common symptoms including general feeling of fatigue (53%), mood changes (47%), broken sleep (46%), temperature fluctuations (42%) and additional stress (40%).

For those who had experienced symptoms, consequently career concerns included:

- Concerns about performance at work (51%)
- Concerns about progression at work (43%)
- Concerns regarding perceptions of their symptoms (47%)

As mentioned, one of the greatest challenges is that women experience and report menopause symptoms very differently. A US study found that Black, Asian and Latin women may go through menopause earlier than white women, with more intense and prolonged symptoms[36]. Migrant women have also reported more symptoms than women living in their country of origin[37]. Neurodivergent women with ADHD who already have lower levels of dopamine may experience more impaired cognitive function[38]. LGBTQIA+ individuals may face additional stress during menopause due to societal stigma, lack of tailored healthcare, or social isolation[39]. It is also important to remember that some women claim to experience no symptoms at all with some describing only wholly positive experiences of menopausal transition[40].

We have already met Charlotte, who was exhausted and perimenopausal with several other mid-life challenges including caring responsibilities. Let's consider the experience of Katherine, 46, a senior director with a hard-won reputation in a male-dominated building services organisation.

> A year prior to coming for coaching, **Katherine** had been promoted to a senior director role and was the only woman at this level. She had had a difficult conversation with her boss and was feeling exceptionally angry and frustrated by him. She was also angry with herself, worried that she had let her emotions get to her and snapped at her boss. She wasn't sleeping and noticed herself making mistakes. The week before she had read the wrong report for a board meeting and was utterly mortified. She thought she might be getting early onset dementia. As one of the few women at her level, she was very conscious of her image and reputation. She thought she was a bit young for the menopause and wasn't sure about taking HRT. She hadn't had time to book a medical appointment, and she thought that her GP would be useless anyway.

The experience of Katherine is not uncommon for women who lack awareness of the physical as well as emotional and cognitive symptoms of menopause. A report by Gen M suggests that those who describe themselves on a career high when entering perimenopause are the most significantly unprepared for its impact (90%)[41]. This furthers the case for the role of employers in raising awareness.

Some of the physical symptoms associated with menopausal transition such as hot flushes may be more widely known than some of the emotional, psychological and cognitive symptoms that some women might experience[42]. Some of the latter can include anxiety, stress, depression, irritability, low self-esteem, loss of confidence, fatigue, memory lapses and slower processing[43,44]. Many women commonly refer to some of the cognitive issues experienced as brain fog. (See the section on 'Strengths of Menopausal Women', Table 8.2, for a list of work skills that may be impacted temporarily and those that may be enhanced.)

Studies are not definitive in terms of the relationship between symptoms and what are primary and secondary effects. For example, does lack of sleep cause or exacerbate some of the emotional and cognitive issues[45]? We know from research into the sleep cycle that it is the final part of the cycle, the deeper sleep, that is essential for cognitive repair and emotional regulation[46].

Let's take Ruth, 51 and her experience of perimenopausal symptoms which were physical, cognitive and emotional.

> **Ruth**, 51, found herself sitting in a business development meeting with her male colleague and a male client feeling anxious, faint, hot and sweaty. She was extremely conscious of how this was impacting her physical appearance which contributed to feelings of overwhelming anxiety and a sense of panic. Her brain fog meant that she struggled to find the right word in presenting options at one stage. It got to the point where she was so anxious that she would faint that she had to excuse herself from the meeting. They didn't win the work and Ruth blamed herself, feeling unable to share what she was experiencing with her male colleague. Ruth found herself becoming increasingly anxious about going into the office for meetings and wherever possible would work at home and organise meetings virtually.

The client-facing nature of Ruth's role was adding to her stress and anxiety and she did not feel she would be supported at work. She was willing to go to significant lengths to hide this from her employer which took increased effort mentally and emotionally, which further depleted her.

Over the Bloody Moon and Kantar research confirms that many women fear the career consequences of drawing attention to their experiences, with 44% too embarrassed to ask for support, 69% not talking to anyone, and only 3% disclosing symptoms to managers[47].

Other countries such as Ireland[48] and Canada[49] have also published data suggesting that less than 12% of women would talk to their managers about menopause.

However, when women have dared to share their experiences with a manager who offers empathy and reminds them of their strengths, I have noticed the significantly positive impacts on women's feelings and experiences. Let's take the example of Jacinta, whose menopausal transition was raising significant questions about how she saw herself at work. She was finding it difficult to equate how she saw herself with what she believed a director should be.

> **Jacinta**, age 49, came to career coaching at a time where she could move into a Director of Customer Services role, but she wasn't sure about taking this step. She recognised that she couldn't leave her organisation for financial reasons but wanted to work out how to explain she couldn't take on the role. She just felt she wasn't up to it. She felt overwhelmed in her current role and like an impostor. She described physical symptoms of migraine, plus emotions of anxiety, forgetfulness and having lost her sense of who she was. When given some time to reflect in coaching, it struck her that her years of experience were valuable, that she had much to give and wanted to be able to share her learning with others. Jacinta started to confide in some colleagues. As well as the HR Director, she also spoke to her mentor to help find the words to explain to her male manager what she was experiencing. She also saw her GP who prescribed HRT. Her manager listened without judgement and asked what she needed to make it work. He reminded her of what he felt she had to contribute to the role. Six months later after working more flexibly for a period, and attending a women's group to share her experiences, Jacinta said the combination of HRT and support from her manager had made an overwhelming difference and she now felt better able to cope. She decided she was ready to step into the new role and they would plan a phased approach together.

Research by Claire Josa has found a connection between menopause and previously dormant impostor syndrome[50], which may have been the case for Jacinta. However, the compassion and support from her manager positively offset some of the psychological issues that were getting in the way of her next career development opportunity.

This leads to a very important aspect: menopause is ultimately *an identity transition*. Helping women to focus on what they might gain positively during and beyond this life stage can support them through this transition. From a career development perspective, this could mean helping them to recognise their strengths and the value they offer to employers as Jacinta's manager did.

Menopause as an Identity Transition

Bridges Transition model[51], has been discussed in detail elsewhere in this book (Chapters 1 and 7), describing the psychological process of transition that takes place alongside physical changes. Bridges suggests psychological transition begins with a loss and an ending and only ends when the individual fully identifies with a new beginning. Unfortunately, the part in the middle can be destabilising and disorientating characterised by a mix of emotion.

For some women, the menopausal transition will be more challenging than others, and whilst some women claim to experience few physical symptoms, they may still experience some of the emotional and psychological elements associated with their responses to this phase in their lives. Table 8.1 attempts to map out what some women may experience in terms of the emotional and psychological aspects of menopausal transition.

Table 8.1 Menopausal transition, drawing on Bridges' Transition model

Endings (Loss)	Neutral Zone (Emotions)	New Beginnings (Gains)
• Reproductive years	• Confusion	• Renewed energy
• Youthfulness	• Fear	• Commitment
• Feelings of attractiveness	• Anxiety	• Focus

(Continued)

Table 8.1 (Continued)

Endings (Loss)	Neutral Zone (Emotions)	New Beginnings (Gains)
• Confidence	• Relief	• Empowered
• Self-esteem	• Grief	• Freedom
• Self-worth	• Overwhelmed	• Resilience
	• Angry	• Courage
	• Irritable	• Assertiveness
	• Low mood	

The model is not linear, and women will experience transition at their own pace dictated by contextual factors, but if organisations support some of the uncertain, disruptive parts of the transition as captured in the neutral zone – by having strengths-based career conversations and offering more balance and flexibility during this part – they might psychologically be able to move into recognising the gains more quickly and successfully.

Before drawing out the strengths further that women may gain during menopause, I want to first highlight some of the fears and barriers that get in the way of women talking about the menopause.

Typical Assumptions and Biases: What Gets in the Way of Conversations About Menopause?

There is a Catch 22 here. One of the challenges is that women may have deeply embedded fears of talking about menopause, linked to stereotypes and negative bias. Yet research continually highlights the importance of *self-disclosure* by women in sharing their experiences[52]. We don't want to ask women if they might be menopausal or create cultures where women are expected to announce their menopause! Rather, that they feel the topic is culturally safe and accepted in the way that pregnancy has become normalised as part of workplace conversations about career.

Ilona's case below highlights someone who was very fearful of sharing with her manager because she was worried it would be career limiting now and in the future.

> **Ilona** was in her mid-forties and suffering from physical symptoms relating to her perimenopause, including heavy periods that were making it very difficult for her to physically be in the office during certain times of the month. For her, the pandemic and flexible working had presented a lifeline. However, her manager now expected the team to be in the office the same three days each week. Due to the unpredictability of her menstrual cycle, Ilona could not always plan when she would need to work at home. She believed visibility in the office was critical for her future development. However, it was taking its toll on her mental health as she was finding she needed to take sick days each month rather than work at home which was adding significantly to her anxiety and impacting her relationship with her manager regardless. He felt very confused and baffled by what was going on.

Ilona felt she could 'never discuss' these issues with her manager. Culturally she was from a background where nobody discussed menopause, and I was one of the first people she spoke to in the safe space of coaching. Her organisation had no menopause policy. However, it did have a women's Employee Resource Group (ERG) to support employees on diversity and inclusion issues. I encouraged Ilona to attend, and, through the group, she found some vital allies. This gave her some strength to explain to her manager that she had some 'health' issues relating to menopause, without having to divulge specifics, and they agreed she could work at home when she needed to and dial into meetings when needed. Crucially, he also asked her regularly if he could support her in any other ways. He also changed the message to the team encouraging regular visibility in the office but communicating that if health and family reasons meant it was easier to dial in, there was no issue.

Women often fear these conversations for the following reasons:

- Not wanting their line manager to think their performance was impacted
- Embarrassment

- Having a male or younger manager
- Concerns over confidentiality.

Studies have highlighted repeatedly that women's fears of the perception of others about menopause is a huge barrier impacting them psychologically and making their experiences worse.[53] Fear is usually linked to biases relating to gender, age and competence. They are often systemic and affect women and men, but they can be particularly prevalent in stereotypes of older women[54]. Lucy Ryan suggests that gendered ageism plays a role in how older women's bodies are seen and how this links to perceptions regarding competence. She also draws out what she calls the Decline Myth; the idea that older women are in decline and are no longer thriving or ambitious[55].

Some of the unconscious biases that may exist in relation to menopausal women might include:

- They are no longer ambitious
- They are less leader-like
- They are hysterical and irritable
- They are less emotionally stable
- They are less confident
- They don't perform as well as others
- Menopause is a permanent state
- Menopause is negative

It is unlikely that most people are consciously aware of these views, but these deeply held beliefs may play out in decisions and assumptions made about women's careers, such as whether to promote them, offer developmental projects or how they wish to work. McKinsey has highlighted the impact of micro-aggressions in the workplace particularly towards women[56]. Seemingly innocuous or even well-meant comments such as 'You look tired today' might have a profoundly negative impact on a menopausal woman.

Numerous studies support that these biases do exist in our cultures and organisations, particularly in male-dominated environments, such as the police and army where menopause might result in negative comments, sniggers and jokes[57]. However, government research also found that menopause discrimination was widespread across many sectors[58,59]. Brewis et al. suggest that the main challenges in tackling menopause at work are 'these stereotypical perceptions of what older female workers are able to do, and the belief that menopausal symptoms are permanent rather than temporary aspects of ageing' [60].

One US study by the *Harvard Business Review* (HBR) created a workplace experiment exploring the perceptions of a middle-aged woman described as having menopausal hot flush symptoms, a middle-aged woman without symptoms, and a middle-aged man to compare who was seen as most leader-like[61]. Negative stereotypes were found with participants reporting that the menopausal woman seemed less confident and less emotionally stable than the middle-aged man *and* the non-menopausal women.

What is particularly noteworthy, however, is that *when women have led the conversation* and disclosed their symptoms, they are viewed more positively and with respect. The same HBR study found that when others told them that a woman was menopausal, they rated her as less-leader-like. However, when the woman herself disclosed the symptoms, they scored her as much more leader-like. It seems fundamentally important to challenge women's own perceptions and fears, and the stories that they may be telling themselves about the menopausal stage of life. As the extensive study by Noon found, women do not want to be known as 'walking hot flushes!'[62]

The HBR authors suggest that educating people in organisations about menopausal symptoms won't overcome deeply held biases but creating environments where women can take control of the conversation for themselves without fear of repercussions is critical to changing attitudes. Additionally, raising awareness of the strengths offered by menopausal women and their career needs, as well as the language we use to talk about menopause, is also critical to tackle this at a deeper level. I highlight some of the strengths of mid-life women before moving to consider more practically what organisations can do.

Strengths of Menopausal Women

Jacinta notes that:

> A year into my new role, I feel like a new woman. I am sleeping better and have really been able to shape the role and team in the way that I want to. I have lots of energy and ideas and have signed up to be a mentor to others in the organisation. I feel more resilient than previously. Things that would have stressed me before, now feel like a welcome challenge. I am much less afraid to push back than before and say no. I also feel better able to set some boundaries about how I work and I am able to delegate more effectively.

This section draws attention to strengths that may be enhanced *because* of menopausal transition and offer increased value on top of women's other existing skills and strengths. This is important in demonstrating the trade-off between skills and strengths that may be temporarily impacted with those that might be gained or enhanced. As described in Table 8.1 above, the emotions and psychological experience of the menopausal transition may further cloud women's abilities to realise and value their strengths, requiring some help and support to recognise this.

Contrary to fears and biases that menopause represents the ending for women of this age, if we consider the idea of the 100-year life[63], and Avivah Wittenberg-Cox's related concept of the four quarter-lives[64] mentioned elsewhere (Chapters 2 and 3), menopausal women are only half-way through! Women at this stage of life often describe wanting more and to 'step-up', feeling that they have much more to give (70% in Lucy's Ryan's sample)[65], so it is important women and employers recognise these strengths.

Several studies suggest that women's performance improves during menopause[66]. Some studies have also supported that post-menopause, women's performance may be superior to that of younger women with women reporting feeling revitalised[67,68]. I mentioned earlier the concept of menopausal zest, a new-found energy for work and life. Indeed, Eleanor Mills at Noon has coined the term Queenagers to reflect this period of revitalisation and sense of freedom many women acquire[69].

The menopausal transition offers women valuable time to reflect on what they want from work and life, and they may well develop their skills of self-assertiveness during this time. Jack et al. suggest they may confront 'organizational sexism and ageism and a sense of liberation'[70].

Mainiero and Sullivan's Kaleidoscope Career Model[71] (see Chapter 6) suggests that although balance features more prominently in the lives of mid-career women, which likely overlaps with the peak of perimenopausal symptoms, it is in fact authenticity that begins to feature more prominently in the later stage of their career (overlapping with their post-menopausal selves). They wish to construct work aligned to who they are with a renewed sense of commitment to their careers. They are coming into their prime when there is less mid-life pressure including menopause with which to contend.

The power that mid-life women have to offer as role models within organisations is also vitally important. Chapter 4 on later life workers highlights that both later life men and women are motivated by mastery and learning (*Artisans* in the Bain model) and by seeing their actions make a positive impact in someone else's life (*Givers*)[72]. They bring humanity and life experience to employers. It is particularly important for younger women to identify with senior older female role models in positions of leadership.

I summarise in Table 8.2 some of the strengths that may be enhanced during and beyond the menopausal transition, contrasted alongside some of those that women might describe as being temporarily impaired.

Table 8.2 Strengths offered through menopausal transition

Skills and Strengths That May Be Temporarily Impacted	Enhanced Skills and Strengths Post-Menopause
• Attention to detail	• Creativity
• Organisation	• Resilience
• Confidence	• Empathy
• Memory	• Compassion
• Concentration	• Wisdom
• Patience	• Renewed commitment to career and goals
	• Increased confidence
	• Role modelling to younger colleagues
	• Assertiveness
	• Adaptability
	• Conscientiousness
	• Flexibility
	• Innovation
	• Freedom

To ensure that these valuable strengths of mid-life women are not lost during the menopausal transition, employers might consider the practical things that can be done to positively influence women to continue to develop and contribute within their careers during this life stage.

What Employers and Managers Can Do

There is no one-size-fits-all approach to creating a menopause programme of support but I share some ideas in this section of what some organisations have found useful. One important point is to reflect on the approach that complements other ways in which the organisation supports the careers, health and working lives of *all* employees. Conversations about menopause may be undermined by a lack of supportive conversations about wider career and other life issues.

In designing a menopause offering, it is important to consider what can be done so that women will genuinely feel they can discuss menopause without it being career limiting. This means thinking about ways to create the infrastructure to ensure that women will feel psychologically safe to instigate a conversation about menopause if they want and need to do so. Employers might also consider how the approach links to performance management criteria and policies on flexible working.

In addition to ensuring physical comfort such as better ventilation and air conditioning, research consistently highlights that women want to be supported in the following key areas[73]:

1 Greater awareness and understanding amongst managers
2 Flexibility in how they work
3 Information/advice about menopause and coping strategies at work
4 Informal support for example from a women's network or employee groups

Not all employers I spoke to have a menopause policy, but many have offered support in other ways drawing on the four areas mentioned above. In addition, several had adapted their employee healthcare provisions to include specialist menopause support, recognising that many women find it difficult to gain medical help from their GP.

There are many things that can be done at the organisational level.

What Can Be Done at an Organisational Level?

Raising Awareness

To create cultures where menopause can be discussed openly, employers can raise awareness of how menopause *might* impact women. This is helpful to women, their managers and wider colleagues. Organisations such as Mansfield Building Society offer voluntary menopause workshops where individuals can learn about symptoms as well as mandatory training for managers. They find that male colleagues now voluntarily attend the menopause workshops motivated to learn more.

Other organisations I spoke to were also raising awareness through webinar sessions and introducing the topic in women's networking or well-being forums. Many organisations found that it was predominantly women attending these sessions and were keen to encourage more men to attend.

Senior Sponsors

Several organisations highlighted the importance of sponsorship from the executive team suggesting that this played a critical part in ensuring that the tone and expectations of the dialogue were being modelled from the top of the organisation.

> What helped was the Exec Team openly championing the work. One of our Directors was the liaison to the Exec Team, and he wrote to all managers in his division, encouraging them to attend the webinars and to educate themselves. This really raised the profile and expectation, and he actively praised managers where he saw them doing that and leading by example. (Learning Specialist)

Another organisation also shared the importance of encouraging other women, particularly senior leaders, to share their stories of menopause. In one organisation, the Chief People Officer volunteered to do this with an overwhelmingly positive reception.

Menopause Champions

Menopause Champions or Menopause Mentors can make a critical contribution to cultural and systemic change. These are trained individuals who offer a safe space outside of line management or HR to share experiences and give emotional support and practical signposting. It is a similar concept to Mental Health First Aiders or Allies. Menopause Champions often also play a key role in setting up workplace support groups.

Other organisations without dedicated menopause champions have ensured that women know that they can speak to well-being champions, internal counsellors or the EAP service. One particularly innovative example I came across was where a reverse mentoring scheme was used to help educate younger colleagues about menopause.

Employee Resource Groups and Menopause Cafés

As mentioned previously, support groups such as Employee Resources Groups or Menopause Cafés have been found to play a vital role in reducing the impact of negative symptoms. Lesley Salem describes the positive impact that these forums can have:

> Employee Resource Groups or cafés help champion a culture where menopause is normalised in the workplace. This helps to remove stigma, removes stress, shame and fear and in turn people feel more positive about their menopause experience and symptoms often subside. In addition, they recruit senior sponsors which helps raise visibility, demonstrating allyship, and can help with investment / fund raising on awareness events. (Lesley Salem, Over the Bloody Moon)

Other organisations are drawing on existing well-being circles to draw on the concept of group support. These types of forums also add richer context to employee surveys helping to identify areas of improvement around systems, processes, equipment and uniform.

Flexible Working

Being able to work flexibly when symptoms are at their worst can make a huge difference to women. For example, one HR Director whose organisation does not have a formal policy described the following ways of supporting a colleague struggling with perimenopause:

> One of our Senior Managers in a European role is struggling with perimenopause symptoms and is in fact quite young to be doing so. She joins our Menopause Cafés regularly and finds these

useful. We have also enhanced our private healthcare offering with specialist support and this has really helped her explore possible medications. We have also let her work 50% of the time to allow her to settle with the new medication and allow her time when she is feeling exhausted. It has all worked well and enabled us to still see business benefits whilst she as a person gains the support required.

The HR Director suggested the combination of access to specialist healthcare, working flexibly as well as being able to share her experiences in the Menopause Café have made a huge difference to the experience of her colleague who had been considering leaving the organisation.

The example demonstrates the importance of policies that reflect and complement an organisation's wider approach to health and flexible working. Providing women with the autonomy to work flexibly from home or work reduced hours if symptoms are impacting them at work can make a huge difference. Drawing on the techniques of job-crafting mentioned in Chapter 3 can empower them to design their approach to their role in a way that suits them during this life stage.

Importance of a Joined-Up Approach

Lesley Salem points out that organisations who are doing this well ensure a consistency and continuity to what they do. This reinforces that the organisation takes the conversation seriously. Regular touchpoints help to embed awareness. For example, one large tech organisation has a virtual session every two months for their women's network. Lesley says that involving men is critical and some employers are also offering male-only sessions on menopause, so they also have a safe space to ask questions.

Some organisations, such as Mansfield Building Society, as described in the case below, agree with this regular and consistent approach. They found it useful to *trial* what worked in their organisation before introducing a formal policy.

Bob Crowe, Learning and Development Specialist, says that this was of particular importance to demonstrate that the policy was not a mere tick-box exercise. Bob is a Menopause Champion along with four of his colleagues:

> When we introduced the policy, we were very clear that we wanted to provide genuine guidance and that this was not a tick box exercise. We are fortunate that we have a very inclusive culture and values which made this much easier to achieve. Management support, in comparison to many organisations in financial services, has a much more empathetic feel in our organisation. (Bob Crowe, Learning and Development Specialist, Mansfield Building Society)

Mansfield Building Society

Mansfield Building Society started their journey with menopause in 2021, recognising that 75% of their colleague population is female and 55% of those are potentially menopausal. They view menopause as a key part of their diversity and inclusion strategy to support their female employees.

Workshops for managers on 'Managing the Menopause' as well as 'Managing My Menopause Workshops' for women were introduced prior to the creation of a formal menopause policy.

Their menopause policy incorporates elements of Trust and Confidence, Signposting, Paid Menopause Leave, Education, Training and General Support.

They have five trained Menopause Champions and have an alliance with Henpicked and the charitable organisation the Menopause Café through which regular community colleague conversations are encouraged. Menopause workshops also run throughout their Learning at Work weeks during the year.

At Mansfield Building Society, management training on menopause is mandatory, whereas the workshops for women on managing their own menopause are entirely optional recognising that not everyone may feel they need this support. Bob says that feedback has been overwhelmingly positive with managers saying they now feel far better equipped on how to approach a conversation if it arises. Women themselves have also reported gaining more knowledge from the workshops than in countless medical visits. One female colleague also shared that she now felt much more comfortable and confident and no longer felt she had to pretend to be ill with Covid symptoms.

A Menopause Inclusive Framework

Lesley Salem has put her learning of what works well in organisations into a five-pillar Menopause Inclusive Framework helping employers to think about the key areas that they need to pay attention to.

A Menopause Inclusive Framework for Employers

1. Commitment (Exec support, policy, reasonable adjustments, well-being strategy)
2. Awareness (Intersectionality, diversity, inclusive, involving men, safe spaces)
3. Capability (All people managers have *mandatory* training)
4. Support (Employee networks, mentors, champions, managers)
5. Culture (Is this being embedded into everyday conversations?)

Source: Developed by Over the Bloody Moon

Lesley believes manager training on how to approach conversations about menopause is essential given the importance that the manager can play in validating a woman's experience. This is important due to increased risk of grievances as well as a significant risk of undermining the other efforts such as having champions and running workshops[74]. However, it is also fundamentally important because of the discomfort managers may feel with this topic. They need guidance on how to approach these conversations and what is appropriate in terms of responses and the language they can use. The following checklist may be helpful to consider an organisation-wide approach:

Checklist for Organisations

1. What resources exist to educate women and managers on menopause?
2. Do employee forums exist where colleagues can safely discuss their experiences of menopause? (e.g. Menopause Cafés or Well-Being Circles.)
3. Have managers attended training on menopause awareness?
4. Who can champion menopause at senior levels in the organisation?
5. Does the organisation's healthcare offer specialist menopause provision?
6. What does the Employee Assistance Programme (EAP) offer to menopausal women?
7. Could menopause champions or mentors contribute to cultural change?
8. Can a mid-life career conversation be offered to all employees?
9. Are women and managers empowered to find flexible working solutions?
10. Is there scope for women to use job-crafting techniques to design their own roles?

Managers are at the front line of delivering the organisation's menopause policy and can make a huge difference.

Ideas for Managers on the Ground

In my research, some organisations highlighted mixed responses from managers varying from high levels of engagement to extreme embarrassment. It is hardly surprising that they lack awareness, knowledge and confidence on this topic. Yet despite women's fears of talking to their manager, research supports that managers can make the biggest difference[75].

Line managers are not there to be menopause experts, but to listen, to show empathy and to signpost to other resources. They are certainly not there to ask colleagues if they are menopausal but to find ways to signal that there is a safe space there should they wish to raise the topic. The phrase 'listen to learn, not to respond' is used elsewhere in this book. Asking your colleague what they need and finding collaborative solutions can make the difference.

Positive examples shared included:

- Managers highlighting the value of attending menopause webinars at team meetings.
- Encouraging all staff to attend webinars.
- Explaining the value of understanding the impact on staff, colleagues and the communities they work with.
- Using a coaching approach of open questions and listening to really hear and encourage women to share their experiences (if they want to).
- Reassuring them that any discussion is a safe and confidential space.

Another particularly inventive example I came across was a manager who had suggested to his menopausal colleague that they use codewords during meetings: to signal that she felt unwell due to her menopausal symptoms, she would use a word he would recognise so she could easily excuse herself but in a way that wouldn't impact or be recognised by others.

The Importance of Regular Career Conversations

Regular and ongoing dialogues play a vital part in creating cultures where women will feel that they can share openly and safely if they feel that menopause is negatively impacting them. This is much easier if they are already engaged in regular, ongoing dialogues about their careers with their managers.

The four-stage framework to career conversations invites colleagues to talk openly about where they feel they are in their present career before helping them to work out incremental steps towards their career development. Encouraging them regularly to talk openly about a range of concerns that might be impacting their career provides this safe basis from which to tackle a conversation on menopause.

It is a different topic, but the skills used are the same. Managers can demonstrate that they are there to hear and not judge through really listening with care and empathy. Empathy enables the other person to feel that they have been heard. For example, instead of managers feeling that they must understand, an empathic response might be to say, 'It sounds as if these symptoms are really causing you frustration/exhaustion/difficulty'. Respecting and acknowledging through undivided attention, care and listening is what will feel more validating for women sharing their experiences. In addition, managers can ask, 'What might make a difference?' and 'What support could be put in place'?

Some of the Following Phrases Might Help

- It sounds a really difficult time for you right now.
- I am so pleased you feel you can share this with me. Thank you for talking to me.
- Have you got any thoughts on any ways in which I can support you through this?
- Could we work together to trial some things to see if they might help?

The following checklist could be useful to managers:

Checklist for Managers

1. Review organisation's menopause policy.
2. Signpost relevant menopause resources to *all* team members.
3. Attend menopause training (if available).
4. Encourage *all* team members to attend menopause workshops.
5. Schedule regular career conversations with all team members.
6. Attend career conversations training (if available).
7. Review flexible working arrangements within the team.
8. Enable a team-wide dialogue on strengths and sharing of ideas to play to strengths.
9. Communicate that any issue a team member wishes to raise is fully confidential.
10. Enable an environment where it is normal to talk about *all* life issues that impact work.

Career Tools to Support Conversations

There are a few tools explored further in Chapter 11 that might also be useful to support career conversations with menopausal women:

- **Using My Strengths** – to raise awareness of strengths and consider the ways in which individuals can use more of strengths in everyday work
- **Energy Raisers** – to consider the amount of time spent on various activities and to try to align them with more 'energy-raising' activities linked to strengths
- **Work–Life Balance Commandments** – to help consider ways in which they can construct work and life in a way that works best for them

Conclusion

It is an exciting time for both menopausal women and the organisations who can benefit from their strengths and talents. Menopause is no longer taboo, and increased visibility and sharing of experiences is empowering more women to speak up. The progress made within organisations in such a short space of time is significant and incredibly heartening. Menopausal women are no longer invisible.

> For most organisations, it's about keeping the drumbeat going. Not a once-and-done approach, but a constant listening and engagement, making sure significant cultural change is fully embedded right across the organisation. You might have a policy but not everyone knows it's there. We live in world of scrolling; people flick past things and think they're not relevant to them. Most of our employers who have received The Menopause Friendly Accreditation have policies and guidance in place, but they realise it can be a sensitive subject which takes time to engage people in. (Deborah Garlick, CEO, Henpicked)

Key Definitions Used in This Chapter

During this chapter, I have used the definitions of menopause, perimenopause and menopausal transition as defined by the WHO:

- Menopause is one point in a continuum of life stages for women and marks the end of their reproductive years. Natural menopause is deemed to have occurred after 12 consecutive months without menstruation.
- 'Perimenopause' is the phase leading up to the menopause, from when these changes in the menstrual cycle are first observed and ending one year after the final menstrual period.
- I use the term 'menopausal transition' in this chapter to cover both the perimenopause and menopause and to represent the period of overall transition experienced by women.
- I also acknowledge that 1) not everyone identifying as a woman will experience menopause and that menopause can be experienced

by people of all genders (and therefore use the terms *woman* and *women* inclusively); and 2) that menopause can be a consequence of surgical or medical procedures including menopausal hormonal therapy.

Acknowledgements

This chapter has benefitted greatly from input from Lesley Salem, CEO and Founder of Over the Bloody Moon, a social enterprise which supports individuals and employers with menopause in the workplace. Lesley gave her time generously in being interviewed for this chapter. It also gained from the unwavering support of Bob Crowe, at Mansfield Building Society, Learning Specialist and Menopause Champion who wholeheartedly believed in the importance of writing this chapter, and who demonstrates through his commitment to championing menopause at work that this is not just an issue for women.

Notes

1 Brewis J, Beck V, Davies A, Matheson J. *The Effects of Menopause Transition on Women's Economic Participation in the UK.* Department for Education; 2017.
2 www.fom.ac.uk/health-at-work-2/information-for-employers/dealing-with-health-problems-in-the-workplace/advice-on-the-menopause
3 www.who.int/news-room/fact-sheets/detail/menopause#:~:text= Most%20women%20experience%20menopause%20between, changes%20in%20the%20menstrual%20cycle
4 www.fawcettsociety.org.uk/menopauseandtheworkplace
5 CIPD. *Menopause in the Workplace: Employee Experiences in 2023.* Chartered Institute of Personnel and Development; 2023.
6 https://assets.publishing.service.gov.uk/media/65e1bc003f69450 011036077/shattering-silence-menopause-12-month-report-march-2024.pdf
7 https://helptogrow.campaign.gov.uk/menopause-and-the-workplace/
8 CIPD. *Health and Wellbeing at Work.* Chartered Institute of Personnel and Development; 2023.
9 https://menopausefriendly.co.uk/membership-and-accreditation/#what-it-means-to-be-menopause-friendly
10 https://content.app-us1.com/LoWoN/2023/09/26/5478cd21-0135-48d2-969e-606e2616dd90.pdf

11 www.overthebloodymoon.com
12 https://menopauseintheworkplace.co.uk/
13 Ryan L. *Revolting Women: Why Midlife Women Are Walking Out, and What to Do About It*. Practical Inspiration Publishing; 2023.
14 Brewis J, Beck V, Davies A, Matheson J. *The Effects of Menopause Transition on Women's Economic Participation in the UK*. Department for Education; 2017.
15 Riach K, Rees M. Diversity of menopause experience in the workplace: Understanding confounding factors. *Current Opinion in Endocrine and Metabolic Research*. 2022;27:100391.
16 https://menopauseintheworkplace.co.uk/articles/menopause-tribunals-lessons-learned-that-should-be-heeded/
17 www.peoplemanagement.co.uk/article/1839328/37k-awarded-office-manager-told-everybody-gets-menopause-%E2%80%93-just-it
18 www.equalityhumanrights.com/guidance/menopause-workplace-guidance-employers
19 Hardy C, Griffiths A, Hunter MS. What do working menopausal women want? A qualitative investigation into women's perspectives on employer and line manager support. *Maturitas*. 2017;101:37–41.
20 Brewis J, Beck V, Davies A, Matheson J. *The Effects of Menopause Transition on Women's Economic Participation in the UK*. Department for Education; 2017.
21 www.menopausecafe.net/
22 Hardy C, Griffiths A, Hunter MS. What do working menopausal women want? A qualitative investigation into women's perspectives on employer and line manager support. *Maturitas*. 2017;101:37–41.
23 Beck V, Brewis J, Davies A. Women's experiences of menopause at work and performance management. *Organization*. 2021;28(3):510–20.
24 https://content.app-us1.com/LoWoN/2023/09/26/5478cd21-0135-48d2-969e-606e2616dd90.pdf
25 www.bbc.com/news/education-27071947
26 www.overthebloodymoon.com/_files/ugd/f1a9b3_1c852b7b2e6c40d68ac4f07c9737b9cc.pdf
27 www.mayoclinicproceedings.org/pb-assets/Health%20Advance/journals/jmcp/JMCP4097_proof.pdf
28 https://menopausefoundationcanada.ca/
29 Steffan B. Managing menopause at work: The contradictory nature of identity talk. *Gender, Work & Organization*. 2021;28(1):195–214.
30 www.agelesspossibilities.org/blog-1/menopausal-women-with-zest
31 Ryan L. *Revolting Women: Why Midlife Women Are Walking Out, and What to Do About It*. Practical Inspiration Publishing; 2023.
32 Blickenstaff, JC. Women and science careers: Leaky pipeline or gender filter? *Gender and Education*. 2005;17(4):369–86.
33 Ioannidis C, Walther N. *Your Loss: How to Win Back Your Female Talent*. Aquitude Press; 2010.

34 www.mckinsey.com/featured-insights/diversity-and-inclusion/women-in-the-workplace?cid=other-eml-mtg-mip-mck&hlkid=9a1f4792f9f041d2a7f58ca3b8c05779&hctky=1926&hdpid=159f1f2a-db7f-431b-8068-cd51058123dc
35 www.vodafone.com/sites/default/files/2021-10/vodafone-menopause-toolkit.pdf
36 Reeves A, Elliott MR, Karvonen-Gutierrez CA, Harlow SD. Systematic exclusion at study commencement masks earlier menopause for Black women in the Study of Women's Health Across the Nation (SWAN). *International Journal of Epidemiology*. 2023;52(5):1612–23.
37 Stanzel KA, Hammarberg K, Fisher J. Challenges in menopausal care of immigrant women. *Maturitas*. 2021;150:49–60.
38 www.additudemag.com/menopause-hormones-adhd-women-research/#:~:text=Menopause%20and%20ADHD%3A%20Conclusions,range%20from%20mild%20to%20severe
39 https://menopausefriendly.co.uk/menopause-and-lgbtqia-time-for-an-inclusive-conversation/#:~:text=Health%20and%20wellbeing%3A%20LGBTQIA%2B%20individuals,can%20be%20exacerbated%20during%20menopause
40 Hvas L. Menopausal women's positive experience of growing older. *Maturitas*. 2006;54(3):245–51.
41 https://gen-m.com/wp-content/uploads/2020/12/Generation-Menopause-The-Invisibility-Report.pdf
42 Reynolds F. Distress and coping with hot flushes at work: Implications for counsellors in occupational settings. *Counselling Psychol Quarterly*. 1999;12(4):353–61.
43 Faubion SS, Enders F, Hedges MS, Chaudhry R, Kling JM, Shufelt CL, Saadedine M, Mara K, Griffin JM, Kapoor E. Impact of menopause symptoms on women in the workplace. *Mayo Clinic Proceedings*. 2023;98(6):833–845.
44 www.theguardian.com/society/2023/jan/12/not-just-hot-flushes-how-menopause-can-destroy-mental-health
45 Brewis J, Beck V, Davies A, Matheson J. *The Effects of Menopause Transition on Women's Economic Participation in the UK*. Department for Education; 2017.
46 www.ncbi.nlm.nih.gov/pmc/articles/PMC2656292/
47 www.overthebloodymoon.com/_files/ugd/f1a9b3_1c852b7b2e6c40d68ac4f07c9737b9cc.pdf
48 www.legal-island.ie/articles/ire/features/supplementary/2022/october/irish-employment-law-in-briefmenopause-special-october-2022/#:~:text=The%20Menopause%20Hub%20and%20Ibec,reason%20for%20menopause%2Drelated%20absence
49 https://menopausefoundationcanada.ca/
50 www.bbc.com/worklife/article/20220517-the-link-between-imposter-syndrome-and-burnout

51 Bridges W, Bridges S. *Transitions: Making Sense of Life's Changes*. Hachette UK; 2019.
52 Bochantin J. 'Long live the mensi-mob': Communicating support online with regards to experiencing menopause in the workplace. *Communication Studies*. 2014;65(3):260–80.
53 Brewis J, Beck V, Davies A, Matheson J. *The Effects of Menopause Transition on Women's Economic Participation in the UK*. Department for Education; 2017.
54 Irni S. Cranky old women? Irritation, resistance and gendering practices in work organizations. *Gender, Work & Organization*. 2009;16(6):667–83.
55 Ryan L. *Revolting Women: Why Midlife Women Are Walking Out, and What to Do About It*. Practical Inspiration Publishing; 2023.
56 www.mckinsey.com/featured-insights/diversity-and-inclusion/women-in-the-workplace?cid=other-eml-mtg-mip-mck&hlkid=9a1f4792f9f041d2a7f58ca3b8c05779&hctky=1926&hdpid=159f1f2a-db7f-431b-8068-cd51058123dc
57 Griffiths A, Cox S, Griffiths R. *Women Police Officers: Ageing, Work & Health*. Institute of Work, Health & Organisations; 2006.
58 https://committees.parliament.uk/publications/8995/documents/152634/default/
59 Brewis J, Beck V, Davies A, Matheson J. *The Effects of Menopause Transition on Women's Economic Participation in the UK*. Department for Education; 2017.
60 Beck V, Brewis J, Davies A. Women's experiences of menopause at work and performance management. *Organization*. 2021;28(3):510–20.
61 https://hbr.org/2022/12/research-workplace-stigma-around-menopause-is-real
62 www.noon.org.uk/meet-the-queenagers-executive-summary/
63 Gratton L, Scott AJ. *The 100-Year Life: Living and Working in an Age of Longevity*. Bloomsbury Publishing; 2016.
64 www.forbes.com/sites/avivahwittenbergcox/2021/11/10/lifes-4-quarters—and-how-the-map-shapes-the-road/
65 Ryan L. *Revolting Women: Why Midlife Women Are Walking Out, and What to Do About It*. Practical Inspiration Publishing; 2023.
66 Social Issues Research Centre. Jubilee women: Fifty something women- lifestyle and attitudes now and fifty years ago. www.yumpu.com/en/document/read/45114468/jubilee-women-social-issues-research-centre/9
67 Gaston JB. The female reproductive. In: Firth-Cozens, J, West, MA, editors. *Women at Work: Psychological and Organizational Perspectives*. Open University Press; 1991. p. 66.

68 Vicki Kafanelis B, Kostanski M, Komesaroff PA, Stojanovska L. Being in the script of menopause: Mapping the complexities of coping strategies. *Qualitative Health Research*. 2009;19(1):30–41.
69 www.noon.org.uk/meet-the-queenagers-executive-summary/
70 Jack G, Pitts M, Riach K, Bariola E, Schapper J, Sarrel P. Women, Work and the Menopause: Releasing the Potential of Older Professional Women. La Trobe University; 2014. www.menopause.org.au/images/stories/education/docs/women-work-and-the-menopause-final-report.pdf
71 Mainiero LA, Sullivan SE. Kaleidoscope careers: An alternate explanation for the 'opt-out' revolution. *Academy of Management Perspectives*. 2005;19(1):106–23.
72 www.bain.com/insights/what-type-of-worker-are-you-future-of-work-report-interactive/
73 Hardy C, Griffiths A, Hunter MS. What do working menopausal women want? A qualitative investigation into women's perspectives on employer and line manager support. *Maturitas*. 2017;101:37–41.
74 Hardy C, Griffiths A, Hunter MS. Development and evaluation of online menopause awareness training for line managers in UK organizations. *Maturitas*. 2019;120:83–9.
75 https://publications.parliament.uk/pa/cm5802/cmselect/cmwomeq/1157/report.html

Chapter 9

Creating a Successful Programme of Career Support

Rob Nathan

Organisational Culture

Referring to the WHO paper mentioned in Chapter 1, which highlighted the link between 'decent work and mental health', it seems imperative that the culture, values and practices of the entire workplace contribute to the well-being, engagement and retention of employees. Equipping managers with the skills to offer holistic career conversations contributes a significant amount to that aim but needs to be offered in an environment that reinforces its aims. To achieve this, there are several considerations that need to be addressed to reinforce operational and strategic messages during the entire career journey an employee has with the organisation.

We are indebted to Anne-Birgitte Albrectsen[1] for allowing us to share this very useful model below. Their research at LEAD in 2023 pointed to 15 factors that contribute to a 'Holistic Model for the Attractive Workplace' (see Figure 9.1).

Key to the Model:

1 *Reputation:* Do you have a good reputation? Is the organisation positively mentioned in the media? Is the organisation recommended by its employees? Do you actively work on employer branding?
2 *Recruitment:* Do you have a professional recruitment process that ensures even the candidates who are not offered a position would recommend that process to others? Is there alignment

The Holistic Model for the Attractive Workplace

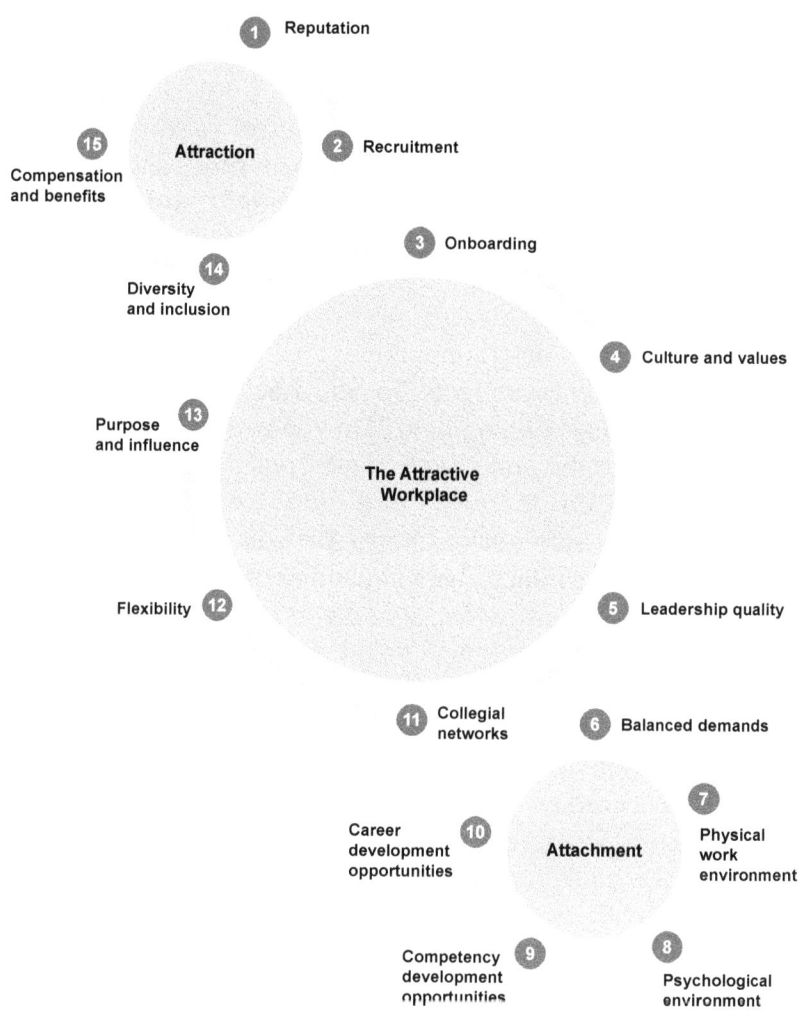

Figure 9.1 The holistic model for the attractive workplace

Source: Qvick CN, Elmholdt CW, Pedersen CS. *Hjælp vi mangler kollegaer! Sådan skaber du fremtidens attraktive arbejdsplads [Help! We need colleagues: Creating the Workplace everyone wants]*. Hans Reitzels Forlag; 2024

between the jobs you describe in jobs postings and the reality that employees encounter?
3. *Onboarding:* Do you have a systematic onboarding process that is tailored individually and ensures both professional and social onboarding?
4. *Culture and values:* Have you formulated explicit values that can serve as the foundation for the desired culture. Are these values upheld in reality?
5. *Leadership quality:* Is there coherence in the leadership chain vertically and horizontally? Are time and resources allocated for leadership development and leadership evaluation?
6. *Balanced demands:* Do you focus on preventing and managing work pressure and stress? Are demands and resources in balance? Is there social support?
7. *Physical work environment:* Do you have up-to-date physical facilities and digital equipment? Do you actively work on health promotion and the prevention of workplace accidents?
8. *Psychological environment:* Are you working to create a psychologically safe environment? Do you focus on preventing and addressing conflicts, bullying and abusive behaviour?
9. *Competency development opportunities:* Do you allocate resources for competency development that enables both personal and professional growth for individuals? What is your practice for supervision, feedback, peer learning and apprenticeships?
10. *Career development opportunities:* Are there clear and attractive career paths for different profiles? Are there opportunities to take on new challenges and more responsibility?
11. *Collegial networks:* What do you do to strengthen the collegial cohesion in the workplace, fostering relationships where employees connect with each other? How do you support the creation and maintenance of meaningful professional and social communities?
12. *Flexibility:* Do your employees have flexibility, in terms of working hours, place of work and employment arrangements? Is there the opportunity for hybrid and remote working?

13 *Purpose and influence:* Do you systematically work to combat meaningless bureaucracy and rules? Are there opportunities to make a positive impact? What do you do to empower and increase employees' influence in their work?
14 *Diversity and inclusion:* Do you have a diverse organisation in terms of gender, age and expertise? Are you doing enough to create an inclusive workplace?
15 *Compensation and benefits:* Do you offer a competitive compensation package and attractive employee benefits that match industry standards?

Note that this model points to the need for employers to pay attention to both strategic and operational considerations, and at every stage of the employee's career journey. For example, successful career support needs to be underpinned by development opportunities throughout the organisation (points 9 and 10). The model includes several factors known to contribute to employee engagement, such as purpose and influence (13). This refers to an absence of unnecessary bureaucracy and the presence of opportunities to make a positive impact.

A psychologically safe work environment (8) implies an active attempt to eradicate abusive and bullying behaviour. I would add that career support works best when individuals feel they can talk openly about their doubts and concerns, rather than feel compelled to put a gloss on their situation.

Collegial networks (11) refers to the need to create and sustain cross organisational networks and communities, and foster opportunities for individuals to connect with each other. Examples include 'lunch and learns', volunteer groups, intranet-based groups of common interest, inter-organisation groups, ERGs.

Balanced demands (6) and flexibility (12) indicate a culture which appreciates the holistic needs of employees, and develops ways to acknowledge the need for flexible working arrangements and for managing work pressures and potential excessive stress.

Finally, career support needs to be available from the beginning – from the recruitment phase through proper onboarding and lived behaviours that match stated values.

So, an effective strategy of career support would be implying to employees the following messages:

- We can't offer you a career for life – but we want you to contribute and develop for as long as you stay with us.
- We shall get to know our people very well, and try to make the best possible use of their abilities and aspirations where they fit with business needs.
- We shall make sure that our employees understand the business so they can have several realistic options in mind.
- We will make developmental opportunities accessible.
- We shall work with our employees as partners in the management of their careers.
- We will provide a range of career supports, from regular line manager conversations to confidential coaching and mentoring, together with accurate and up-to-date learning and career development resources.

Unfortunately, there has been the view that line managers are not sufficiently confident to conduct effective career conversations[2]. We know of many instances when employees would rather have a conversation with someone away from their direct line; this is seen as more open and less constrained by a focus on performance. Nevertheless, there is the perception that it is a line manager's responsibility to be open to a career conversation, which focuses on future aspirations and not just the evaluation of performance.

Being able to separate the evaluation of performance from an empowering conversation focused on the employee's aspirations can be quite difficult for some managers. A significant factor is the belief that these conversations matter, and the consequent willingness to provide a safe space for the employee to talk openly about the way they see things going. The employer needs to support this approach with a clear positive statement; they may be mandated or at the very least expected to take place.

Key Factors for a Successful Internal Career Support Programme

In 2021, CCS produced a report[3] summarising research into those factors considered critical by employers for creating a successful career support programme. These were some of the key factors:

1 Alignment with Business Strategy

In those organisations where business aims were linked to career management interventions, there was involvement and endorsement by the highest level of HR and General Management. There was planning that linked business processes such as a monthly mobility forum with ongoing career conversations by line managers or tailored career coaching by professionally trained HR and other managers.

The Case of Saint-Gobain

In 2011, CCS was approached by the HR Director for Saint-Gobain UK & Ireland, who wanted to create a career coaching programme for 'talents'. As an organisation who promote career development and internal mobility between functions, brands, businesses and countries, Saint-Gobain wanted to support its employees to gain clarity of direction of their personal strengths and interests and to build and drive their own career development. The organisation hoped to increase engagement, internal mobility, and strengthen their talent pipeline. They were seeking to develop a highly professional internal service that would benefit both the organisation and the individual.

Since 2011, over 40 Career Coaches have been trained and a cross section of line managers. The programme is still in place at the time of writing (2024). Surveys indicated that 81% of those receiving career coaching said it has had a positive effect on their engagement and commitment to the company; 66% said that career coaching had opened their eyes to further development opportunities within the company.

2 Availability of Relevant Information

One organisation encourages employees to be proactive in seeking out the information they need for career development. This 'Raise Your Hand' scheme allows any employee to signal digitally their interest in a role. Their name is shared with a HR colleague from their current business. The HR colleague will then follow up with the employee who has expressed an interest in moving. There are a number of things that may then happen: options may be discussed in the current business; if unsure of options the person may be offered career coaching, or their name and details may be shared at the weekly mobility call with other colleagues to see whether anyone has a role currently available, or whether it's worth the employee meeting someone to learn more about where opportunities may be created in the future.

3 Clarity of Purpose of Career Conversations

For career conversations to play a significant part in any organisation, there needs to be clarity about their purpose and alignment with the aims of the business – 'not just another HR process' as one general manager put it to a gathered HR team. There also needs to be a clear differentiation between career conversations and other kinds of support, such as performance coaching, mentoring and counselling.

4 Managers as Enablers of Career Development

Managers were not perceived as having the confidence or competence to engage in an open career conversation. To encourage employees to know about, and make use of, the many available resources, the line manager needs to be able to facilitate an effective career/development conversation. Many do not and would rather HR or Learning and Development take that responsibility.

Questions for Reflection

- How is career management aligned with career development in your organisation?
- How would you define a 'career conversation'?
- How could creating a 'coaching culture' lead to constructive career conversations?

- What information would it be useful for employees to have access to which would build their confidence to make development moves?
- How could your organisation give the message that career conversations are taken seriously?
- How can people be recognised for lateral development in your organisation?
- How could your organisation train managers to accept that a properly carried out career conversation would contribute to the well-being and engagement of employees?

Successful Career Conversations: A Shared Responsibility

There has been a lot of emphasis in recent years on encouraging employees to manage their own career development. This earlier emphasis has now been developed by focusing on a shared responsibility between the employee, the manager and the organisation. Without this wider support, self-managed career development is unlikely to achieve much success.

When we work to enable employers to foster effective career support, we ask them to complete a four-part grid stating the responsibilities towards career development of the different parties involved. Table 9.1 shows what one employer came up with.

Table 9.1 Responsibilities of different parties in career development

Employee – Driver	Manager – Coach
• Take ownership and initiative	• Coach team member to take ownership of their career and development
• Seek to understand self and options	• Discuss and input into development plan
• Get support when needed	• Keep up to date with career and development opportunities
• Use internal tools and resources	• Discuss potential opportunities
• Develop plans and take action	• Share network with team
	• Consider the person's wider life context

(Continued)

Table 9.1 (Continued)

Employer – Enabler	Shared Responsibility
• Develop, implement and communicate strategies that impact career development • Provide access to tools and up-to-date resources	• Link employee goals to business needs • Develop employee strengths • Identify organisation-wide opportunities

Table 9.2 Blank grid of different parties in career development

Employee – Driver	Manager – Coach
Employer – Enabler	Shared Responsibility

The above chart demonstrates that there is an open acknowledgement of individual and shared responsibilities, and career development is seen as a collaboration between the employee, their manager and support from wider organisational systems, such as Learning and Development, and opportunities for growth and learning across the organisation.

You might like to draft such a quadrant, imagining that it would be appearing on your intranet. Do use the blank grid in Table 9.2.

Adopting a COURT Mindset

To give managers the confidence and competence to support employees through career conversations, we regularly teach a practical four-stage framework on our training programmes. But, to ensure such a framework is effective, it is helpful to adopt the kind of mindset indicated by the following COURT qualities:

C uriosity
O penness
U nderstanding
R eflective
T ime generous

Curiosity is about being interested in a person's situation – wanting to know about a person and their whole life, without allowing any judgement to intervene in the conversation. It combines with *Openness* to a person, a frankness which implies 'I am here to listen to you'. An *Understanding* approach involves an acceptance of the person and what they might be experiencing in their whole life. Someone who demonstrates *Reflective* listening is doing so to learn and not to respond. This needs an approach which is *Time generous*.

Once this mindset is established, the skills of listening and the application of the framework described below become much easier to implement. Skills training alone is not enough.

A Simple and Practical Framework for Conducting Career Conversations

On a recent Career Conversations training programme we ran for managers, one participant, on viewing a demonstration of the process, said afterwards 'That was not a *career* conversation'. Which is the nub of the problem. People expect career conversations to be about promotion and progression up the proverbial ladder. The truth is that, for many organisations, either the ladder no longer exists, or it does not serve people's needs, as they get stuck at the top of their grades and may see themselves as having 'nowhere to go'. If managers and employers are to retain people and the skills and experience they bring, it is vital that *development across* the organisation is not only discussed but supported by the organisation's resources and infrastructure. For many employers, a values shift is required, so that managers are enabled to have the conversations which lead to the outcomes they and their team members would value.

Helen Tupper and Sarah Ellis described[4] the support managers need:

> Managers need help with three things. First, they need help shifting the focus of career conversations from promotion to progression and developing in different directions. Second, they need help creating a culture and structure that supports career experiments. Finally, managers need to be rewarded not for retaining people on their teams but retaining people (and their potential) across the entire organisation.

The four-stage Career Conversations framework described below is designed to give managers the confidence and competence to have such career *and* developmental conversations:

Stage 1: Opening the conversation
Stage 2: Where are you now?
Stage 3: Future focus
Stage 4: Resourcing action

Stage 1: Opening the Conversation

Managing expectations: A critical consideration for any person conducting a holistic career conversation is the management of expectations. Managers are not there to solve the problem, but they do need to acknowledge and respect the whole person who shows up at work. Such acknowledgement can go a long way to contributing to a sense of feeling heard, validated and thus normal.

There are several reasons why managers are reluctant to even begin career conversations. They often don't feel comfortable with guiding such a conversation, they don't want to open a can of worms and they may have their own feelings and life situations which, impacting upon their own stress, make it hard to be 'present' and non-judgemental in a career conversation. They also may find it difficult to separate their view of their team member's performance from a conversation about that same person's aspirations. As one person said on a recent training course: 'we should listen to learn, not to respond'.

So, setting the expectations of such meetings is critical and allows all parties to feel contained by the agreed boundaries. These include confidentiality and a clear understanding of the purpose of the conversation, which is an opportunity to explore how the team member sees things going and an exploration of their aspirations. It is **not** the time to review performance. Together with very good listening skills, it is possible to build sufficient trust to have a genuinely useful conversation, for the individual and the employer.

The example of Philip below shows how a manager trained in the core skills of career coaching enabled a colleague to avert a poor, and probably mistaken, career decision.

Philip was 45 and had worked for a major UK bank for 15 years.

He had recently split up from his wife after 20 years of marriage. At work, he provided a key technical role in the business, having skills and knowledge at his fingertips that had taken years to acquire. Following a couple of thwarted attempts to gain promotion to a management position, Philip felt let down and quite angry. He threw his energies into developing his passion for things Italian – learning the language, cultural visits and more.

He approached the company's Learning and Development manager to seek information about a business language course.

During the meeting, Philip's anger towards the employer came out. He seemed on the brink of leaving. The Learning and Development manager saw that Philip's anger was driving his decision. His training told him that he should not encourage people to 'act' when in the grip of strong emotions. So, he encouraged Philip to return for a further meeting, and gave him a couple of Career Tools to act as a focus for discussing his interests and values.

It was during the next meeting that Philip revealed that his deepest anger was towards his ex-wife, rather than the employer. The discussion arising from the Career Tools strengthened Philip's self-belief, and clarified how important were his needs to be valued as an expert.

Philip agreed to use the company's Employee Assistance Programme to address his angry feelings further. He also committed to identifying ways of gaining further recognition for his technical expertise and set up an immediate meeting with his line manager.

So, the Learning and Development manager essentially listened to Philip, and gave him space to be heard. He did not panic at the expression of strong emotions, did not react defensively on behalf of the employer and enabled Philip to get further help once the problem had been identified. Crucially, Philip felt supported, and the employer did not lose a valued employee.

Active listening: This is often mentioned as a critical skill for managers and leaders to develop and display but impartial listening is extremely challenging for managers whose very position vis-à-vis their team members is far from impartial. They need to hold two sometimes ambivalent and possibly conflicting positions, one which requires them to judge and monitor performance, and the other to listen in an unbiased way to their team member's aspirations. This requires not just skills training but also a sharp self-awareness, as managers too have feelings, stresses and aspirations of their own, which can impact their ability to remain impartial. Below are a few useful questions a manager could use to stay as impartial and self-aware as possible:

- What do I know about this person, both in and out of work?
- What stressors exist for this person different from others in my team? How are they dealing with those stressors?
- What motivates and engages them when they come to work?
- When discussing aspirations, would it be more productive to focus on the shorter term or longer term?
- How does this individual team member view me?
- Who else might be well placed to support this person?
- How can I separate this career conversation from judgement and assessment of performance?

Stage 2: Where Are You Now?

It is always wise for both the manager and the team member to prepare for any career conversation. Having set the purpose of the conversation, and agreed clear boundaries, it is now time to ask the most appropriate open question such as 'how do you see things going at the moment'? Active listening is underpinned by asking open questions, reflecting back in a timely and reasonably accurate way, while allowing sufficient pauses for the other person to respond.

Scaling: The Scaling technique is enormously useful in enabling someone to gauge their situation. For example: 'If you imagine a scale of 1–10, where 10 means you are ecstatic about the way you see your career is going, and 1 means you feel hopeless about it, where are you now?'

It is important to accept and respect whatever number the person gives. It is *their* scale, and that is what matters. If someone is, say, below 5, it can sometimes be useful to ask something like 'and what tells you that you are an x and not lower?'

Stage 3: Future Focus

Using the chosen scale point, now ask this question: 'supposing you move 1–2 points up the scale, what is different?' Try and use what is called 'future present' language, such as 'What are you doing? What problems are you working on? What skills are you using? What results are you getting? What contribution are you making to the department/function/business?' The conversation should *not* focus on how to get to a 10. Nor should you judge the person's scale. Where they place themselves is the base to work from and moving 1–2 points up the scale is usually doable and within reasonable sight.

Stage 4: Resourcing Action

Now it is appropriate to look at ways to fill any gaps to get to the future state, and explore the skills, experience, knowledge, relationships and behaviours needed to reach 1–2 points higher up the scale. Encourage your team member to make any actions as specific as possible. You can enable them to develop more specific actions with a simple question such as 'and how will you do that?'

The Development Grid example below in Table 9.3 shows how it is possible to create a tiered approach to detailing actions, in increasing levels of specificity. The example of Bopal divides the chosen action areas into 'Training', 'Building Relationships', 'Leadership' and 'Research'.

> Bopal is an ambitious technical specialist who has been turned down for promotion to a managerial role. He has recently received feedback that he does not come over as decisive or assertive enough at meetings, and he feels this has been a key reason. From his career conversation with his manager, he decides to do something about demonstrating his assertiveness. His manager helps him to refine his general commitment to being more assertive to offering him the opportunity to deputise for him in an upcoming meeting where he can demonstrate his technical knowledge while leading the meeting.

Table 9.3 Example Development Grid

Development Goal	Training	Build Relationships	Leadership	Research
Increase my assertiveness during meetings	I will ask for feedback to better understand my strengths and areas to work on	I will build stronger relationships with colleagues to gain support before meetings	I'll offer to deputise for my manager at meetings	I will ensure I have researched data to support my decision making and recommendations
	I will prepare a list of specific areas I want feedback on	I will find areas of common interest with peers	I'll find a meeting where my analytical and technical knowledge could be useful	I will consult and seek input from key stakeholders prior to making recommendations
	I will attend an assertiveness training	I'll contact two of them before our next team meeting	I'll put the case to my manager for my development	I'll prepare by creating a few key slides outlining the rationale for the decision
	I will read and get ideas from the book *The Art of Everyday Assertiveness*		I'll prepare a couple of ideas to ensure the meeting goes productively	

Note that each action step increases in its level of specificity as the steps progress down each column. Thus, 'I will ask for feedback' becomes 'I will prepare a list of specific areas I would like feedback on', and so on.

Identifying Skills and Strengths

This book takes the view that strengths can be gained from any life experience, positive or negative. Sometimes, people need the support of a manager to enable them to bring their 'best self' to work. The Career Tool 'When I'm at My Best' (see Chapter 11) is a great way of enabling a person to identify not just the conditions they need to thrive, but also the strengths and skills they can display when these conditions are met.

The case of Grace describes the benefit of the 'When I'm at My Best' Career Tool:

> Grace had recently returned from maternity leave after her first child. She had been Assistant Site Manager of a manufacturing plant. She was highly thought of as a potential leader, and her manager was looking forward to putting her forward for the Leadership Development Programme. In their career conversation, Grace expressed some doubts about whether this was the right move for her, partly because of the time commitment of a more senior role. She talked about how her view of life and priorities had changed since having her first child. Her manager decided to give her the Career Tool 'When I'm at My Best'. It emerged in their next discussion that she worked best as a 'doer' and, for now, they decided she should stay in an operations role.

There are many strengths-based questionnaires available. They include Clifton Strengths[5] and the Strengths Profile[6]. Any strengths-based questionnaires describe the optimum use of the strengths and the tendency to over-use that strength. For example, the optimum use of the 'analytical' strength can become 'pedantic', 'decisive' can become 'dictatorial'. Readers may find one of these questionnaires a useful focus for discussion. The 'Strengths and Skills Grid' shown in Table 9.4 can be used by managers and coaches to enable someone to extend their awareness of the skills and strengths they may have

Table 9.4 Strengths and Skills Grid

Attitude-Based	People-Based
Enthusiasm	Directing others
Self-awareness	Collaborating
Flexibility	Customer service
Self-starting	Networking
Humour	Organising people
Determination	Influencing
Resilience	Developing others
Calm	Connecting others
Patience	Relationship building
Courage	Resolving conflict
Persistent	Presenting and explaining
Curious	Showing empathy
Optimistic	Compassionate
Improver	Listening
Ideas-Based	**Detail- and Action-Based**
Generating ideas	Analysing
Experimenting	Problem solving
Brainstorming	Making decisions
Implementing ideas	Planning and arranging
Future visioning	Organising and structuring plans
Strategic thinking	Prioritising and scheduling
Critical thinking	Results focused
Improving and adapting to new situations	Managing complexity
Writing creatively	Researching
Creating events	Proofreading and fact checking
Expressing ideas through body, face and voice	Time management
Reading for ideas	Data analysis
Open to new ideas	Logical reasoning
Design thinking	Project management
	Attention to detail

used in their life and work experience to date. I usually explain that a 'skill' is something which can be learned and developed (e.g. listening), and a strength is more the way a person approaches a situation (e.g. determination).

Guidelines for Effective Career Conversations

The four-stage framework described above works – it is simple to understand, and yields results quickly. It also provides a shared appreciation of how to conduct an effective career conversation. You might like to use the Manager's Checklist below as a guide to structuring the preparation, delivery and follow-up of any career conversation.

A Manager's Checklist for Effective Career Conversations

Setting Up the Meeting

It is important that any preparation sets the tone of the meeting, and how it differs from other kinds of interaction, such as a performance review, and what will be the role of the manager and the team member. Something on the lines of: 'this will provide us with the opportunity to reflect on how things are going and for me to support you in thinking through your aspirations and any options for development'.

- ☐ Set up the meeting with advance notice
- ☐ Share that the purpose of the meeting is to discuss development
- ☐ Ask my team member to come prepared with thoughts on what is going well and development ideas
- ☐ Prepare my thoughts on positive feedback and possible development ideas

During the Meeting

- ☐ Ask my colleague what they would like to gain from the discussion – what do they expect?
- ☐ Put them at ease

- ☐ Ask open questions, listening carefully and reflecting back and summarising what they said
- ☐ Encourage open discussion about options
- ☐ Provide positive feedback
- ☐ Balance the conversation between individual and organisational need

Closing the Discussion

- ☐ Leave enough time to bring the discussion to a close
- ☐ Decide together whether we need to meet again or whether speaking to someone else is useful
- ☐ Think widely about ways to support development, mentoring, secondment, on-the-job training etc.
- ☐ Discuss actions we will both take so that responsibility is shared
- ☐ Agree a realistic timeframe

Follow-Up

- ☐ Ensure information has been shared and passed on
- ☐ Ensure introductions to other people who can support development are made
- ☐ Agree a date for future progress review
- ☐ Reassure my team member I am there to support whilst allowing them to drive this

The Questions People May Want to Discuss

A career-related conversation should not wait until the situation has reached a crisis. Unfortunately, there is often little incentive to have such a discussion, as the work demands take priority. Enlightened employers build in the facility to have career discussions on an ongoing basis.

Below are listed some of the career-related issues people may want to address:

- I have just returned after maternity leave, and don't feel I am being given the same level of work I had before (see Chapter 7).

- I have been in this role for five years, and it feels like I am not developing. I feel frustrated.
- I don't think my skills are being used sufficiently well. Actually, I'm not sure what my skills are anymore.
- I don't feel I can keep up with the younger people here – they are so tech savvy and I'm not.
- After several years' break, I returned to work but feel my confidence has been dented (see Chapter 6).
- I've lost my mojo – I used to be really excited and motivated about the work.
- The job is taking too much of my time outside of work.
- I've been turned down for three promotions and wonder what I'm doing wrong.
- I've recently had a diagnosis of ADHD. I'm not sure it is wise to tell people this as it may go against me (see Chapter 5).
- My family circumstances have recently changed which means that I'm going to have to turn down certain work opportunities. I think this would only be temporary, but can we discuss ways to mitigate potential damage?
- I'm finding it really hard to concentrate since I've been back at work after the death of my husband.
- I feel like I'm losing my confidence and am starting to question my ability to deliver in my role. I can't understand why I'm finding it more challenging than others do.

These are just a few examples. Some areas for discussion may be primarily work-related. Others are precipitated by an event outside of work or could be an undiagnosed neurodivergent condition or health related issue. Most likely it is a combination of several things at once. Whatever someone is going through, employers can go a long way to recognising and responding to their employees *holistically*. This book recognises that typical life experiences, phases of growth, life stages and motivation, as well as disinclination and disengagement, and physical and mental conditions, are all experienced in a very personal and individual way. It is important to avoid generalising about what someone might be going through, even though some of the writing about life stages may suggest the kind of questions and transitions which people *may* experience at different points in life.

Potential Outcomes of Career Support

Employers sometimes express the concern that, by providing career support, dilemmas will be raised which may cause the individual to leave the organisation. Whilst this is an understandable fear, effective career support can lead to a 'win–win' outcome: it not only gives people the tools to enable them to do what employers want, that is, be 'self-directed' in their career management, but also respects the rights of individuals to be autonomous. Sometimes that means an individual will decide to leave the organisation, but that is relatively rare. If it does happen, it may well prevent the organisation from further months or even years of under-productivity. More likely, as the case of David shows, individuals will feel connected to their work, valued for their contribution, engaged with the organisation and motivated to contribute. Their willingness to apply and increase their capability will be enhanced. In turn, the organisation's capability to meet future demands will be enhanced by its ability to retain existing staff and to attract high-quality applicants, thereby unlocking the value chain which links personal success, business results and shareholder value.

David is 34 and works for one of the top accountancy firms. He is regarded sufficiently well to be considered 'partnership' material. Of late, David has expressed doubt about his future in the organisation – he has long nurtured a wish to run his own business. He enjoys football coaching and refereeing at the weekends. He has also just become engaged.

David is just not sure he wants the commitment that partnership will mean. His motivation has also gone right down, as he is overworked and has insufficient support, partly because several others in his department have left the organisation in recent months.

His line manager realised the importance of giving David the time to talk over his feelings and aspirations, without any overt agenda to persuade him to stay.

> As a result, David's motivation for his current work increased – he became clearer that he enjoyed the management aspect of his work. He requested, and received, reassurance that he could work fewer hours, and have more support, in order to be freer to manage the work of others. He was still not convinced that he should develop to partnership level, but felt happier to 'go along' with things for now.

Although David's employers clearly had their own agenda, they were sufficiently realistic to allow him the autonomy to make up his own mind about his future. Allowing him this autonomy demonstrated their respect for his opinion and right to make up his own mind.

Providing wide-ranging career supports can bring many benefits to the employer, the manager, the individual and the organisation's culture:

Employer

- Increasing the commitment of individuals to stay and engage
- Encouraging people to develop who otherwise might fester and become stuck
- Building the capability to meet future demands
- Creating ambassadors for the business – a sense of pride and engagement
- Reducing staff turnover, thus saving huge recruitment costs
- Enhancing 'competitive advantage' and employer reputation

Manager

- Really getting to know team members – their strengths, motivators, values, needs
- Team members more willing to proactively manage their career and development
- Team members being more open to lateral development
- Increasing motivation and productivity of team
- Gaining satisfaction from developing team members

Individuals

- Feeling valued as an employee
- Gaining clarity about possibilities for development
- Reducing the risk of burnout, boredom or frustration
- Feeling empowered in their career and development decisions
- Finding meaning and purpose in what they are doing
- Identifying career and development goals and ways to achieve them
- Increasing willingness to manage their own career and development
- Feeling supported and validated as a person, and not just as an employee
- Bringing more of their 'whole self' to work

Culture

- Building a culture that values diversity
- 'Walking the talk': stated organisation values are lived in practice

Notes

1 Qvick CN, Elmholdt CW, Pedersen CS. *Hjælp vi mangler kollegaer! Sådan skaber du fremtidens attraktive arbejdsplads [Help! We Need Colleagues: Creating the Workplace Everyone Wants]*. Hans Reitzels Forlag; 2024.
2 Career Strategy Insights. *CCS Report*. CSS; 2022. https://career-counselling-services.co.uk/career-strategy-insights-tool/
3 Career Strategy Insights. *CCS Report*. CSS; 2022. https://career-counselling-services.co.uk/career-strategy-insights-tool/
4 Tupper H, Ellis S. *The Squiggly Career*. Portfolio Penguin; 2020.
5 www.gallup.com/cliftonstrengths/en/252137/home.aspx
6 www.strengthsprofile.com/en/

Chapter 10

Conclusion

Rob Nathan

Writing any book is a journey. Often that journey is taken alone and the challenges of creating the work you intended and hoped for have to be tackled alone. We have had the good fortune of not just being a team of close colleagues but, through the experience of co-creating a book we all believe in, learning from a combination of research, co-critiquing and sharing of knowledge, resources and experience. It has truly been a co-creation. The acknowledgements at the start of the book also celebrate the many people who have supported us individually and collectively with their patience, encouragement and critical eyes.

This journey is part of our evolving story. And a good story is often marked by a change in the key characters, their views, relationships or actions. Since we embarked on this project at the beginning of 2024, there has been extensive learning from each other's expertise – Tamsin has opened all our eyes to appreciating the constant challenges that face neurodivergent people and how managers can recognise their battles as well as their strengths. Becoming a parent and continuing to engage with career development has long been fraught with obstacles, and Frances has shared her deep experience of what works both for employers and new parents. Gilly's primary research for the chapter on older workers focused on the needs of people at this stage of life, and examples of best practice within organisations responding to those needs. Kate's experience working with Career Returners has reminded us of the practical benefits to employers of taking time over the way returners are re-integrated into the workplace and of the strengths and benefits those returners bring to employers. And her passion for giving voice to women and men to talk openly about the menopause has been an eye opener, as we have realised how much good work is already going on in the UK.

Managers are regularly beleaguered to do more, often with insufficient resources. We may forget they are people too, who are managed as well as managers. Yes, they need to listen, but they also need to be listened *to*. They are judged on the performance of their teams, and it is easy to lose sight of the fact that they need their people in good mental, physical and emotional shape to deliver. The responsibility for providing the infrastructure to deliver the healthy and attractive work environment that contributes to both the well-being of employees and their ability and energy to give the required results, over time, lies mostly with the employer. See Chapter 9 for a description of the Holistic Model for the Attractive Workplace. That responsibility cascades down the line and enables managers to feel sufficiently supported to pass on support to their teams via the strengths-based career conversations we have described throughout this book.

Career development needs to be viewed in the context of the entire organisation and its culture. Careers and career development are important, for employers and individuals. And people bring their whole selves to work. Work fulfils psychological, social and economic needs and can provide meaning and a sense of purpose. Employers and managers can make a huge difference to the experience of the work of their teams, which in turn can influence those people to give their best.

Employers who are reading this book might consider raising the profile of 'Careers' and 'Career Development'. In addition to a Chief People Officer (CPO), the position of Chief Careers Officer (CCO) would elevate the importance of careers in the organisation. The CCO would sit at or near Board level, and would have the oversight, insight and data to influence a range of policies and to enable people to access the information and resources they need for career development.

Employers need people to develop, so they can reap the rewards of utilising the employees they have rather than going down the expensive route of recruiting externally. But many people are ill-equipped to successfully manage and develop their careers on their own, as they may become siloed in a narrow specialism, and limited by an inertia fuelled by a fear of failing in a new and unfamiliar role. Or they are too valuable for their manager to lose, and so not encouraged to develop.

Hiring, developing and retaining productive people is a constant challenge, not just for large organisations, but also for SMEs. Tight labour markets have led to a shortage of skilled and experienced employees. As one managing director of a successful SME with 100 employees told us:

> I see that with an extremely tight labour market, lack of any educational establishments or apprenticeships in our work area, a more holistic approach to career development is going to be key to staff retention and our future success, and indeed survival.

The precarious nature of even the successful SME quoted above, where the question of survival is ever apparent, suggests that all employers need to treat their employees as 'whole people' if they want to care for their bottom line, whether that be profit or efficiency.

We summarise here a few points that have been highlighted in different parts of this book, with some reminders, tips and ideas employers and managers can take in response to these points.

Employers:

- Raise the profile of 'Careers' in your organisation, in a way that the practices on the ground match the messages coming from leaders.
- Create and communicate a clear career and development policy that joins up with the entire employee experience and employer value proposition of your organisation, from recruitment onwards.

- Offer a range of ways your employees can access opportunities for development.
- Offer career support via a variety of touchpoints: many people can conduct effective career conversations: line managers, colleagues, peer managers, workshop facilitators, non-line coaches, external coaches, cross organisation career mentors.
- Give people access to confidential support, plus the information and resources they need to develop across, or up, the organisation.
- Be mindful of how the organisation's culture facilitates or inhibits the development of a diverse workforce.
- Ensure that opportunities for socialising are not limited to after-work drinks. Consider facilitating a range of social interactions before, during and after work.
- Offer flexible working as default and provide as much autonomy around core working hours as possible (e.g. 10am–2pm).
- Provide part-time roles that offer meaningful work that allow people to develop their career capital.
- Introduce inclusive measures of performance that support non-linear career progression.
- Improve psychological safety – develop a culture where people are not afraid to admit and learn from their mistakes by introducing zero tolerance for micro-aggressions.
- Respect employee time outside of work, allowing them to rest and re-energise.
- Provide opportunities for internal and external mentoring.
- Consider the impact on employees who leave the organisation. They will talk to others of their experience of working in your organisation. Whether via a formal ex-employee group or alumni, or via informal networking, the word will get around about what it was like to work in 'that organisation'.

Managers:

- Adopt the COURT mindset (see Chapter 9) and give regular time to your team members to discuss how they see things going, and not just focus on operational targets.

- Listen to learn, not to respond. Empathy is a powerful way of demonstrating compassion and allowing employees to feel validated in the workplace.
- Apply a simple coaching framework (see Chapter 9) and use relevant Career Tools wisely and sparingly – they are not a substitute for time and attentive listening (see Chapter 11).
- Be open to whatever might be going on in a person's life – but be mindful of setting boundaries – your role is not that of a counsellor. So, it is key to know a range of people you can refer to. You may have access to an EAP or other counselling, medical or well-being support. But many organisations do not have these available, so you will need to be aware of community resources which may provide professional help.
- Look for the strengths people bring to work, including those that may not be visible in the workplace.
- Know your limits and respect other people's. Some people are not comfortable talking about emotions or their personal life, and it is not the place of the career supporter to pry and probe. It is also important to realise when the person's non-work concerns may need more specialised help.
- Remember that when anyone in the team is going through a difficult time, they may not be able to bring their best self to work. Sensitive support, including a non-judgmental listening ear, can go a long way to maintaining loyalty and speeding a return to productive work.
- When vertical development is unlikely, consider ways to enable team members to craft an individual approach to their work, making use of their unique set of skills and strengths.

We hope that this book has been interesting, enjoyable and insightful. We hope it has given you frameworks and tools to coach individuals *holistically* about their career and its development, and we also hope that you will continue your own learning journey. Please join us for one of our free Career Tools Taster sessions, run online a few times per year. Just follow this link: www.career-counselling-services.co.uk/free-introductory-career-tools-workshop/

Further Resources

External Coaching

At times, it may be appropriate to get support from an external coach. The following are accrediting coaching bodies, whose websites give access to accredited coaches:

The Association for Coaching: www.associationforcoaching.com
International Coaching Federation: https://coachingfederation.org/find-a-coach
European Coaching and Mentoring Council: www.emccglobal.org/directory/

Coach, Career Coach and Career Conversations Training

The ILM offers a range of training: www.i-l-m.com/learning-and-development/coaching-and-mentoring-qualifications
Career Development Institute: www.thecdi.net/
Career Counselling Services: https://career-counselling-services.co.uk/accredited-career-coach-training/
The Maternity Coach: https://thematernitycoach.com/maternity-coach-training/

Chapter 11

Career Tools

We are pleased to provide a selection of Career Tools (see Table 11.1 for the full list, followed by the tools themselves in Figures 11.1–11.15) which we commonly use in our career coaching and training. Since 1996, we have trained thousands of managers and coaches to use these tools in a professional and ethical way. Tools are what they say on the tin: they are designed to improve the quality of career conversations. In themselves, they may have limited value, as the results and subsequent reflections ideally need to be talked through, as part of a wider conversation, rather than as a one-off exercise with no follow-up discussion.

Who Can Provide Career Support?

This book is for anyone conducting career conversations in the workplace, in addition to line managers. Many Human Resources and Learning and Development specialists are trained to provide support, although the impartiality of their position can be compromised when asked to comment upon a person's suitability for a role. Our own research showed a poor view of line managers' competence and confidence to have career conversations. They may get drawn into a conversation about performance and their views are often influenced by the demands of the work, and less on the individual's aspirations. To build cohorts providing more objective career support, some organisations have trained career mentors, volunteers from across the organisation who offer confidential career discussions. Others have introduced Performance Coaches or others outside the direct line who are responsible for reviewing an individual's performance and aspirations, outside of day-to-day operational requirements. The list below is not exhaustive:

- Internal dedicated career support service – provided for people wishing to assess the direction of their career, or to support people leaving the organisation.
- Trained pool of line managers across the organisation – offering career discussions for employees at the annual or bi-annual review, and throughout the year.
- Learning and Development specialists – linked to career discussions with line managers.
- Human Resources professionals – as part of their work supporting 'talent development'.
- Trained career mentors, across the organisation.
- Internal coaches – support on a range of career and development considerations.
- Internal 'performance coaches' and other managers, outside of any line responsibility, for enabling effective performance.
- External career coaches – offering confidential career support to 'take stock' of talents, skills, experience, values and motivation and plan direction.
- Executive, performance and development coaches – focusing on performance development and 'First 100 Days' coaching.
- Workshop and Training Facilitators (e.g. on Leadership Development programmes) where career questions are raised.
- Outplacement services – career assessment and job search support for individuals whose jobs are redundant.

Guidelines for Using Career Tools

For an introductory practical virtual workshop to using Career Tools, follow this link to our free Workshop: www.career-counselling-services.co.uk/free-introductory-career-tools-workshop/

- Use only in conjunction with a one-to-one career conversation or on career workshops.
- Ensure that you have read through the entire exercise before giving it to someone, and ideally complete it yourself.

- It is a principle of good practice that anyone completing a Tool has access to a supportive conversation to debrief and make sense of it.
- That conversation should encourage the person to reflect on their whole life and not just their work experience.
- Choose a Tool you believe the person will be successful in completing.
- Ensure that the person 'owns' the exercise (that is, does not treat it as 'homework' to be handed in for assessment).
- Ask the person: 'How did you find doing the exercise?' in other words, don't assume they've done it or that they found it immediately beneficial.
- Remember that, if the person does not complete an exercise, they may have thought about what it asks for but not been able to commit this to paper. Give them time to talk it through.
- Encourage the person to talk through the tool with a 'good listener': this could be a coach, friend or colleague.

Table 11.1 Holistic Career Tools

Tool	Rationale
11.1 Work Values	To deepen understanding of what is important
11.2 When I'm at my Best	To remind someone of the strengths and skills they use when they are thriving
11.3 Skills	To identify motivated skills that may be transferable
11.4 Satisfying Achievements	To highlight moments of personal satisfaction and the skills and strengths used and gained
11.5 Addressing Blocks to Learning	• To identify key blocks and bridges to learning and development • To increase motivation for learning by adding some bridges and challenging any key blocks
11.6 Addressing Skills and Knowledge Gaps	To identify the skills, knowledge and experience needed to achieve career and development objectives
11.7 Job Satisfiers	To pinpoint those core elements needed in a future work role
11.8 Energy Raisers	To commit to specific activities which raise and sustain energy during the working day

(Continued)

Table 11.1 (Continued)

Tool	Rationale
11.9 Using My Strengths	• To identify the strengths currently used • To identify opportunities to use some of these strengths more frequently
11.10 Work–Life Balance Commandments	To create some clear boundaries about acceptable levels of commitment to different parts of a person's life
11.11 The CCS Work Engagement Wheel	To focus a career conversation on which areas of engagement are met and which need attention
11.12 Planned Happenstance	To identify those ways to develop curiosity and other 'Planned happenstance' skills
11.13 Creating My Stakeholder Map	• To generate a map of key stakeholders • To increase awareness of who is in your network and how you might mutually benefit
11.14 Supporting Parents in Their Careers	Conversation checklist for managers
11.15 Supporting Neurodiversity Personal Playbook	Preparation exercise to support career discussions about career needs

Tool 11.1 Work Values

Objective

To assess those values most important to you in work.

Introduction

People work for different reasons. Most of us work for money, but the amount of financial security and income regarded as important by people will vary. We all 'help' others less fortunate than ourselves from time to time, but some people value doing this for most of their time. Most of us like a challenge from time to time, but some find significance when faced with challenge after challenge.

Instructions

1 The table overleaf lists a number of work and non-work values. Think about how important each value is to you in a work context. Rate each one on a scale of 1-10.
1 = of no importance at all and 10 = of the utmost importance.

2 Are your main values where you would have expected them to be? Are you currently meeting your most important values at work? If these are not being met at work, are you finding an outlet for your values in your leisure, home or community life? Have your values changed significantly in the last few years?

3 Rate the values again, but this time how much each is currently being met (Scale: 1-10, where 1 = not at all; 10 = completely). If you rate a value low in importance (eg 2), and it is however being met, then rate it high on the scale (eg 8). This indicates the degree of difference between what you value and how you see your current situation.

4 Complete the 'Action' column with 'Y' or 'N' according to whether you might want to take action. If unsure, leave blank until you have talked through your thoughts.

Value	Your Rating 1-10	Currently Being met 1-10	Action Yes/No
1 To belong to a team. To have close relationships with colleagues. To work in a supportive environment			
2 To do something useful for society. To make a difference			
3 To help, care for and nurture others To show compassion			
4 To earn a good salary. To be paid what I am worth			
5 To be financially secure. To have stability of employment			
6 To achieve important things			
7 To take risks. To embrace change			
8 To be responsible and accountable for results and quality			
9 To engage in demanding tasks. To test my abilities			
10 To be recognised as an expert. To apply and develop skills in a particular area. To be consulted for my expertise			
11 To influence the thoughts and actions of others. To lead people			
12 To be recognised and valued for my contributions To get positive feedback for good work			
13 To engage in complex tasks requiring an intellectual grasp of several issues			
14 To have variety of activity, people and location			
15 To decide how I spend my time. To have control over what I do. To make my own decisions			
16 To make my distinctive mark. To appreciate difference, uniqueness and individuality			
17 To develop and create new ideas. To be innovative and imaginative. To create my own projects/enterprise. To be original			
18 To have professional and personal growth. To learn new skills and knowledge			
19 To have work that fits in with other parts of my life			
20 To have a role that commands respect			
21 To be busy most of the time			
22 To enable people to develop and grow			

1 List here your top six values and your bottom three values:

Top Values	Bottom Values
1	1
2	2
3	3
4	
5	
6	

2 Write below the **3 KEY POINTS** emerging from this exercise:

1	
2	
3	

Tool 11.2 When I'm at My Best

Objective

To identify the key factors which are essential for you to thrive.

Instructions

1 On one column of a page, list up to six specific times in your life (work or personal) when you've really felt or been 'at your best' (ie thriving, 'in the zone')

2 Then note in the other column the key factors that seemed to contribute to your feeling 'vital', 'on top of things' or 'at your best':

- Was it because you were utilising particular strengths or talents? What were they?
- Did it have something to do with the environment?
- The people?
- The particular activities?
  Etc. etc.

Try to detail, as best you can, the essential factors that seem to contribute to your being 'at your best'.

3 Now note below any patterns emerging in both your chosen examples and the key factors which enabled you to thrive or be at your best.

"When I'm at My Best" Patterns	
My Examples	Comments / Surprises / Implication

Tool 11.3 Skills

Objectives

- To identify and evaluate your skills.
- To identify those skills you currently use the most.
- To identify those skills you most want to use (your Motivated Skills).

Introduction

We all under-estimate our potential and our skills. We tend to forget that, something we were able to perform competently ten years ago, but have stopped doing, could be resurrected to an acceptable level after a short practice period (e.g. I.T. or language skills). You may be particularly susceptible to this kind of self-doubt if you have either a perfectionist streak or a short memory!

It is also easy to be trapped into thinking that your skills are suited only to the employment sector you know. This is not true! Your skills may well be portable. It is true that the context in which you use the skill may be different, and the activities may be labelled differently in another function. But, in essence, the core skill is the same.

We also tend to focus too much on paid employment skills, and forget or play down those skills used in leisure and home pursuits. Skills gained in part-time or temporary jobs may be minimised. This exercise will jog your memory and get you thinking about all the areas where you may have gained skills.

Instructions

1. Make a list of all the 'jobs' you have ever done outside of paid employment, or your main career path, e.g. I organised a Charity Pantomime . . . was PTA Secretary . . . did a Christmas Post job twice . . . got myself and two friends to Australia . . . and worked there 3 months . . .

1	4
2	5
3	6

2 Before completing the following table, think about your use of the skill in as many different contexts as you can. Rate yourself using the followings scales:

Skill Competence	Skill Motivation	Skill Use
	I want to use this skill	I currently use this skill
1 = Weak	1 = Hardly ever	1 Never
2 = Undeveloped	2 = Occasionally	2 A little
3 = Adequate	3 = Quite a lot	3 Sometimes
4 = Competent	4 = A good deal	4 Quite a lot
5 = Very Competent	5 = Most of the time	5 A lot

	Competence Rating 1-5	Interest Rating 1-5	I use this skill 1-5
People / Interpersonal Skills			
1 Resolving conflict			
2 Coaching – helping individuals develop competence by building on strengths			
3 Appreciating strengths in others			
4 Listening with full attention, taking time to understand what is being said. Asking appropriate questions			
5 Persuading others to change their minds or behaviour			
6 Bringing others together to reconcile differences			

7 Delegating			
8 Organising people - supervising			
9 Opening conversations			
10 Sharing skills in a team			
11 Teaching, training			
12 Inspiring and motivating others			
13 Leading others			
14 Demonstrating empathy/ Being aware of others' reactions. Understanding why they react as they do			
15 Interviewing for facts			
16 Talking to others to convey information			
17 Others (add your own)			

	Competence Rating 1-5	Interest Rating 1-5	I use this skill 1-5
Information / Data Skills			
1 Estimating – putting data together to predict the future			
2 Planning – identifying key tasks to be done			
3 Writing concisely. Paraphrasing effectively			
4 Understanding written documents			
5 Analysing, dissecting, sifting through information; evaluating alternatives			
6 Problem solving – considering alternative courses of action			
7 Diagnosing, looking for problems, identifying causes			

8 Understanding the implications of new information for decision making			
9 Organising, classifying, arranging resources to be classified effectively			
10 Researching, gathering information and data from many sources			
11 Making rapid mental calculations			
12 Using computer applications to create spreadsheets			
13 Writing computer programs			
14 Using computers to manage databases			
15 Using computers to create visual presentations			
16 Using generative AI programs			
17 Managing financial resources. Budgeting			
18 Examining and observing detail accurately			
19 Using logical reasoning to evaluate the strengths and weaknesses of alternatives			
20 Others (add your own)			

	Competence Rating 1-5	Interest Rating 1-5	I use this skill 1-5
Physical Skills			
1 Assembling things – building, constructing			
2 Finding out how things work			
3 Manual dexterity			
4 Muscular and hand-eye co-ordination			

5 Using hand tools			
6 Using machine tools (e.g. sewing machine drill etc.)			
7 Fixing, repairing things			
8 Quick physical reactions			
9 Handling things with precision and speed			
10 Crafting things or materials			
11 Keeping physically fit			
12 Others (add your own)			

	Competence Rating 1-5	Interest Rating 1-5	I use this skill 1-5
Creativity Skills			
1 Improvising, adapting to novel situations			
2 Writing creatively			
3 Creating events, learning situations			
4 Composing tunes, lyrics			
5 Thinking of new ideas and alternatives			
6 Expressing ideas through body, face, voice			
7 Reading for ideas			
8 Keeping your mind open to new ideas			
9 Having insight, using intuition			
10 Sizing up a person or situation quickly and accurately			

11 Working creatively with shapes and spaces			
12 Developing others' ideas			
13 Conveying feelings or thoughts through sketching, drawing or painting			
14 Using colours creatively			
15 Others (add your own)			

3 If you wish, ask at least three friends or colleagues to rate you for each of the skills. This can increase the objectivity of the ratings.

4 Complete the final column "I use this skill . . ." Write below the six skills you use the most.

1	4
2	5
3	6

5 Which skills would you like to use:

More of	Less of
1	4
2	5
3	6

6 Write below your top "Motivated Skills" - these are the skills you have rated as 'Competent' or 'Very Competent' and which you want to use 'a good deal' or 'most of the time'.

My top Motivated Skills are:

1	5
2	6
3	7
4	8

7 Write here the category or categories your top Motivated Skills fall into, i.e. Interpersonal / People, Data, Physical or Creative:

1	3
2	4

8 Write down your reflections on this exercise in the space below. Were there any surprises? Eg. Did your Motivated Skills fall into the 'Interpersonal / People' category, but you would have expected them to fall into 'Information / Data'? Did your colleagues/friends rate you differently? And for which skills? Did you tend to underestimate yourself? And for which skills? Do you perform the same skill very differently in different situations? And with different people? And in different roles? (i.e. work/leisure, supervisory/supportive). When you are "at your best" (see exercise 11.2) which skills come out. Are the skills you want to use the ones you are using the most

Reflections on Skills Exercise

Tool 11.4 Satisfying Achievements

Objectives

To establish patterns of:

- Achievements you have found satisfying.
- What you found satisfying about those achievements.
- Skills and strengths you used in those achievements.

Instructions

1 Divide a page into two columns. Down one side of the page write between two and six achievements from your work and non-work life. Consider the beginning, any low point or challenge, the peak of your achievement, and the nature of the outcome or ending. What did you do to get through the difficult or challenging parts?

2 Down the other half of the page, write down:
   - what you found satisfying, and
   - what skills, strengths and other qualities you used in each achievement. (refer to your Motivated Skills list in exercise 11.3).

3 Ask a good listener to read the exercise and to highlight any patterns of achievements and skills/strengths which you may have missed.

4 List the patterns overleaf and complete the comments column. Were there any surprises? What are the implications of these patterns for you?

Achievement Patterns	
A Achievement	Comments / Surprises / Implications
B What i Found Satisfying	
C Skills, Strengths & Qualities Used	

Tool 11.5 Addressing Blocks to Learning

Addressing blocks to learning and development

Objectives

- To identify key blocks & bridges to learning and development.
- To increase motivation for learning by adding some bridges and challenging any key blocks.

Introduction

People may avoid taking their learning forward for a variety of reasons:

- fear of failing
- a previous bad experience of learning
- a self-limiting belief such as 'people of my age/background/experience don't/can't/shouldn't do that'
- a long gap since undertaking any study
- a lack of knowledge of what is on offer
- confusion from the huge range of choice on offer
- lack of awareness of where and how to get funding
- feeling under-confident if the course involves IT skills and demotivated by jargon (eg online forums)
- uncertainty whether the course will really help their career
- an unclear vision of the future, and thus what skills, knowledge and experiences are needed to get there.

Instructions

1. Write down your ideal learning goals or outcomes. Then rate how important each goal or outcome is to you and your development: 1 = not at all important. 10 = extremely important

My Ideal Learning & Development Goals	How Important 1–10
Example: Be better at presenting to large groups	7

2 Bridges and Blocks are the real resources you have or lack in relation to a goal.

Examples of Bridges:
Skills
Knowledge
Interest, motivation
Clarity of vision
Support from others
Role models (others you respect who have done similar things)
Contacts in the area of interes
Previous experience (eg of study)
Your own personal qualities (eg openness to change)
A career development or learning goal you are committed to

Specific Blocks may include:
Lack of knowledge of where and how to get funding
Fear of new methods of learning
Anxiety about how well you will do
A self-limiting belief that you are 'not the right type' (eg too old/young/under-qualified/wrong background)
Not confident in IT skills, or a lack of IT skills
Unsure if the learning style will suit you
Confused by the number of courses on offer
A previous bad experience of learning
Time, or the perception of it
Commitments and dependents
A previous or current routine which does not allow time off for study
Accreditation routes are not available in the way I prefer to learn.

Instructions

1 Make a list in the box below of your key Blocks and Bridges for your top one or two learning goals. Be specific: eg indicate which skills you have (or lack)
2 Discuss this with your Career Coach, with the aim of adding bridges and challenging some key blocks
3 Write down your actions for building on your bridges and minimizing the impact of any blocks

Learning Goal example: Eg Be better at presenting to large groups
Key Bridges
1 I've done it a couple of times before and it was Ok
2 I have two colleagues I really admire who present well
3 I've taken risks before and survived!
Key Blocks
1 Fear of looking foolish is the main one

Learning Goal 1:
Learning Goal 2:

Key Bridges
Learning Goal 1
Learning Goal 2

Key Blocks
Learning Goal 1
Learning Goal 2

Actions I will take
Building on my Bridges
Learning Goal 1
Learning Goal 2

Managing any Blocks
Learning Goal 1
Learning Goal 2

Tool 11.6 Addressing Skills and Knowledge Gaps

Objective

To identify the skills, knowledge and experience you need to develop to achieve your objectives.

Instructions

1 For each of your career development objectives, decide which ones require new skills, knowledge or experience. Write these below:

	Career / Personal Development Objective	Skills, Knowledge, Experience Required
1		
2		
3		
4		

2 Read the following list of ways in which you can develop your skills and knowledge:

- Using contacts to 'open doors'
- Deputising for your boss or a colleague
- Secondments
- Take on a project
- Job swap
- Work shadowing
- Same job in different location
- Full or Part-time Study
- Webinars, online learning or web-based course
- Short training course (in-house or open course)
- Residential courses (weekend and holidays)
- Joining 'groups' (eg. Professional/Linkedin, pressure groups) which may offer training and professional development
- Voluntary work
- Your next job!
- Discussion with people doing the job with the knowledge you want
- Reading journals / newspapers
- Others:
  - _____
  - _____
  - _____

3 Discuss with a good listener the most appropriate, available and attractive ways in which you can acquire the skills / knowledge you need.

Notes

Tool 11.7 Job Satisfiers

Objective

To evaluate the elements of job satisfaction most important to you.

Instructions

1 List below in any order those elements of work you must have in your next job. Be specific. You could think of 'tasks' (what you will do), 'people' (who with), 'environment' (in what type of organisation) and 'rewards' (pay, working conditions, etc.) If you have completed a Personal Summary, you may find it useful to refer to it.

   Examples:

   - Minimal management responsibility
   - Using my creativity
   - Improving people's lot in some way
   - Little routine
   - Working with intelligent, non-conformist people
   - A small, forward-looking organisation
   - No less than £50k at current rates

Try and keep your list to 12 elements. Write them below:

My Elements of Job Satisfaction	
1	7
2	8
3	9
4	10
5	11
6	12

2 Look again at the Job Satisfiers you have listed in the previous table. Answer the question: 'Which is more important to me - number 1 or 2?' If you answer number 1, circle the figure '1' in the first column. Then proceed for every pair of Job Satisfiers - 1-3, 1-4, 1-5 and so on, until 11-12. Work quickly. Some 'satisfiers' may overlap, but nevertheless make a choice.

1-2	2-3	3-4	4-5	5-6	6-7	7-8	8-9	9-10	10-11	11-12
1-3	2-4	3-5	4-6	5-7	6-8	7-9	8-10	9-11	10-12	
1-4	2-5	3-6	4-7	5-8	6-9	7-10	8-11	9-12		
1-5	2-6	3-7	4-8	5-9	6-10	7-11	8-12			
1-6	2-7	3-8	4-9	5-10	6-11	7-12				
1-7	2-8	3-9	4-10	5-11	6-12					
1-8	2-9	3-10	4-11	5-12						
1-9	2-10	3-11	4-12							
1-10	2-11	3-12								
1-11	2-12									
1-12										

TOTAL CIRCLES FOR EACH JOB SATISFIER

1	2	3	4	5	6	7	8	9	10	11	12

3 Count up the number of circles for each Job Satisfier. This is your 'weighted' score. Write down the scores next to each Job Satisfier.

4 List your **3 top Job Satisfiers:**

3 Top Job Satisfiers
1
2
3

Tool 11.8 Energy Raisers

Objectives

- To become more conscious of the specific activities which raise and sustain my energy during the working day.
- To decide which energy raisers to do more of.

Introduction

You may be aware of those activities that raise your energy. But you may have become so caught up in your work demands that you lose sight of what does you good. This exercise will remind you and enable you to take action to raise and sustain your energy.

When your energy is raised, you may experience the following:

- more alert
- less tired
- stamina
- more creative
- more fluent
- more aware of your strengths
- better 'mood'
- more able to focus on positives
- sense of humour

Instructions

1 Complete the table below, using the blank spaces to add your own energy raisers

This is an energy raiser for me	When did I last do it?	Would I like to do it more? Yes/No
Intellectual/Learning Eg Go to a lecture, read business book or article, read self improvement book **Add your energy raisers:**		
Physical Eg Do Pilates, Yoga, gym, stand up rather than sit, run, go for a walk **Add your energy raisers**		
Social/Connecting Eg Meet a non work friend, meet with work colleagues out of work hours, join a networking group **Add your energy raisers**		
Creative Eg Do something new each day, try a different approach, brainstorm/mindmap ideas, draw, write **Add your energy raisers**		
Self development Eg Meet with coach/mentor, self development course, get feedback on performance and/or goals, talk to someone who challenges you **Add your energy raisers**		
Spiritual, emotional, relax Eg Meditate, listen to music, sing, laugh, relaxation exercise, nature **Add your energy raisers**		

Time management *Eg Get to work early, make a to-do list, delegate* **Add your energy raisers**		
Positive focus *Eg Make a list of your achievements, positives for today, give positive feedback, 'gift' others something* **Add your energy raisers**		
Represent *Eg Attend a conference/event, represent your employer, sit on a committee* **Add your energy raisers**		
Others: add your own		

2 Write any reflections you have on your responses above to discuss with your coach

My reflections on what raises my energy and what I might do more of. Give examples.

Tool 11.9 Using My Strengths

Objectives

- To understand a core principle of Positive Psychology.
- To increase your energy by focusing on what works well.
- To adopt 'strengths spotting' to identify the strengths you use.
- To identify opportunities to use some of these strengths more frequently.

Introduction

Using a strength will strengthen you. Using a weakness will weaken you. This is a central tenet of Positive Psychology. You can take a simple questionnaire which will identify some of your key strengths: see StrengthsFinder (available from Amazon).

In order to spot a strength (in yourself or others), it is important to notice:

- the activities which attract you (even when tired)
- the topics and skills you learn quickly
- the areas you perform well
- what you prioritise
- when you are 'at your best''.

When you focus your attention on strengths, notice how your voice tone, body language and energy change. And ask for feedback (perhaps initially from your coach).

Instructions

1 Refer to the 'When I'm at my best' exercise 11.2. If you have not done it, think of a time you were 'at your best' or 'in the zone'. Write here some of the key strengths you used during this time.

Key strengths from "when I'm at my best'

2 Strengths Spotting:

Over the next week or so, make a conscious effort to notice the strengths you use.
*Eg I love cycling. Strengths: physical stamina, fitness, determination.
I learn software packages quickly. Strengths: IT skills, openness to the application of new ideas
What I perform well: preparing presentations. Strengths: visual acuity
What I prioritise: keeping up relationships at work. Strengths: listening, connecting with others
When I'm at my best: being pushed to perform better. Strengths: risk taking.*

	Activities	The Strengths I Use
Activities which attract me + The Strengths I use		
What I learn quickly + The Strengths I use		
What I perform well at + The Strengths I use		
What I prioritise (by choice) + The Strengths I use		
When I am 'at my best' + The Strengths I use		

4 Complete this Reflections box to discuss with your coach.

My reflections on which strengths I would like to use more

Tool 11.10 Work–Life Balance Commandments

Creating your own work-life balance Commandments

Objectives

- To realise that work-life balance is very personally defined.
- To identify what matters to you right now.
- To create your own work-life balance 'Commandments'.

Introduction

Only you can define what is being 'balanced' or 'out of balance'. It will depend on so many individual factors. Rather than go along with text book suggestions of how to balance your life, we suggest you take some time to work out what are your own 'commandments'. These are the rules you won't budge on, because the elements that underpin them are so important to you.

You might want to consider whether you are a Separator', an 'Integrator' or a 'Juggler'.

Separators: Prefer to keep work and personal life distinct, setting clear boundaries between the two.
Integrators: Blend work and personal activities, comfortable with intermingling the two throughout the day.
Jugglers: Manage multiple demands from work and personal life simultaneously, often in a dynamic and reactive way.

We suggest you complete these exercises before continuing:

- Work Values (exercise 11.2)
- When I'm at my best (exercise 11.3)

Instructions

1 Write down the key ingredients for your commandments.

The key ingredients for my Work-Life Balance Commandments (ie what I will not compromise on)
My Work Values (priorities)
My key motivators
When I'm at my best (the conditions for me to thrive)
My preferred Work-Life Balance style is: Separator/Integrator/Alternator see https://solutions.brighthorizons.co.uk/resourceroom/work-and-you-blogs/are-you-an-integrator-separator-or-alternator

Career Tools 383

2 Below, draft up to five 'Commandments' to discuss with your coach. Base these on what you have written above.

My Work-Life Balance Commandments (draft). Begin each Commandment with "I will….." or "I will not…."

Tool 11.11 The CCS Work Engagement Wheel

Introduction

We all want to feel engaged with our work and our employer. The pandemic underlined the importance of bringing our 'selves' to work and not necessarily maintaining a clear demarcation between our work and non-work selves.

For some people, having a sense of purpose and bringing one's 'best self' to work are critical. For others, strong social relations matter the most. It may be that stability and security are crucial for others' sense of wellbeing and commitment.

Completing the Wheel

Use the WE Wheel as preparation for a purposeful conversation. This could be with a coach, colleague or your line manager. You also might like to talk it through with anyone who is a good listener.

Use the 1-10 scale in the following way:

1 = not at all met
10 = completely met.

When you have marked your wheel, take a separate piece of paper, and now mark 1-10 for any or all of the following:

1. How important is each of the ten factors to you? (1= not at all important; 10 = highly important)

2. How would you score each factor for say, two years ago? (choose a date appropriate to you)

3. What point on the scale would you like each factor to be in say, one year from now? (choose a point in the future appropriate to you)

In the box below, write your reflection and insights from completing the WE Wheel.

```
Reflections and Insights:



```

In the next box, write down what you would like to discuss with your coach/manager.

```
What to discuss with my coach/manager:



```

386 The Holistic Career Coaching Handbook

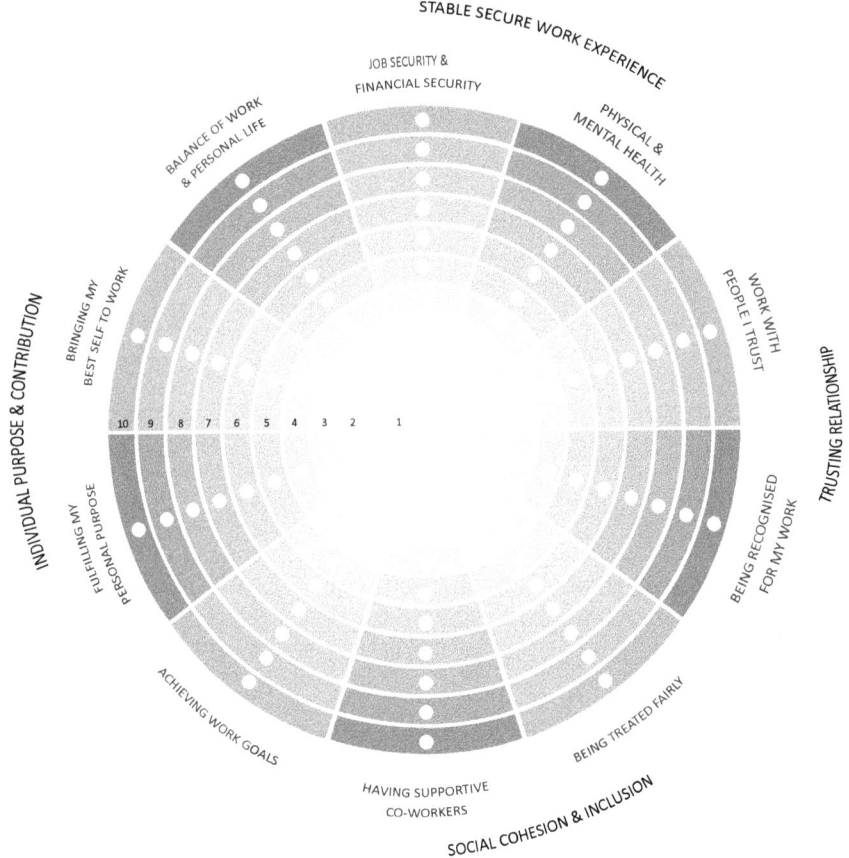

Tool 11.12 Planned Happenstance

Objectives

- To know about the value of a 'planned happenstance' approach to managing change in career management.
- To know the career competencies of planned happenstance.
- To identify ways to develop your openness to new opportunities.

Introduction

Planned Happenstance is an approach to career management which can actively assist you in responding to a changing work environment. Because we cannot predict the future, it does not mean that we should abandon having any plans. It does mean, however, that we should allow our plans to be flexible and adopt an open mind.

Examples of situations where a planned happenstance approach could be useful:

- Someone changing career who needs to explore new opportunities
- Someone who wants to develop in their chosen career but where the path is not clear cut or laid out
- Someone thinking about moving function or department and who needs to know more about what the work involves

There are five career competencies that have been identified as part of a planned happenstance approach. They are:

- Curiosity: exploring new possibilities
- Persistence: exerting effort despite setbacks
- Flexibility: changing attitude according to circumstances
- Optimism: viewing new opportunities as possible
- Risk-taking: taking action in face of uncertain outcomes

Of course, a 'balanced' approach is wise. We are not suggesting that taking any risk is a good thing. But you do not need to be completely certain about the outcome before taking action. These competencies will enable you to respond to changes with more of an open mind, and a preparedness to consider possibilities, as an ongoing strategy. So you become more proactive rather than just reacting to changes when they occur.

Instructions

1. Give an example of when you have demonstrated each of the five Planned Happenstance competencies at work (you may find it useful to refer to your Career Timeline, if you completed one).

Competency	Example
Curiosity	
Persistence	
Flexibility	
Optimism	
Risk-taking	

2. Rate yourself for each of the competencies on a 1-10 scale. 1= I never demonstrate this competency. 10 = I demonstrate this whenever it is needed.

Competency	My rating 1-10
Curiosity	
Persistence	
Flexibility	
Optimism	
Risk-taking	

Now, asterisk * which competencies you would like to develop more.

3 Note down some ideas about ways you could begin to develop the competencies you marked above. *Eg Look at your examples in 1, which have paid off; consider role models who show these competencies; people who could encourage you.*

Planned Happenstance Competency	How I could begin to develop each competency
Curiosity	
Persistence	
Flexibility	
Optimism	
Risk-taking	

Tool 11.13 Creating My Stakeholder Map

Objectives

- To generate a map of key stakeholders.
- To increase awareness of who is in your network and how you might benefit each other.
- To increase motivation to spend time on building relationships.

Introduction

Networking involves giving and seeking support, feedback, information, contacts, ideas and insight. It can be an ongoing process or for a particular purpose. It involves building 'chains of helpfulness'.

We often forget just who is within our 'network' of contacts. Or we too narrowly focus our attention on where we see our contacts. For example, consider the many different roles we play (eg parent, supplier, customer, colleague, manager, social/sports/club/professional/ neighbourhood group member, online groups, volunteer) and past groups we have belonged to (employment, university). These are just some examples of where your networks exist.

Instructions

1. Write in the adjacent box some examples of what contacts can potentially do for you and you for them:

Examples of what contacts can do for each other Eg exchange information about new opportunities, provide introductions, give advice on experience needed

2   Write down below all the 'groups' you belong to, or have belonged to. Include online and face to face groups, and the roles you have in these groups

---

Groups I belong to and roles I have

---

3   Now complete a 'Personal Network Map' in the box on page 392 listing the names of people you know from each group. Use the Key below to show how particular people may be helpful:

    S = Supporters and Encouragers
    I = Information and knowledge holders
    M = Mentors (whom you can talk to in confidence about concerns or decisions)
    G = Gatekeepers (who can connect you with others) Any others?

4   Asterisk one or two of these people who could help you or to whom you could be of assistance, now or at some time in the future.

My Personal Network Map

Tool 11.14 Supporting Parents in Their Careers

Supporting Parents: Conversation Checklist for Managers

This guide contains suggestions for things to cover in your conversations with your employee as they prepare for parental leave and return to work. It is designed to accommodate up to a year parental leave. If they are taking less time off, adjust the timings accordingly. It is not an exhaustive list, so do add your own questions that suit your own individual situation and organisation's policy.

After hearing the news

Suggested topics to cover	My questions
Confirm your company policy and what they are eligible for.	
What support is available?	
How should they manage time off for antenatal appointments?	
Planning a risk assessment	**Notes**
When would they like to take their annual leave?	
When would they like to start their leave?	
How long are they planning to take for leave?	
What are their work priorities before they go on leave?	

Planning and preparing for parental leave (with pregnant employees)

Suggested topics to cover in regular meetings	My questions
Any new health and safety risks?	
Any pregnancy related changes needed to working patterns?	
Any additional support she may need to fulfill her role?	**Notes**

Planning the handover (as early as possible)	
Suggested topics to cover	**My questions**
How will you cover their work while they're away?	
Involving them in recruiting their replacement.	
When their replacement will start, including hand over and hand back.	
Preparing their hand over notes.	**Notes**
Who are the key contacts who need to know they are going on leave?	
What will they do on their KIT/SPLIT days? (if applicable) Agree payment for the work they do.	
What to do if their baby/child comes early?	

Planning the handover (continued)	
Suggested topics to cover	**My questions**
Arrange a final performance review before they leave, even if this is outside the regular timing. This can review their performance and set objectives for when they return. If applicable check your company policy on performance related bonuses if these are due to be awarded while they are on leave.	
Confirm their return to work job description.	**Notes**
Confirm their return to work plan	
Who will be in their support network while they're away.	
Creating an update file for them for when they return to update them on key projects or any organisational changes that happen while they're away.	
Confirm statutory leave and payment of statutory pay.	

The last week	
Suggested topics to cover	**My questions**
Final review of the handover plan - what do they have left to finalise? Are they redirecting emails, setting up an out of office?	
How soon and how often would they like to hear from work (other than your requirements to keep them up to date with new opportunities, restructures etc) and how would they like you to contact them?	
When are they likely to work their KIT/SPLIT days? Can they pencil anything in now?	**Notes**
Who do they need to stay in touch with while on leave?	
Do they have all the equipment they need to stay in touch with work while on leave? Will they still have access to everything or will their account be suspended while they're off?	
Finalise arrangements with HR to confirm support, benefits and timings.	

While they are away, dependent on communication arrangements	
Suggested topics to cover	**My questions**
Confirm when they will be returning to work, making it clear they can change their mind or take full amount of leave. If they want to return earlier than the end of their full leave they need to give 8 weeks notice.	
Do they want to use any accumulated annual leave before they return? Can they use this to ease their return to work?	
What working pattern would they like to return to? Speak to your HR contact to confirm arrangements if necessary.	**Notes**
What will their priorities be when they return?	
How can their KIT/SPLIT days help support their return?	
Confirm their return to work job description.	
Have there been any changes at work?	
[For mothers who have given birth: Are they continuing to breastfeed when they return to work? Where can you offer them to do this and store their pumped milk?]	

2 weeks before they return	
Suggested topics to cover	**My questions**
Confirm their return to work date and make sure it's in everyone's diary.	
Will their logins / work pass still work?	
Will you be there the day they return? If not, who will be their point of contact for any issues?	
How will the hand back work for their cover?	**Notes**
Confirm their priorities for their first week back.	
What changes to the workplace or team do they need to be made aware of?	
Confirm what they should you do if their child can't go to childcare and requires them to look after them?	

The day before they return

Suggested topics to cover	My questions
Check in that everyone is set for their return.	
Has anything changed since you last spoke that they need to know about?	
Confirm their start time / who will be there to welcome them back if not you.	**Notes**

The first day back	
Suggested topics to cover	**My questions**
Confirm everything is working and if they need support with anything.	
Confirm their priorities for their first week back.	
[For mothers who gave birth who are are continuing to breastfeed.: Confirm where they can express milk.]	**Notes**

End of the first week (and weekly catch ups)	
Suggested topics to cover	**My questions**
How has their week gone?	
Is there anything they need your support with?	
Clarify their priorities.	**Notes**
How can you help support their career development ideas?	

End of the first month	
Suggested topics to cover	**My questions**
How has their first month back gone? Ask about their career development plans How can their priorities for the next couple of months help support their career development ideas?	
	Notes

After three months

Suggested topics to cover

Focus on their career development plan and how their work and priorities support this.

My questions

Notes

Tool 11.15 Supporting Neurodiversity Personal Playbook

Personal Playbook

The Personal Playbook aims to give a template to clearly articulate what you need to work at your best. It is a personal document, but one that should act as a starting point for a discussion about how you work together as a team.

This is a **personal document for you** to build up throughout your time with us. It can be very helpful to your team and the broader organisation if you can share elements of this that will help us to better support you, but it **remains your own confidential document**. Feel free to use it as a starting point for a broader personal record of what helps you at work – consider creating a physical or online folder collating positive feedback emails, specific articles or insights – whatever you can pull together over time that helps you.

We hope that over the course of the next few weeks through your onboarding process (and beyond) you will develop a good understanding of how we tend to work together as a team. If you feel that any policies, systems or procedures are unclear, please contact *[Enter the name of the person responsible for clarifying]*.

We've outlined a few different reflective questions here as a starting point to help you build your profile, but please adapt in any way that is helpful for you.

While we will do all we can to try to accommodate your preferences there may be situations where team members have conflicting needs. If this should happen, please be assured that we will do all we can to resolve in a way that works for everyone as far as is possible.

Name	
Role	
Team	
Manager name	
Parts of my role that I am most confident in delivering	
Strengths and experiences that I'm bringing that will help me to deliver	
Parts of my role where I would appreciate additional support	
What support would help? Who would be a part of your ideal support network?	
What skills, strengths or interests do you have that we might not know about you from your original application that could be useful to explore in your current role or within the wider organisation? [*This is an interesting question to ask when considering organisational skills capacity, and future development goals / projects*]	
What strategies help you to approach a task that you're finding hard? (Tick all that apply)	☐ I like to talk it through with my manager ☐ I like to talk it through with someone else ☐ I like to work it out visually ☐ I like to think it through myself ☐ I like to think on the move ☐ Other (please specify)
How do you prefer to receive work/task requests? (Tick all that apply)	☐ Verbally face-to-face ☐ Verbally by phone ☐ Over email ☐ Other (please specify)

Are there any provisions that would support you in your work? (Tick all that apply)	☐ Access to assistive technology e.g. mind map tools, speech to text / text to speech software (please specify) ☐ Coloured screen overlays ☐ Use of headphones when doing focused work ☐ Access to quiet place to work ☐ Access to sit/stand desk ☐ Other (please specify) _____
What helps you to re-energise when you are feeling low? (Tick all that apply)	☐ A conversation ☐ Movement break ☐ Change of task ☐ Change of scene ☐ Other _____
What is your ideal way to connect with people informally? (Tick all that apply.)	☐ I prefer not to ☐ One person at a time ☐ Group activities ☐ Day time activities ☐ Evening activities ☐ Other _____
Are there any specific activities that you enjoy doing with others in a work socialising context?	
What else, if anything, can we do to support you to do your best work?	

Thank you so much for taking the time to complete this. Please do share anything else that might be helpful with your manager as part of your onboarding process.

Index

55 Redefined 94
70-20-10 guidelines 14

Access to Work scheme 147
Acker, Joan 187
acronyms 210
active listening 8, 100, 328–329
additional needs 254–255
Addressing Blocks to Learning exercise 363–367
Addressing Skills and Knowledge Gaps exercise 368–369
ADHD 109, 111–112, 116, 118, 121–125, 127, 129, 136, 138, 151, 154, 288, 335
adoption 219, 230, 235–236, 269, 271
Adoption UK 229, 235
age-diverse teams 51–52, 68, 97, 102, 175
ageism 45, 52, 65, 79, 298
Albrechtsen, Anne-Birgitte 316
alpha pattern careers 13
anxiety 8, 29–31, 39, 42, 52, 120, 126, 132, 144–147, 191, 205, 218–219, 228–229, 239, 242, 257, 270, 284, 289–291
archetypes of workers 72–75, 89
artificial intelligence 89, 102
assistive technology 145–146, 150
assumptions and biases: of career returners 171, 183–189, 211–212; of menopausal women 293–7; of mid-lifers 45–47; of neurodiverse individuals 115–119; of older workers 62–63, 90–92; of parents 255–260
AstraZeneca 133
Atos 95
Attrition Triangle model 173–174
autism 111–112, 114–121, 123, 125–126, 129, 131–132, 136, 138, 142, 144, 148–149, 153, 255
autonomy 22, 25, 39–40, 53, 56, 63, 85, 124–125, 264, 303, 338, 343
Aviva 95
away days 154

Barclays 95
bereavement 40, 170, 279, 335
beta pattern careers 13
biases *see* assumptions and biases
BMW 95
boundaries 56, 141, 250, 253–254, 268–269, 327, 344
boundary management 253–254
brain ageing 260
brain fog 44, 144, 289–290
brain training 47
breastfeeding 145, 245, 401
Brewis, Jo 279, 282, 296

410 Index

Bridges, William 11–12, 191, 205, 220, 292, *see also* Transition model
Brown, Brene 39
bullying 21, 91, 120, 318–319
burnout 40, 43, 56, 129, 132, 220, 253, 255, 268–269
business networks 239–240
Butler, Steve 51–52

career break penalty 183–185, 211–212
career capital 231, 233, 239–240, 263–264, 343
career conversations 7–10, 23, 35–36, 48, 51, 55, 71, 80, 87, 90, 99–160, 283, 293, 308–309, 316, 320–337, 341, 345–347
Career Counselling Services 2, 5, 53, 158, 210, 321
career metaphors 15–16
career returners 2, 170–213, 285, 340, *see also* returning to work; assumptions and biases 171, 183–189, 211–212; importance of to employers 173–177; integration of 199–210; lived experiences of 177–183; self-limiting beliefs of 190–193; strengths of 193–199, 340–341
Career Returners (organisation) 171–173, 177, 184, 189, 194–197, 201–203, 205, 210–212, 340
career support programme, creating 316–339
Career Tools 2, 128, 153, 155, 210, 309, 328, 346–408
Careers After Babies report 172, 223, 247
Carlson, Carole 44
Cattell, Raymond 47
Centre for Ageing Better 64, 66, 81, 93, 103
Chartered Management Institute 66, 90
childbirth, fear of 227
childcare 64, 170, 172, 178–179, 182–185, 191, 198–199, 219–220, 223, 225, 244–250, 253, 261, 263, 265, 270, *see also* parents
Cisco 96, 104, 196, 206
clichés 97–98
Clifton Strengths 207, 332
Club Landoy 93, 98
collegial networks 317–319
Collie, Jonathan 65, 97
communication 36, 54, 83, 100, 103, 127, 136, 140–141, 151, 153, 237–239, 261–262, 267–268
commuting 19, 23, 130, 143, 154, 246
company culture 25, 46, 53, 102, 147, 249–250, 316–321, 339
compensation and benefits 317, 319
confidence 11, 36, 131–132, 185, 190–191, 200, 202–204, 206–209, 220–221, 232–233, 240–241, 322–323, 325–326
Connelly, Chip 83
Cory, Giselle 102
COURT mindset 325, 343
Covid-19 1, 9, 19, 43, 80, 116, 176, 196, 266, 280–281, 294
creativity 27, 39, 46–47, 102, 131, 133, 195, 197, 253, 358
Crenshaw, Kimberlé 113
crisis 3, 18, 22–25, 38–39
Crowe, Bob 304
crystallised intelligence 47

Danker, Karen 191, 194, 197
Dark, Jessica 113

Decline Myth 295
demand avoidance 126–127
depression 8, 11, 39, 42, 120, 132, 228–229, 247, 257, 289
Development Grid 156, 158, 210, 330–331
Dinwiddy, Ian 225–226, 248–249, 258, 265
disability 93, 114, 118, 140
discrimination 10, 45, 79, 115, 283, 296; microaggressions 115, 224–225, 264
diversity 31, 51–52, 68, 90, 98–99, 143, 172–173, 175–176, 193–194, 197, 202, 285–286, 317, 319, see also neurodiversity; age-diverse teams 51–52, 68, 97, 102, 175
divorce 40, 59, 279, 327–328
Dunne, Maureen 139
Dweck, Carole 101
dyscalculia 109, 111–112, 138
dyslexia 109, 111–112, 122, 136–138, 146, 198
dyspraxia 111–112, 118, 138, 142, 144

early career 18–36; importance of to employers 28–30; myths associated with 30–31; quarter-life crisis 3, 22–25
Edwards, Rob 130–131
eldercare 42–43, 49, 81–82, 170, 172, 279, 282
Ellis, Sarah 326
embarrassment 80, 100, 228, 283, 290, 294, 307
emotional intelligence 58, 138, 259, 262
emotional maturity 67
emotions 10, 21, 23, 67, 125–127, 129, 218–219, 242–243, 289, 292, 297, 327–328

empathy 14, 18, 23, 31, 40, 48, 100, 117, 137, 138, 171, 194, 204, 261–262, 291, 307–308
Employee Assistance Programme 302, 306, 344
employee resource groups 96, 133, 140, 143, 148, 150, 159, 161, 265, 270, 294, 302, 319
Encompass Equality 46, 281
#EndtheCareerBreakPenalty campaign 211–212
Energy Raisers exercise 309, 374–376
engagement 2–6, 10, 35, 38, 52–56, 63, 134, 156, 280, 307, 316, 319, 321, 384–387
environmental design 144–145, 317–318
equality 45–46, 224, 244, 263
Equality Act (2010) 80, 90
Equality and Human Rights Commission 283
ethnicity pay gap 173
executive functions 113, 115, 122–124, 129–130
exit interviews 1, 23, 287
expectations 59, 118, 150, 156, 220–221, 225, 301, 326–327
EY 96, 133
eye-contact 117, 152

family, see also parents; work–life balance: adoption 219, 230, 235–236, 269, 271; childcare see childcare; concerns regarding 209; eldercare 42–43, 49, 81–82, 170, 172, 279, 282; parental leave see parental leave; pressures 243
Farrell, Chris 65
fatherhood bonus 256
FDM 205–206

Fertility in the Workplace 233
fertility rates 64
fertility treatment 219, 230, 233–235, 271
flexibility 21–22, 75–76, 80–81, 85, 91, 103–105, 143, 145, 172, 182, 184, 196, 223, 234, 246–247, 249, 252–253, 256, 264, 266–267, 270, 284–285, 302–303, 317–319, 343
fluid intelligence 47
Fossat, Michael 67, 71, 75, 94
Francke, Ann 66
freelance work 130–131, 170
Frolander, Martin 97
future focus 33, 158, 326

gender ambition gap 256
gender differences 18, 25, 42, 45–46, 81, 93, 121, 172–174, 176, 179–183, 199, 219–220, 223–224, 240–241, 244, 252, 255–257, 262, 271
gender pay gap 173, 176, 223
gender-based brain drain 173–174
Gothard, Bill 39
Gratton, Lynda 212
groupthink 85

happiness 3, 41–43, 59, 218
Harvard Business Review 296
Hays 81, 83, 88
Henpicked 281
Herzberg, Frederick 20
HireVue 96
hiring process 147–150, 207, 264, *see also* recruitment
hot-desking 145
HRT 289, 291
Human Development Index 271
hybrid working 82, 142, 154, 189, 196
hyperfocus 112, 124, 138, 143

Ibarra, Herminia 191
imposter syndrome 80, 92, 100, 191
inner critic 190–193
Inspiring Dads 225, 258
intelligence 47, 111, 121–123; emotional 58, 138, 262
Intelligent Careers theory 196–197
intergenerational teams *see* age-diverse teams
interpersonal skills 8, 62, 67, 75, 194–195, 355
intersectionality 92–93, 110–111, 113–115, 164, 282
IT skills 88–89, 101
IVF *see* fertility treatment

Jackson, Mark 38–39
jargon 210
job crafting 56–59, 99
job satisfaction 20, 81, 196, 370
Job Satisfiers exercise 371–373
job security 19, 29, 43
Josa, Claire 292
Junoverse 97

Kaleidoscope Career Model 12–13, 181, 298
Kierkegaard, Soren 109
Kirby, Amanda 113, 140
Kline, Nancy 146

later career *see* older workers
layoffs 1–2, 10, 43, *see also* redundancy
Le Marie, Sibylle 98
leaky pipeline 174, 223
learning 2, 13–14, 87–89, 96, 99, 101–102
legacy 15, 70, 80, 83, 105
LGBTQIA+ individuals 228–229, 288
life expectancy 42
life stages 12–15

lifelong learning 96, 99
line managers 46, 94, 100, 125, 143, 150–151, 202, 212, 230, 240, 243, 248, 250, 265, 281, 307, 320–322, 343, 346–347
listening 2, 8, 35–36, 60, 67, 100, 151, 199, 307–308, 310, 325, 327–329, 344

male menopause 14
Mansfield Building Society 300, 303–305, 311
Manual of Me 153–154
masking 120–121, 140, 285
maternal wall 256
Maternity Coach 5, 218, 231–232, 240, 244
maternity leave 170, 180, 222, 235, 240–241, 247–248, 270, 335, *see also* parental leave
Mavius, Sarah 197, 205–206
McCall, Davina 281
McDowall, Almuth 150–151
McKinsey 52, 81, 174, 224, 286, 295
Mead, Margaret 285
meeting culture 146–147
menopause 5, 45, 170, 279–311, 341; assumptions and biases 293–297; definition of 310–311; impact on careers 288–293; importance of discussing 283–288; strengths of menopausal women 297–299
Menopause Café concept 284, 302–303
Menopause Champions/Mentors 301–302, 304
Menopause Friendly Accreditation 281, 310
Menopause Inclusive Framework 305–306
mental health 8, 20, 30, 53, 82, 120, 132, 150–151, 224, 228–229, 235–236, 242–244, 249, 254, 294, 301, 316, 335
mental load 244
mentoring 33, 38, 50–51, 55, 69, 75–76, 82–85, 97–98, 104, 143, 205, 265, 297, 301–302
Mercer 96
microaggressions 115, 224–225, 264
micro-managing 157
Microsoft 206
mid-life crisis 3, 38–39
mid-lifers 38–60, 279, 282, 297; assumptions and biases 45–47; career dilemmas 48–49; career needs of 43–45; menopause 5, 45, 170, 279–311, 341; strengths of 49–51; work engagement 52–54
Mills, Eleanor 297
miscarriage 227
motherhood penalty 256
Motionspot 144
motivation 2, 5–6, 27–28, 53–54, 62, 67, 69–71, 88, 95, 100, 196, 205, 280, 329, 336–338, 347
Motivation and Hygiene Factors of Job Satisfaction 20
Multiverse 97–98

National Union of Teachers 285
necessity entrepreneurs 130–132
neurodiversity 2, 40–41, 109–164, 255, 288, 335; assumptions and biases 115–119; career support and development 139–165; definition of 111–113; experiences and perspectives 119–133; and intersectionality 113–115, *see also* intersectionality; strengths 112, 118, 133–139, 155–156
neuroinclusion 111, 119, 133–134, 139–165

NHS 69–70, 91, 228
Noer, Daniel 43

occupational downgrading 200
OECD 64, 66, 68, 244
older workers 62–106; assumptions and biases 62–63, 90–92; benefits of employing 67–69; benefits to 69–71; definition of 63–64; demographic need for 64; desire to work 64–66; needs of 71–90
onboarding 149–150, 172, 190, 317–318, 320
Opportunity Now 176
organisational culture *see* company culture
Over the Bloody Moon 281, 290
overwhelm 25, 43, 56, 145, 150, 199, 238, 243, 255, 265, 269–270, 290–291

parental leave 10, 170, 180, 219, 222; managing careers after 248–255; preparation for 229–233, 393–405
parents 12, 217–273, 340, *see also* childcare; adoption 219, 230, 235–236, 269, 271; assumptions and biases 255–260; becoming 227–229; of children with additional needs 254–255; effect on careers 229–248; fertility treatment 219, 230, 233–235, 271; getting the best out of 262–271; importance of supporting new fathers 225–227; importance of supporting new mothers 223–225; neurodiverse parents 255; pregnancy 219, 224, 227–228, 231–234, 237, 247–248, 251, 254, 256–257, 269, 293; solo parents 265, 269–270; strengths of 5, 218, 260–262; transition to parenthood 220–223
part-time work 71, 74, 82, 91, 95, 102, 103, 189, 196, 225, 246–247, 249–251, 253, 258, 264, 282, 343
paternity leave 222, 229–230, 262, 266, *see also* parental leave
pensions 69–70, 103
performance coaches 322, 346–347
perimenopause 279, 289, 294, 302, 310
PERMA Model 54
Personal Playbook 153, 157–158, 406–408
person–environment fit theory 137, 158
phased-retirement 71
physical health 20, 65, 69–70, 81, 170, 226, 335
Planned Happenstance exercise 24, 48, 128, 387–389
Plumbly, Claire 129
population growth 64
postnatal mental health 228–229
praise/criticism ratio 53–54
pregnancy 219, 224, 227–228, 231–234, 237, 247–248, 251, 254, 256–257, 269, 293
priorities 3, 9, 12, 18, 157, 161, 208, 233, 241, 255, 258, 332
productivity 52, 65, 68–69, 71, 89, 102, 119, 128–129, 134, 142–144, 162, 223, 252, 262, 271, 283–286, 337
progression 7, 19, 40, 74, 125–126, 128, 158, 231, 250–251, 256–257, 264, 280, 288, 325–326, 343
promotion 59, 63, 85, 100–102, 130, 184, 226, 232, 234, 240, 250, 257, 259, 264, 325–327

pro-retirement 65
psychological safety 5, 114, 163, 250, 264, 343

quarter-life crisis 3, 22–25

race 113–114, 173–174, 228–229, 282, 288
Rauch, Jonathan 41, 67
reasonable adjustments 141–142, 153, 161–162, 271, 305
recruitment 22, 52, 66, 69, 94, 147–150, 187, 201–202, 207, 223, 316–317, 320, 338, 342
redundancy 10, 42, 59, 103, 186, 188, 235, 247, 347, *see also* layoffs
rejection sensitivity dysphoria 125–126
reliability 67
remote working 142, 154, 248, 250, 318
reputation 316–317
re-skilling 87–89, 94–95, 98–99, 101, 201
respect for experience 75–80, 101
retention 31, 54, 56, 134, 175, 194, 263–265, 279, 285–286, 316, 342
retirement age 62, 65, 68–69, 71, 79, 93
returning to work 5, 10, 12, 170–213, 218, 231–232, 237–238, 241–245, 247, 252, 257–259, 261, 265, 285, 335, 400–405, *see also* career returners; parental leave
returnship programmes 201, 204, 212
Robinson, Oliver 20, 24–25
role models/modelling 94, 160, 163, 194, 196, 198–199, 223, 249, 264, 280, 286, 298–299

Root, James 63, 67, 71, 85, 104
Ryan, Lucy 282, 295, 297

Saga 96
Saint-Gobain 321
Salem, Lesley 283, 303, 305
sandwich generation 282, *see also* mid-lifers
Sanofi 96
Satisfying Achievements exercise 361–362
scaling technique 329–330
Schneider Electric 94–95
Schwartz, Shalom 85
Scott, Andrew 212
second shift 244
secondment 170
self-employment 130–131
self-limiting beliefs 190–193, 257
sensory overload 144–146
Singer, Judy 111
skills 1–2, 21, 27, 50, 57, 87–89, 170, 186–187, 194, 209–210, 261–262, 332–335, 354–360; re-skilling 87–89, 94–95, 98–99, 101, 201; up-skilling 42, 70, 87, 89, 189–190, 205–206
Slaughter, Anne-Marie 181–182
sleep deprivation 244–245, 281–282, 288–290
small and medium-sized enterprises 204, 281, 342
social culture 137, 154–155
social media 24, 29, 85, 88, 98, 104, 227
societal pressures 243
solo parents 265, 269–270
'Squiggly Career' metaphor 16
Stakeholder Map exercise 392–394
Standing, Lucie 96
stereotypes 30–31, 62–63, 65, 90–92, 116, 200, 257, 264, 293,

295–296, *see also* assumptions and biases
stigma 115, 119, 288, 302
strengths 2, 9–10, 207; of age-diverse teams 51–52; of career returners 193–199, 340–341; identifying 332–334; of menopausal women 297–299; of mid-lifers 49–51, 55; of neurodiverse individuals 112, 118, 133–139, 155–156; of parents 5, 218, 260–262
Strengths and Skills Grid 56, 139, 155, 333
Strengths Profile 332
strengths-spotting 55, 156, 379
stress 25, 44, 67, 129, 147, 219, 228–230, 233, 239, 245, 247, 262, 284, 288–290, 319, 327
suicide 42
support networks 50, 212, 240, 265, 267, 408
supported hiring 201
Swissray 96

talent shortages 173
Timewise 81
Toffler, Alvin 24
tools 2, 128, 153, 155, 210, 309, 328, 346–408
Tourette's Syndrome 111
Transition model 11–12, 192, 194, 197, 205, 220–223, 292
traumatic births 227
trust 53, 126, 148, 152, 161
Tupper, Helen 47, 326

underemployment 130, 132
unemployment 42–43, 65, 90, 131–132
UNICEF 245
Unilever 96
up-skilling 42, 70, 87, 89, 189–190, 205–206
Using My Strengths exercise 307, 377–380

volunteering 154, 185, 194–195, 198–199
vulnerability 21, 46, 122, 140, 235, 242–243, 262, 279

Warner, Ed 144
well-being 20, 27–28, 35, 43, 50, 54–55, 69–70, 95–96, 104, 142, 160–162, 220, 224, 227, 235, 244, 286, 301–302, 305, 316, 344
'When I'm at my Best' exercise 36, 155, 210, 332, 353
Wittenberg-Cox, Avivah 44, 47, 297
Work Engagement Wheel 53, 384–386
Work Values exercise 350–352
work–life balance 1, 27, 35, 43, 48–49, 56, 59, 81, 98, 182, 210, 224, 246–247, 250, 252–253, 273, 309, 382–384
Work–Life Balance Commandments 210, 309, 381–383
work–life integration 182
World Economic Forum 64
World Health Organization 8, 245, 316

For Product Safety Concerns and Information please contact our EU representative GPSR@taylorandfrancis.com
Taylor & Francis Verlag GmbH, Kaufingerstraße 24, 80331 München, Germany

www.ingramcontent.com/pod-product-compliance
Ingram Content Group UK Ltd.
Pitfield, Milton Keynes, MK11 3LW, UK
UKHW020827220425
457528UK00028B/185